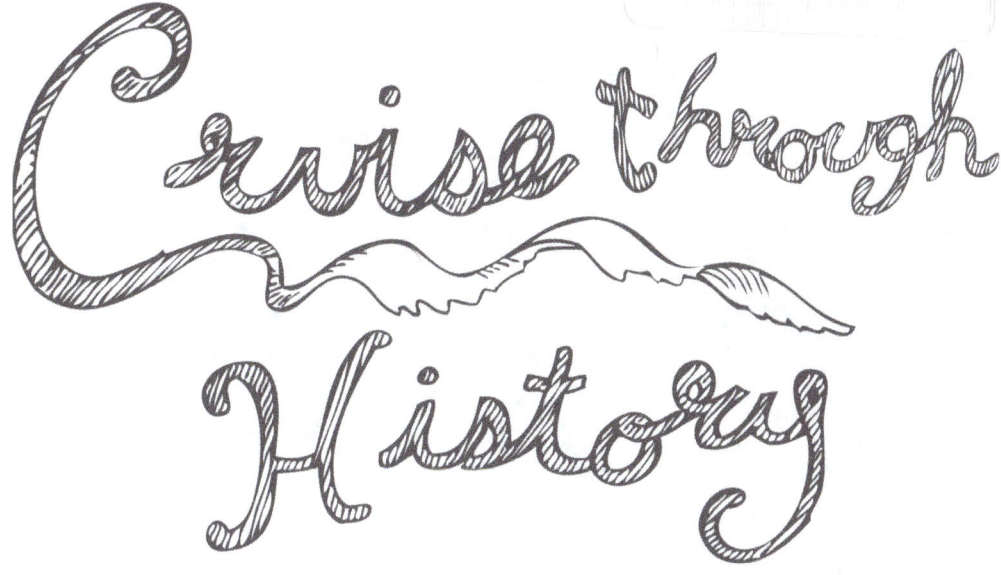

Cruise through History

ITINERARY 12

PORTS OF THE NORTH SEA

Hanseatic League, Iceland & Greenland

SHERRY HUTT

Copyright © 2020 by Sherry Hutt

All rights reserved. No part of this book may be reproduced or transmitted in any form or by any means, electronic or mechanical, including photocopying, recording, or by any information storage and retrieval system without the written permission of the author, except where permitted by law.

Bound: ISBN: 978-1-942153-19-1

Epub: ISBN: 978-1-942153-18-4

TABLE OF CONTENTS

Preface 5
Acknowledgements 9
Introduction: Vikings and Merchants Create Cities 11
Map of Itinerary XII Ports of the North Sea 14
Timeline of Stories 15

Belgium
    Brugge: Medieval World Metropolis 17
    In Flanders Fields 31
    Poppies of Remembrance 45

Netherlands
    Amsterdam in the Golden Age of World Commerce 57
    Walk through Amsterdam with Rembrandt, Keyser & Clusius 73
    Tulips, Chocolate and Diamonds 91

Norway
    Viking Ships, the Fram, & Kon-Tiki in Oslo 105
    Vigeland's Dream for Oslo 121
    Nobel at Peace in Oslo 133
    Oslo Fjords 147
    Art and Artists of Bergen 157
    The Secret Life of Trolls 173
    Birchlegs and Baglers Battle for Bergen 181
    Saga of Olav Nilsson and the Fall of Hansa 193

    Trondheim: Nidaros Cathedral – The Power of Place 215

    Flam and the Fjords 235

At Sea

    Search for a North East Passage 257

    Vikings Playing Chess 271

Russia

    Murmansk: The First 100 Years 289

    Archangel's Marvelous Merchant Adventurers 303

    Archangel Part II: 1918 323

Iceland

    In Reykjavik Celebrate the World's Oldest Democracy 337

Greenland

    Mapping Greenland in the Fram 359

    Discovery of the End of the Old and Beginning of the
    New World 373

Index 387

PREFACE

Cruise through History is a collection of short stories grouped by the sequence of many popular cruise itineraries, rather than by country, or period of history. As the stories move from port to port, they randomly move through time. The stories are all true. They introduce the traveler to the history and culture of a port through the story of a long-ago, or not so long-ago, resident, whose exploits left a castle, a palace, or a lovely site that can be explored on a cruise ship shore excursion.

The host character for each port stop is chosen for their inspiring actions, and the visible culture left behind. Some names will be familiar, presented in these volumes with depth to their personality. Other characters may become like new friends, too long unrecognized. Either way, stories offer a new twist to the school-age history of a place, drawn together to put travels in a fascinating context for the short-term visitor.

No apology is made for choice of subjects. They have been chosen arbitrarily on whim of the author, accumulated from past travels, for your enjoyment. The desire is that the reader will share the fun. No attempt is made to be politically correct, or give a chamber of commerce gloss to stories evident in remnants of the past. Knowledge of history can teach us a great deal about ourselves and the human condition, but only if it is honest and fairly told. No doubt it is the quest for "real" that draws adults to travel as often and for as long as they are able.

The desire to seek knowledge, about distant places and times, fuels international tourism. Many travelers who found history in school to be dull, later in life seek to fill gaps in their knowledge, with personal experience. This book is an opportunity for events of one's life to give rich meaning to the human condition and to enjoy stories of fact for which fiction is no rival.

Praise is due to the many historians and other scholars who have delved deeply into source data to ponder minute details of history for pedagogical pursuits. Such information has been mined here, with attribution, for lively details, which will heighten the traveler's enjoyment of the past. History is a public good. The more it is found to be enjoyable, the more it will be valued.

An apology is due to those who hoped to foster a disciplined scholarship in the author. This is reading for an out-of-the-classroom experience. Footnotes are inserted to give due credit to scholars, who have provided valuable information, and to remind the reader that these stories are true. The presence of source notes is not to feign academic appearance. Editorial sidebars and fun bits are in the footnotes.

When there are gaps in facts, or mysteries remain, they are not supplemented by fiction. Rather, an effort is made to look at the known as a guide to the unknown. The reader can draw their own conclusions, daydream through the gaps, and enjoy the reason that so much popular fiction and movies are drawn from historical facts.

These stories are offered to give historical context to sites often visited as cruise destinations. In these stories, meet the characters who walked the same streets centuries in the past, which visitors walk today. Go beyond castle ruins to envision people who built them and lived there.

Itineraries in this series have stories at each port that seek to inspire cruise travelers to rise out of their deck chairs and investigate a destination with honesty and irreverence, or the potential traveler to rise from the sofa and embark on a Cruise through History©. There is no stigma of a school assignment. Earn an "E" for enjoyment.

Itineraries in the Cruise through History series available and forthcoming-

1. **London to Rome - 2014**
2. **Rome to Venice – 2014**
3. **Ports of the Eastern Mediterranean- 2019**
4. **Ports of the Black Sea- 2020**

5. Ports of Southern Mediterranean – Arabia to Atlantic – coming 2021

6. Ports of East Coast of North America – coming 2020

7. Ports of West Coast of North America – coming 2021

8. **Mexico, Central America and the Caribbean Islands – 2015**

9. **Ports of South America – 2017**

10. **Ports of the British Isles – 2020**

11. **Ports of the Baltic Sea – 2018**

12. **Ports of the North Sea – 2020**

13. Ports of Africa, India and Southeast Asia – coming 2021

14. Ports of the South Pacific – Australia, New Zealand, Indonesia, Polynesia – coming 2021

15. Ports of the Far East and North Pacific – coming 2021

    Cruise through History – Shakespeare as Travel Writer – coming fall 2021

Find all the storybooks at **cruisethroughhistory.com**.

ACKNOWLEDGEMENTS

Writing travel stories began as therapy from the world of Washington, D.C. Thanks are due to the Summer Citizens' program at Utah State University, Logan, and the several cruise lines, book clubs and community associations, which have given me opportunities to share stories with their guests and students.

Much appreciated are those who helped to produce the series, including:

Digby and Rose, publisher, art director, and publicist; Heather Richardson, blog editor; and Lisa Lynn Aispuro, research assistance. Diana Verkamp created the CTH logo. Elizabeth Herrgott at Feast Studios produces video format stories and podcasts, which support CTH in print.

These stories would not be possible without the treasure trove of material in libraries and used bookshops. In this increasingly paperless world, bookstores and libraries provide solace and an opportunity to revive our humanity. Source materials linger on paper for which the web is no match.

Much appreciation is also due to those who apply their skill to preservation and protection of heritage resources in the United States and around the world. The greatest thanks go to my husband, Guy Rouse, who has lugged my camera equipment all over the world for thirty years.

This volume is dedicated to fellow travelers Rita and Joel Rosenshein. Many of the stories in this volume were written while traveling the seas with this lovely couple. They instigated our move to Florida, which made transit effortless to reach a home port for cruises to ports of the world.

All of the photos in this volume are the work of CTH unless noted, accumulated over thirty years. Original art is sourced through Digby Rose Publisher. The photos and art are all property of Cruise through History© and all rights are reserved. No use may be made of the photos, art, or text, the construction of history in stories, without prior permission of the author.

Author and husband at Flam

INTRODUCTION
VIKINGS AND MERCHANTS CREATE CITIES

In this Itinerary of stories found in Ports of the North Sea, kings, queens and generals step down to allow Vikings and merchant contributions to shine. Founding cities, typically the prerogative of royals, have lesser impact in the North Sea, where mastery of the seas was key to power and the ability to control the direction of history. In the ninth through tenth and into the eleventh century, Vikings had mastery of the North Sea. As Vikings found new prime farm land, became Christianized and settled into calm, terrestrial pursuits, commerce flowed freely in the North Sea. Reigning mastery of the North Sea passed from Vikings to merchants. Merchants built cities.

This Itinerary begins in Brugge, Belgium, the first true World Metropolis. Brugge, rather than Bruges is used here, as Bruges was a Dutch moniker and Brugge is Flemish. Brugge was a major center of North Sea commerce, when cities of the Netherlands were still hamlets among shallow waters. So much wealth poured into Brugge from the eleventh century, that merchants were able to build palaces to rival royals of the time. In Brugge, the Dark Ages were never dark. They were filled with gilded housewares, in opulent halls, along streets and canals of elegant homes. In this story follow the rise, abandonment and rediscovery of the most popular visitor site in Belgium.

That Brugge remains unscathed after two world wars is miraculous, given that the city is in proximity to some of the most contested turf in the world, the site of numerous battles over a millennium. In the story In Flanders Fields, revisit history of battles from Romans to World War II. Memorials are part of the landscape, within which a few Medieval era towns remain. Of special note is the red poppy, an icon of remembrance, launched after World War I and inspired by the poem of an army doctor, seeing the reality of battle field trauma.

When Brugge declined in commercial power, a victim of politics, religion and environmental disaster, the silting of its river, Amsterdam rose to take its place. Merchants of Amsterdam built their city around canals, funded by world trade from the Far East. Merchants commissioned great houses, churches and civic buildings, as well as great art. Walk through Amsterdam where Rembrandt painted and Keyser created streetscapes with towers, in an Amsterdam Renaissance of architecture. Fools lived in Amsterdam too, lured by quick profits in tulip bulbs. Tulips and tulipomania, as well as sustained fortunes made in chocolate, and birth of the Amsterdam diamond industry, an outgrowth of religious toleration, are all part of the Netherlands stories.

Vikings step to center stage in stories from Norway. Visit Viking Ships, the Fram and Kon-Tiki in Oslo, where Norwegians built ships, over a millennium, to sail Oslo Fjords, to Flam and coastal fjords up the coasts of the North Sea. Viking technology in rowed and sailing ships are a marvel of the early Medieval world. When Vikings wanted a diversion from sailing and ravaging monasteries in England, they played chess. Examine the aesthetic side of Vikings Playing Chess.

Norwegian fjords have beauty, which cannot be captured in a story. These stories tell of the lives of people who lived among fjords, in the days when Birchlegs and Baglers Battled for Bergen, and Olav Nilsson fought Hansa merchants through the streets of Bergen for dominance in trade, until it became the Art and Artists of Bergen, who made this city a wonderous place for return port visits. The itinerary stops in Trondheim, where a marvel of church art, Trondheim Cathedral, began with burial of a Viking, who was deified and became St. Olav, displaying the Power of Place. Today, in Trondheim ask the question, where is Olav?

In Oslo wander through an entire city park devoted to the sculpture of one artist, Gustav Vigeland in Vigeland's Dream for Oslo. Nobel had dreams too. His dreams were of peace. In Oslo learn the story of Alfred Nobel and the story behind the Nobel Peace Prize. Beware of trolls among the fjords. Before travelling fjords of Norway learn The Secret Life of Trolls.

The North Sea, wonderous and beautiful today, was for people of five hundred years ago a mysterious realm. In 1553, merchants of London formed a company of Marvelous Merchant Adventurers to sail north, in a quest to sail over the top of Norway, Finland and Russia to China and Japan, in order to establish trade routes not dependent upon land travel across the Silk Road, or through the tumultuous Mediterranean. Follow the story of these hopeful merchants, who went no further than the White Sea of Russia and established trade with Tsar Ivan IV, later known as Ivan the Terrible. England opened trade with Russia, which endured for the next three centuries. Other captains, of several nations, continued to Search for a North East Passage, until a Swede, exiled from Finland by a Russian tsar, became a Swedish and Russian hero, in his conquest of the Arctic Sea. In this itinerary, stories of the Search for a North East Passage, tell of the lengths of effort merchants exerted to reach the Far East in a quest to extend trade.

While in the White Sea, visit Archangel, seaport of the Arctic north. The story here is the seldom-told tale of Archangel Part II: 1918. After the end of World War I, Allies of Britain, France and the United States focused troops on tiny Archangel for a never-declared war on Russia. This war, left out of American history books, was all too vivid for young soldiers from Michigan and Wisconsin, sent to advance on Russia, in an effort to rouse peasants to rise and reseat the royal family. This Itinerary sails from the White Sea, back to the North Sea, with a stop at Murmansk, where the story is of Murmansk Convoys in World War II. Built as a military outpost, the story is Murmansk: The First 100 Years.

Next, sail west from the Arctic reaches of the North Sea, to Iceland and Greenland. Iceland, settled by Vikings, is where the story in the capital is: In Reykjavik Celebrate the World's Oldest Democracy. Vikings governed their new land, with an absence of royals, in a system of representative democracy, that became a model for the civilized world. There is so much more to Iceland, than a venue from which to view the Northern Lights. Then sail to Greenland, where the story is mapping Greenland in the Fram.

This Itinerary ends with the question still debated of: Who discovered North America, Leif Erikson, or Christopher Columbus? Read the story of the Discovery of the End of the Old and Beginning of the New World, then come to your own conclusion. The stories in Cruise through History are offered to add depth of knowledge, that will increase enjoyment of travels to ports of the world. Read, travel and enjoy!

CTH

14 | Cruise Through History – Itinerary XII Ports of the North Sea

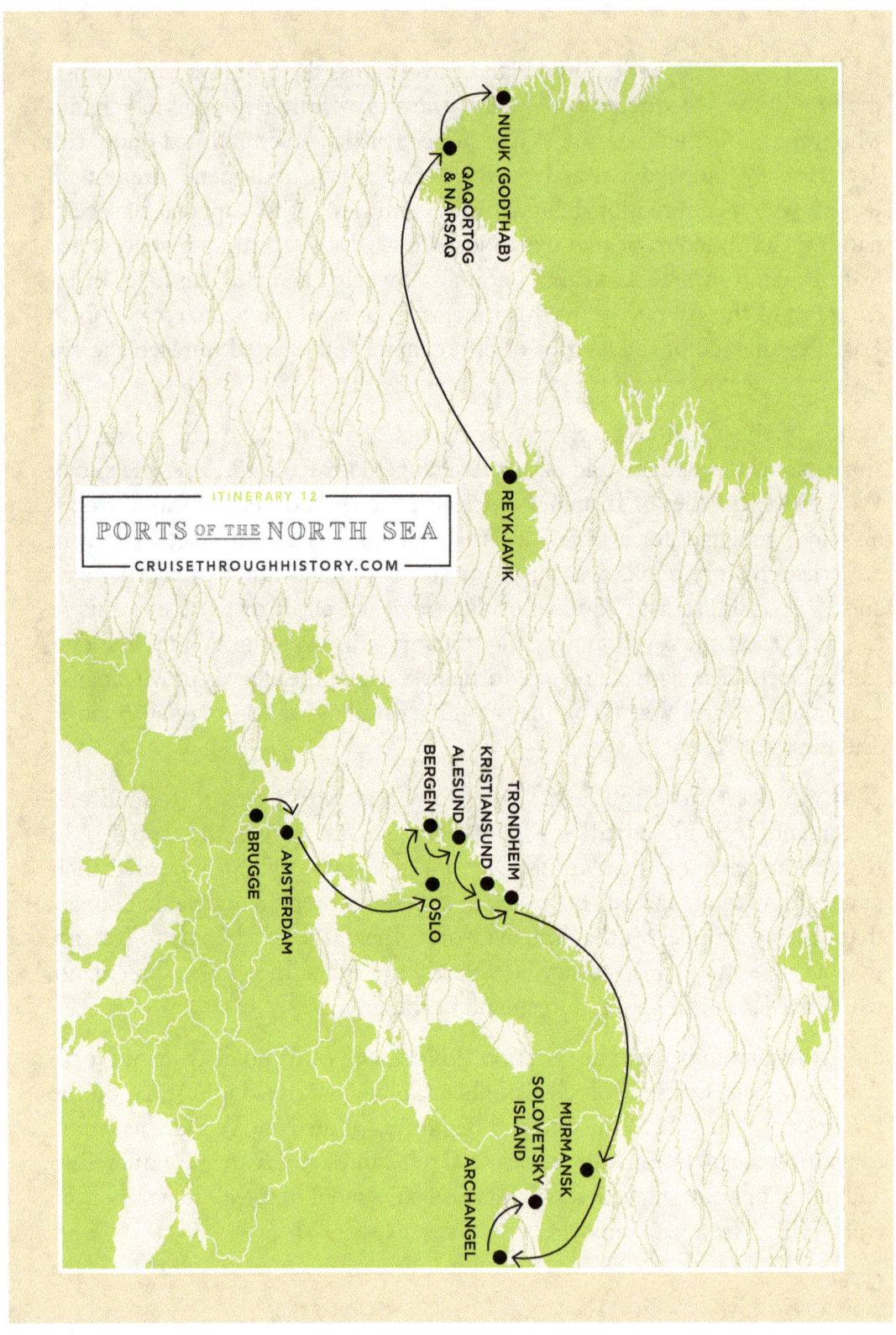

Cruise Through History
Itinerary XII

Timeline | cruisethroughhistory.com

Ancient to Viking Era
Up to – 11th c

Trolls
Viking Ships
Birchlegs
Viking Chess
Reykjavik
Greenland

Medieval to Renaissance
12th – 15th c

Brugge
Amsterdam
Trondheim
Saga Fall Hansa

Age Discovery and Explorers
16th – 18th c

Rembrandt Amsterdam
Flam Fjords
Tulips/Chocolate
Oslo Fjords
NE Passage
Archangel

Recent History
19th c   20th c

Flanders Fields
Poppies
Vigeland Oslo
Nobel
Art Bergen
Murmansk
Archangel 1918
Map Greenland

Brugge Belfry Market Square

BELGIUM
BRUGGE: MEDIEVAL WORLD METROPOLIS

Immediately upon arriving in the city of Brugge, visitors realize this is a special place. Visitors begin walking tours on Market Square, the Grote Markt, where buildings are massive, beautiful and truly old as they are unique. Walking from Market Square down the street to Burg Square, the original heart of the city, the building scape does not change. Everywhere in view are more buildings of the medieval era, thirteenth and fourteenth century, well preserved, numerous and lovely. Look down back streets, in courtyards, across canals; the view is the same. Brugge is a real medieval city, not a reconstruction. It is also, THE medieval city. For centuries of the early medieval era, Brugge was the major seaport of Europe. This is no mere walled medieval town. Brugge[1] was a metropolis.

The story of Brugge is one of international commerce on a grand scale. Sitting at the east to west access of Europe to England, Brugge received spice and silk from the Silk Road. The north to south route of trade brought herring and fur from Norway and Russia, to the extent of the North Sea and Baltic Sea, for transit to France. France sent wine north. Brugge was the economic center of the European medieval world. There were no Dark Ages in Brugge. It was lively and wealthy.

Today cruise visitors to Belgium dock at the commercial port of Zeebrugge. The drive to the city of Brugge is about an hour, about the same time sixteenth century residents of Brugge spent on a barge down the canal from Brugge to Damme, for the same reason. All three cities are, or were, water access economies. When the river Zwin silted, curtailing access to Brugge, Damme was built down river. When Damme was left without water access, the port moved closer to the sea.

---

[1] Brugge or Bruges? Bruges is the Dutch name of the city. Brugge is regarded as Flemish. This volume will use Brugge as the city is located in the Flemish area of Belgium.

The story of Brugge can be told, in part, through its buildings, so wonderfully preserved. Buildings are only the tangible part of the city story. The intangible spirit of residents is also part of the story. Residents of Brugge identified with their city and privileges in city residency. In an age prior to nationalism, when the majority of people worked as peasants on the land of their lord, residents of an independent city of world commerce held freedoms worth fighting to protect. The story of Brugge must also be told through its people; a weaver, butcher, painter and lord, to complete a picture of life in this special place, at the height of its vibrancy.

Brugge was spared destruction in both world wars, despite intense fighting on nearby Flanders Fields. Neutrality of Belgium in World War II did not spare Brugge occupation by German troops. The inland position of the city, its nightmare in an age of sea commerce, rendered it of no strategic consequence in times of international warfare and bombing. Brugge is preserved as a grand city of the medieval era, enjoying a second life as a destination of world travelers. To appreciate Brugge as a gift of insight to life eights centuries past, go armed with a little story of its buildings and its people.

Looking Down Dijver River to Church of Our Lady

City Center of World Commerce

In 50 BCE, Europe was part of the Roman world. Although Julius Caesar kept a headquarters at Trier, today a German city on the Moselle River near Luxembourg, his goal was to look west as far as rivers could take him. Where rivers ended, he built roads. During the time of Caesar, the River Zwin flowed to the North Sea. From the Belgic coast, Caesar went to England, to Colchester. That is another story. On the Belgic side of the Channel, the area of Brugge was a protected port. Belgic Gaul, the future Belgium, was a port in the Roman supply line. Belgic farmers supplied Romans.

Roman dominance in the Low Countries, today Belgium and Netherlands, lasted to around 455 CE.[2] Romans created infrastructure, supply lines and communication links, necessary to control of vast territory. When Roman control receded to Rome, it bequeathed trade routes that endured.

Mundane evolution of trade is too bland a history to introduce such a grand city as Brugge. For an appropriate, colorful, knights in shining armor version, city history begins with Baldwin of the Iron Arm in the ninth century. Baldwin is sometimes regarded as a Frankish adventurer, therefore German. His birthplace is in France.[3] In the ninth century, kings of France had little control over Gaul, much of which was aspirational territory for kings in Paris.

Baldwin became the first Count of Flanders after he abducted Judith, the beautiful daughter of Charles the Bald, king of France.[4] Besides seething anger at Baldwin, for whom Charles sought excommunication from the pope, the other source of grief for Charles was Viking king Rorik, who set up camp on the North Sea coast in the Zwin River Delta. What Charles lacked in hair, he more than compensated for with plenty of savvy. He bestowed on Baldwin, as a wedding present, the Belgic domain on the Zwin, occupied by Vikings. Vikings were an obstruction to North Sea trade.

---

[2] See generally for a deep history of the Low Countries, Paul Arblaster, A History of the Low Countries, second edition, Palgrave/Macmillan, 2012.

[3] Baldwin, 1st Count of Flanders, born around 830 and died of certainty in 879.

[4] See more of the story of Charles the Bald and adventures of Hairy, in Cruise through History Itinerary I London to Rome, 2014, Port of Barcelona, How Hairy and Baldy Founded Barcelona.

Baldwin proved his worth, when he stationed his knights in deserted Roman forts, from which he challenged Vikings to sail elsewhere. He built his nuptial castle at a wide spot on a circle of river, which he called Burg. Trade resumed and Burg prospered. Burg became the heart of Brugge, a metropolis of commerce. The wide spot on the water, *brygghia*, became the port of Brugge, now known as Lover's Lake. The pope and Charles forgave Baldwin. Swans on Lover's Lake came later.

Town Hall (left)Burg Square

By the twelfth century, Brugge was an important founding member of the Hansa League.[5] The Hansa League began in Lübeck, Germany, as an international trade consortium, under the Law of Lübeck, the first code of international law. The League began the Renaissance of commerce in the Baltic and North Sea, effectively ending feudalism for its almost two hundred trading stations. Hansa founded cities, held its own army and transferred power from disparate nobles to merchants with ships. It was a new world. In this world, Brugge was a capital city of commerce.

---

[5] For more on the Hanseatic League, see Rostock of the Hanseatic League, in Cruise through History Itinerary XI Ports of the Baltic Sea, 2018.

Baldwin is honored by edifices on Burg Square, begun with wealth brought to Brugge from its Hanseatic alliance. Baldwin's castle does not survive. His St. Donation Cathedral was dismantled brick-by-brick in the 1790s during the French Revolution, when France annexed Flanders. Miraculously, Basilica of the Holy Blood survived. The Basilica was consecrated in 1150, when Derek of Alsace, another Count of Flanders, returned from a Crusade with a cloth containing the blood of Christ.

Normally, a relic, that is bones of a saint, were required to consecrate a cathedral. The Holy Blood was a relic deserving of a church with immediate basilica designation. Through the ages to today, the cloth, in its glass vial, in a gold holder, has been protected by guardians from the Confraternity of the Holy Blood. The vial is on display at special times. On Ascension Day, the vial of the Holy Blood has an honored place in the procession through the square.

Basilica of the Holy Blood

Palace of Justice

The Basilica of the Holy Blood is a time capsule of the development of the core city from Burg Square to a city center at the much larger Market Square. The first level of the basilica is Romanesque in style, with squat pillars and dark corridors of stone. The second level, built centuries later, is in the Gothic Renaissance of Venice, with emerald stone and gold decoration. Outside, the fifteenth century façade looks more appropriate for a Venetian city than Flemish.

Also on Burg Square are the fourteenth century Town Hall and the still functioning Palace of Justice. The youngest building on the square, the Old Recorder's House, dates to early 1500s. The Town Hall is a masterpiece of Gothic Brick architecture, seen in Rostock and cities of the Hansa era. The façade held rows of statues, many removed in the 1790s by French soldiers. Rather than fill spaces with reproductions, the spaces are left empty.

Inside the Town Hall, or Stadhuis, on the second level is a majestic meeting room, completed in 1402, with a stalactite ceiling of downward spires. If the governing body is important, this Gotische Zaal, Gothic Room, is where they meet. During control by Napoleonic France, a painting of the *Burgomaster receiving Napoleon on his visit to Brugge* was installed in the Gothic Room. The room holds twelve wall murals on which the history of Brugge from 1150 to 1433 is displayed.

Brugge outgrew its first city square, so development wandered down the short Breidelstraat to surround Market Square, the Grote Markt with thirteenth century gabled houses. Market halls were built in the 1200s. Towering above the halls is the iconic Belfry of Brugge, begun in the early 1200s. Climb three hundred and sixty-six steps for a city view from the belfry tower.[6]

Brugge grew to be one of the largest European cities from the twelfth to fifteenth century. The central city expanded along the Djiver River, toward the port at the junction of the Zwin as it connected to the ring river, that fills internal canals. The confluence point, across the freeway from the Brugge Central Train Station today is known as Minnewater, or Lover's Lake. Along the route out of central town to the port, Knights of Saint John erected a hospital in the twelfth century. Knights and town nobles returned to this building from crusades to the Holy Land. Today the hospital continues the historic function. It is also venue of the Memling Museum.

Also just beyond the city center is a tiny, walled city-within-the-city of modest bungalows. This is Beguinage, where widows, and never-married women of Brugge, lived like secular nuns, since 1245, in the security of an enclosure, with the freedom to come and go. Today Beguinage is home to Benedictine Nuns. The tiny town is open for visitors in controlled hours.

---

[6] The Tower view is 272 feet above the square.

Spirited City: Matines, Golden Spurs, Swans and Saintly Women

Monument Market Square

For so many buildings of a city to last eight hundred years required substantial investment by building owners and the skill of craftsmen. As a Hansa city, commerce was primary. Military pursuits of lords and kings, that depleted treasuries and left estates in ruin, were not the activity of merchants of this city of the world. City leaders of Brugge meant their homes to endure.

Builders of edifices of Brugge also possessed a spirit of place, bolstered by the strength of bricks. Brugge was a city where no king was in control. French counts of Burgundy, kings of France or Austria, might consider Brugge in their domain. Their rule did not surmount Law of Lübeck. When pushed to subjugate themselves, people of Brugge rebelled. Their freedom was precious.

French royals pushed tradesmen of Brugge too far at the end of the thirteenth century. In May 1302, they rebelled. Led by Jan Breydel, a butcher, and Pieter de Cominek, a weaver, artisans of several guilds had no patience for lords attempting to control their markets, prices and guild functions. In what has become known as Matines of Bruges, wealthy lords and controlling merchants were killed early in the morning.[7]

Knights of France responded two months later with a mounted army, clad in shining armor. Inexperienced in battle, yet determined, angry tradesmen defending their freedoms and privileges as citizens of Brugge, faced the knights. In the resulting Battle of the Golden Spurs, Flemish fighters were out-armed in the face of charging cavalry. The craftsmen stepped aside, at the last crucial moment, exposing a canal to horsemen unable to stop in mid-gallop. The knights plunged to their death by drowning in a Brugge canal, while encased in heavy armor. According to legend, tradesmen of Brugge retrieved seven hundred pairs of golden spurs from vanquished knights.

Brugge calmed when a city charter was written, affirming rights to produce and trade in the marketplace, to which all kings and lords taking dominion over Flanders were required to sign. The charter was stored safely, visibly and ceremoniously in the Belfry Tower until late in the fifteenth century. On Market Square a monument to Breydel and Cominek was erected in 1902.

More than century later an Austrian Hapsburg Royal, Maximilian, forgot the lessons of Matines and the Battle of the Golden Spurs. People tolerated Maximilian in deference to his much-loved wife Maria of Burgundy. After Maria died in a hunting accident, there was no barrier to hostility of the citizens of Brugge for their overbearing royal.

One of the opulent residences on Market Square, Cranenburg House, was often a party venue for elegant people able to view festivals on the square without mingling with rabble. In 1488, the castle-like mansion became a prison for Maximilian. Angry citizens held Maximilian prisoner in this choice location, so that he could view execution on the square of his Austrian henchmen and favorite courtiers. Once released, Maximilian demanded that swans be maintained on the lake and canals of Brugge, in perpetuity, in memory of his favorite courtiers. Swans are forever present.

---

[7] Matines are early morning prayers in a monastery, hence the name of the revolt.

Hans Memling Museum

Hans Memling arrived in Brugge from Germany in 1450.[8] He was drawn by the reputation of Flemish painters, using pigment in oils to paint precise and intricate works, now known as Flemish Primitives. Painters of works taking months to a year to complete required wealthy patrons, which Brugge held in abundance. Part of Memling lore holds that he was a young soldier treated for wounds in the Hospital of the Knights of St. John in Brugge, which garnered his everlasting affection. There is no doubt that Memling was prolific, prosperous in Brugge and appreciated during his lifetime across Europe for excellent commissions adorning churches.

---

[8] Hans Memling born in Germany in 1430 and died in Brugge in 1494. Patrons included Medici. Memling joined Rogier Van der Weyden (1399-1464), Jan van Eyck (d. 1441), Hugo van der Goes (1440-1482), Petrus Christus (1410-1475), Gerard David (d.1523), Dirck Bouts (1415-1475) and Hieronymous Bosch (1450-1494), as masters of Flemish art.

The prize possession of the Hospital of the Knights of St. John Brugge today is a three-foot-long box, reputed to be the Reliquary of Saint Ursula, a much-revered saint by women of Brugge; nuns and laywomen. In 1489, two nuns at the Hospital requested Memling paint the reliquary. To understand the honor bestowed on Memling, late in his life, is to know the story of Saint Ursula.

Ursula was the beautiful daughter of a fourth century king of Brittany, the Celtic arm of France. The son of a pagan king in England pressed Ursula to marry him. To stall her suitor's advances, Ursula agreed to marry only after she and her intended traveled on a pilgrimage to Rome, where the groom could be baptized by the pope. Ursula traveled with ten maidens, each of whom were attended by one thousand virgins. Ursula, her ten maidens and eleven thousand virgins became well-known as they traveled across France to Rome. In Cologne, an old woman outside a church told Ursula she was traveling to her martyrdom. Ursula stood by her faith.

In Rome, the pope performed baptism on all pagans in the party, then joined Ursula and her companions for their return home. As they neared Cologne, Attila and his infamous Huns attacked the travelers, killing all the maidens and virgins except Ursula. Attila told Ursula he would spare her if she would marry him. She refused. Attila killed her. Citizens of Cologne rose in furry and attacked the Huns.

In 975 a monk, at the Abby of Saint Omer, near Calais, France, wrote the story of Ursula in an illuminated manuscript. Fame of Ursula spread through France. Two centuries later, a mass grave holding the bones of thousands of young women was found near Cologne. The story of Saint Ursula was still popular in fifteenth century Brugge, when two nuns made their request of Memling.[9]

Memling painted the entire story of Ursula, in minute detail on six tiny panels of the reliquary. Included are travels to Rome of the eleven thousand virgins, the stop in Cologne, the baptisms and dark clouds of an ominous

---

[9] Keepers of the Ursula story at the Hospital of the Knights of Saint John in Brugge today suggest that Christopher Columbus named the Virgin Islands in reverence to Saint Ursula.

prediction hovering over the party on their return to Cologne. In Brugge, at the Groeninge Museum near the Hospital, the Ursula story is seen on a larger nine panel work of other fifteenth century artists. The tiny reliquary loses none of the story due to size.

Another favorite saint of women of Brugge was Saint Catherine of Alexandria. Saint Catherine earned her veneration by facing Romans with unshakable faith. Roman generals sent fifty pagan scholars to turn Catherine from her faith. She converted all fifty to Christianity. When Romans bound Catherine and rolled a razor-edged wheel of death toward her, the wheel burst into pieces as it became near to Catherine. Finally, Romans beheaded the lovely young woman for her obstinance. Saint Catherine is remembered in Brugge by the painting of the *Mystic Marriage of St. Catherine*, by Memling in 1479, for the Hospital of the Knights of St. John in Brugge.

Clearly, men and women of Brugge have a legacy of bold action in defense of their freedoms. From the first count of Flanders, who married for love, through the ages of independent artisans, artists and city leaders, Brugge remained a city of commerce, beholden to no sovereign. The city grew, without a planned grid, as a display of wealth brought by individual accomplishment.

Dead City and New Life

Brugge was home to craftsmen, cloth and lace trade and international commerce for five centuries from the eleventh century. Heads of wealthy families became virtual lords of Brugge, in a line of merchant royalty. Representative of the lords of Brugge was the family Gruuthuse, which held the exalted title for two centuries. The Gruuthuse clan members advised dukes of Burgundy, who wielded more power than the French king from 1388 to 1479. Louis Gruuthuse, at age eighty, arranged the marriage of Maximilian of Austria to Maria of Burgundy. Serving dukes and mastering trade made the Gruuthuse clan wealthy beyond royals. The Gruuthuse home and thousands of its accoutrement are now open to the public as a museum.

Swans on Lovers' Lake

The Gruuthuse clan were patrons of the Church of Our Lady, at the end of Djiver canal, just beyond city center, and across the street from the Hospital of Knights of Saint John. Built in the Gothic style of the twelfth century, the church can boast of having the tallest spire in the city at three hundred and sixty feet, and possessing the only white Carrera marble statue by Michelangelo outside of Italy. It is in this church that the effigy of beloved Maria of Burgundy lounges on her mausoleum, above a window in the floor, exposing her tiny, plain coffin.[10] The Gruuthuse home has a window in the home chapel adjoining the church, so the family could view the wealth of the Church of Our Lady as an extension of their home.

The spigot of life was literally turned off for Brugge at the end of the fifteenth century. For most of the fourteenth century, city leaders watched in horror as the Zwin filled with sand. An initial solution was to build an auxiliary port town of Damme, erected from the early fifteenth century, from which goods came to Brugge by canal. By the end of the fifteenth century Brugge was dead.

---

[10] Maria's heart is in Antwerp in the mausoleum of her mother.

Wealthy residents moved east to Antwerp, which later suffered the same fate as Brugge. Catholics in Netherlands came south to Antwerp and Brugge, when Protestants held the north of the Lowlands and revolted from Spanish-Catholic rule. Post-fifteenth century residents of Brugge had little income. Buildings of later eras were modest. Brick Gothic grandeur ended with loss of the Zwin.

The Industrial Revolution of the eighteenth and nineteenth century was seen in interior cities of Belgium and other cities of Europe. Brugge remained an untouched time-capsule of Medieval life. Lack of urban renewal, in the absence of population growth, left Brugge mostly preserved.

Today, benign preservation makes Brugge a visitor favorite. Brugge is not a reconstruction, nor did it require archaeological removal of layers of fill to be revealed. Visitors have such easy access to an experience in a Medieval Metropolis, that the fortune of a new life for the city is taken for granted. Cafes, shops and hotels have a population today that does not quite reach Brugge at its Medieval height, even though streets may seem crowded with tour groups in peak season.

Paintings of Memling, majesty of buildings lining squares, and interiors of churches and the Town Hall impress visitors of today as they did visitors of the fourteenth century. Brugge is a city that celebrated, and took pains to preserve, individual liberty from its inception. The Dark Ages of Medieval times will never seem dark, once a visitor experiences Brugge.

Brugge Architecture

In Flanders Fields

Flanders Fields Tyne Cot Memorial Cemetery

As if by force of some diabolical cosmic energy, one area of real estate has drawn repeated, protracted and bloody battle to its site. This is Flanders Fields. Battles in the formation of modern Europe have come to climax on these fields over a period of two thousand years.

In the broader sense, Flanders Fields comprise the low land, watershed of the Rhine, Maas, Waal, Ijzer and Leie Rivers. Low land rivers empty into the North Sea. Land area crosses modern-day boundaries of France, Belgium, Netherlands and Germany. The principality of Luxembourg falls within this terrain. Beaches run from Normandy in the south, to Dunkirk, Flanders, Zeeland shallows, to north west Germany.

The discrete area known as Flanders is low land of Flemish west Belgium, where people speak Dutch/Flemish. East Belgium, so called Wallonia, is dominated by French speakers. The capital district of Brussels is politically correct bi-lingual. That one small country is so culturally and linguistically divided, such that even beer choice is contentious, begins to describe the ethos of Flanders Fields.

Romans, Franks, who were early Germans, Vikings and Germans have battled for control of the area, or for access to trade across the water-land-water route. French, German, Austrian and Spanish kings historically held feudal control of the rich farmland. During the War of Spanish Succession, France occupied the area. French took the opportunity for a border area during the War of Austrian Succession, then invaded during the Napoleonic Wars at the beginning of the nineteenth century. Germany held some or all of the Low Lands in the twentieth century.

Flanders Fields were the desire of Pepin and his son, Charlemagne. From their control, Saxons fled to England in the eighth century. On these fields Napoleon met his Waterloo. Britain and Commonwealth forces held back German advance during World War I in the infamous Battle of Passchendaele. In World War II, Allied troops landed on beaches of Normandy and headed across Flanders Fields. The last major German offensive of the Western Front, across the Ardennes, included siege of Bastogne, in what became known as the Battle of the Bulge.

After all the battles occurring, with frequency, since 58 BCE, the many cemeteries and war memorials in the area is expected. Unexpected, is the number of reconstructed medieval buildings that have been repeatedly salvaged from piles of bricks. In these buildings, history of the people of Flanders Fields perseveres. These are places visitors enjoy, not to celebrate war, rather, to enjoy the victory of peace over dissention. In this place, human determination is a marvel.

In Flanders Fields some history is brutal. All history is preserved in the name of those who fought for king and country. The message here is that kings and rulers pass in time, while people remain, retake their farms and progress, until next time. Much of this history is available to cruise travelers from the port of Zeebrugge. This is the story of this strategic place.

Strategic Low Countries

To understand why this section of a continent, in all the world, has been the scene of so much bloodshed, consider the geography and geology of the place. Low Country coasts begin where the English Channel opens to the North Sea. The land is flat, as rivers slowly open into deltas of shallows. There is no ring of protective mountains. Perennial floods fertilize ancient soils. This is prime farmland. This is the land of tulips, dykes and endless views of flat green.

Early people traveled by rafts and eventually flat-bottomed boats. Making connections in commerce came early to this part of Europe. By the twelfth century, elaborate buildings on massive village squares were built. Guilds occupied cloth halls and meat halls. Cities of Belgium were more densely populated than cities of England, or much of France or Germany.

Brugge was an early Hansa League city of the thirteenth century, connecting its markets to London, Lübeck and Tallinn. Easily accessible to ships throughout history, Low Country ports were situated at the confluence of trade from the

Silk Road to England, east to west, and from north Baltic and North Sea ports going south to Brugge. South of Brugge, French ports eagerly awaited ships carrying goods from the farthest reaches of the world.

Romans crossing the channel from Europe to England, established supply lines, which became trade links, from the first century of the current era. Lowland looms sent cloth to England and Baltic ports, making Brugge, Antwerp, and even Ypres, early ports of trade across the English Channel and the North Sea in the tenth century. Reputedly, bricks to build the Tower of London in 1278, came from Flemish kilns. When Romans retreated to Rome in the fifth century of the current era, and Europe and England supposedly went into a Dark Age, international commerce enjoyed by Lowland cites brought it to an early Golden Age in the eleventh to fifteenth centuries.

Prosperity in trade gave residents of Brugge a broad view of peoples of the North Sea, rather than an insular sense of kingdom. Early ports of North Sea coasts were a mélange of diverse peoples, speaking various languages, all joined in commerce. Belgium, early to international trade, came late to nationalism. Today, people of Belgium see themselves as people of the world.

Fortress Walls of Ypres

Walls, forts and indicia of land control came after centers of commerce developed, as projects of French and Spanish overlords. French took control in the fourteenth century, Austria in the fifteenth century and Spain in the sixteenth century. The result is that domestic structures, such as homes and guild halls, reflect Flemish or Dutch architecture, while fort walls are the work of French military architect Marshal Vauban, or Spanish builders.

Vauban was the architect for Louis XIV. His designs can be seen across France and Belgium, then replicated in the New World. Classic Vauban design are star-shaped forts of complex layers of walls, creating a protected space within, even when landscape is flat and openly accessible. Spanish military constructions favored high stone walls, of massive squares. In contrast to their military occupiers, tradesmen and guildsmen worked under stair-step lined, steeply pitched roofs, in buildings of several floors with tall windows. An example of Flemish jewel box buildings of light, surrounded by Vauban battlements can be seen in Ypres, known as Ieper in Flemish.[11]

Twelfth century counts of Flanders lived in the ominous, dark stone Medieval castle at Ghent. It was built to protect monks of surrounding abbeys from the last Viking raids. The castle was home to successive overlords, more interested in protecting their personal assets. Today the Ghent Castle is best known for preservation of a Medieval castle and for its torture rooms. The river provides a natural moat. Long, winding streets of tall buildings in Ghent, have no apparent grid.[12] Troops of an aggressor could be lost here, or easily trapped. Vauban style walls were unnecessary. Ghent was too old and developed to be subject to Spanish city planning designs.

City walls of Brugge pre-date the French, as most were constructed by the end of the twelfth century. These walls could hardly be called a fortress. Walls formed a city boundary, as a line to defend from Vikings or pirates. Gates of

---

[11] Ieper is the town in Flanders Fields near where British and German troops drew their line during World War I, which became the Ieper Salient. Ieper, pronounced éper in Flemish, is known to English as Ypres, pronounced as wipers.

[12] John of Gaunt, as Ghent was known in England, was born in Ghent in 1340, third son of English king Edward III.

the city were an opportunity to regulate trade, control newcomers from entry during times of plague, or create a boundary for city government or taxes.[13]

History and demographics of the Lowlands rendered Brussels a natural venue for administrative offices of the twentieth century European Union. English is widely spoken in Brussels, where English language newspapers have large circulation. International currency has always been welcomed in Belgium, since herring of the Hanseatic League was established as a measure in trade.

Battles on Flanders Fields

Ypres Restored

---

[13] Those who lived within a city boundary, known as *bourgs*, for one year were known as *burghers* or *bourgeois*.

Reflecting on Belgium, the great travel writer Arthur Frommer once mused that Belgium was the battleground of other peoples' wars.[14] Never conquering, repeatedly conquered, pillaged and passed between sovereigns of other nations, the land was venue for wars of conflicts of other nations. People of the Lowlands were pawns in conflicts, not of their making, and from which they derived no beneficial interest.

In an early dynasty of kings from the area now known as Germany, known in the post-Roman era as land of the Franks, emerged Clovis and Pepin, the father of Charlemagne. In the fourth century, prior to arrival of Vikings, Frankish kings easily swept through the Lowlands, across Flanders Fields. In their wake, they left a political structure of counts, to lord over peasant farmers.

Counts built castles, such as in Ghent and Namur. They established feudal fiefdoms. Eventually, strong counts rebelled against control from Aachen, Germany. Absent centralized control, counts fought among themselves. Their weak state made towns vulnerable to invasions of Vikings, arriving in the ninth to eleventh centuries.

Vikings disrupted supply centers, undercut wealth of counts, and left the Lowlands open to entrepreneurs. Independent merchants, with a few ships, became the burgeoning Hansa League. The League was the death of feudal Europe, for those with access to port cities.

Wealth in Lowland cities aroused attention of powerful kings of England, France, Austria and Spain. In 1383, King Edward III of England sent his son, the Black Knight, to siege Ghent. In contention with kings of England, kings of France conquered the Low Countries in 1384.

Austria battled France over Flanders Fields in 1477, establishing Austrian Hapsburg rule. By inheritance, the king of Spain received the Lowlands, which became Spanish Lowlands from 1555 to 1701. Spanish king Philip II, former brother-in-law and attempted nemesis to Elizabeth I of England, with his two failed Spanish Armadas, demanded the Calvinist Lowlands be uniformly Catholic.

---

[14] See Arthur Frommer, A Masterpiece Called Belgium, Prentice Hall, New York, 1989, at 3 and 9.

War of religion was the undoing of Philip. Netherlands broke free, remained Protestant and prospered as refuge of Jews and Protestants fleeing the wrath of Philip. Catholic Belgium lost stature in international trade. Amsterdam became wealthy, while Antwerp declined. At this time, the Hansa League was in decline, the victim of competition and independence of port cities.

The next invasion of Flanders Fields came in 1701, when France invaded, to claim turf, while Spain was distracted in the civil war of Spanish succession. The flatlands were periodic battle venues, until 1713, when the Treaty of Utrecht placed the Lowlands back under Austrian rule.

Peace in Flanders Fields was of short duration. Twenty-seven years later, Austria was in flux over its own royal line of succession. France took the opportunity to invade and occupy Flanders Fields. Military occupation enabled French benefits of trade. French royals had other distractions.

Napoleon rose in French ranks through military prowess and ambition. In his march across Europe, Flanders Fields was an early conquest. By 1801, the Low Countries, once again united Netherlands and Belgium, became French.

In his encore military performance, once escaped from prison on the island of Elba, Napoleon lost his charm. On Flanders Fields, at Waterloo, in June 1815, Napoleon was outmaneuvered by the British army of the Duke of Wellington and Prussian army under Gebhard von Blücher. Napoleon's unification of the Netherlands came to haunt him, as the unified nation took the field with seventeen thousand troops. Next stop for the former emperor was the distant island of Saint Helena. In 1831, Belgium and Netherlands became separate nations.

A century later, Flanders Fields were the scene of bloody battles of World War I. British and Belgium troops faced German troops across a line, the Ypres Salient, through the middle of Flanders Fields. Trenches cut across former farmers' fields, were rendered swamps of mud by shelling. Compounding the horror of war, in fear, layers of corpses, cold and wet terrain, was the first use of chemical warfare, when Germans sent chlorine gas searing through trenches.

Slight attention is often given to the role of troops of Belgium in the war. In fact, troops of Belgium King Albert I, known as the soldier king, were instrumental in holding the line of the Salient. Across the line lie France and the English Channel. Belgium held the line for four years.

In a small stretch of land, dubbed Essex Farm by British Commonwealth troops, opposing forces of German troops and Allied troops, of British, French and Belgium forces, were at a short distance across a narrow canal, formerly used to control water on crops. Five major battles occurred at this place. In the first battle, a truce at Christmas in 1914, gave troops the opportunity to sing carols across the lines. At Houplines in France, opposing forces stopped action long enough to play ball, young man to young man, without the politics that later swallowed them.[15]

The Third Battle of Ypres, also known as Battle of Passchendaele, occurred from July 31, to November 10, 1917. Combined casualties of this single battle were at the least over half a million men. The full extent of loss was never fully determined. American troops arrived after the battle.[16]

In fall 1918, British, French and Belgium forces were joined by General John J. Pershing and American troops. The Allies overran their supply wagons as they marched across Flanders Fields. By the time the last ordinance exploded on October 14, one million, seven hundred thousand troops died in Ypres Salient, in combined troop losses of both sides.[17] This did not include the civilian cost of lives. The war was touted as the Great War and the war to end all wars.

Peace was short-lived in Flanders Fields. In 1940, German forces swept across the Low Country, until all in the path from Germany, to include France, was under German occupation and control. The liberation of Belgium was protracted and bloody. In the Ardennes, Germany made its last offensive attempt to reach Antwerp and change the direction of the war to a German victory.[18]

---

[15] Read the passionate story of the Christmas Match, by Pehr Thermaenius, Uniform Press, London, 2014.
[16] Read Lyn Macdonald, Passchendaele, Penguin Books, 1993, 2013 edition, of Michael Joseph's manuscript, They Called It Passchendaele, 1978.
[17] See, Martin Marix Evans, Pitkin Guide of Ypres: In War and Peace, Pitkin Publishing, UK, undated, purchased 2018.
[18] The area of Ardennes includes Luxembourg, Liege and Bastogne.

The action became known as the Battle of the Bulge, fought from December 14, 1944 to January 16, 1945. In the offensive Germany faced predominantly US troops. Strategic aim of German forces was to isolate British forces from American troops, by driving a wedge through Allied forces. Opposing generals were Field Marshal Gerd von Rundstedt and General Dwight D. Eisenhower.

The US army under General George S. Patton reached Bastogne on December 26. From there, Allies launched a counter offensive. Heroics in battles in this eventful month have been subject of novels and movies. In the end, two hundred thousand troops were lost, less than half to the Allies. Strategically on the ground, the battle was not decisive in the war. It was, however, a blow to German morale. Germany was losing momentum and was unable to turn itself toward victory.

For residents of Flanders Fields, once again in the midst of a war fought by super powers to its east and west, and across the Channel, their farms and cities were overrun by a war in which they were an involuntary host. Belgium's people know the extreme cost of war, in full force view. They are least likely to be belligerents.

After the war, once again Belgium rebuilt its economy. The port of Zeebrugge is one of the largest commercial ports in the world today. Cruise ships send busloads of guests to Brugge and Ypres, for a day of immersion in peaceful Flanders Fields.

Fertile Farms and Cemeteries Today

In Flanders Fields, on a visit from the cruise port of Zeebrugge, is an excursion through sites of the Great War. In Ypres, the Cloth Hall is now the Flanders Fields Museum, where poppies are sold and the story of World War I is well told in compelling exhibits. Visitors typically enter the town through the Menin Gate. Completed in 1927, the Menin Gate War Memorial cuts through earthworks of Vauban fortress walls. Carved in the interior vault of the memorial are names of 54,896 troops missing in action, or for whom no known grave site exits from action in Flanders Fields, up to August 16, 1917. Each evening, Last Call is played and a moment of reverence is observed. Relatives of fallen soldiers come to this place to mourn, when there is no other site.

Menin Gate entrance to Ypres

Detail Menin Gate

Names Inscribed in Menin Gate

Beyond Ypres, though Flanders Fields, there are one hundred and seventy-three British Commonwealth, six Belgium, seventeen French and four German cemeteries. Commonwealth casualties occurring from August 16, 1917, to the end of the war, for whom no known grave site exists, are inscribed on the memorial wall at Tyne Cot Cemetery at Passchendaele. There are 34,957 names, additional to those on Menin Gate. Tyne Cot is the largest of Commonwealth cemeteries in Flanders Fields. Headstones are inscribed with maple leaf for the Canadian graves.

Travel through Flanders Fields is a sobering excursion into the past. In Ypres, where Medieval buildings have been reconstructed to their pre-war glory days, visitors enjoy resilience of Belgium's people. Belgium, forced to host humankind at its worst, is voluntary host to visitors interested in understanding a part of history, not to be repeated.

Flags on the Field

Poppies of Remembrance

Poppies of Remembrance

Around the world, little red paper, or felt, poppies are on lapels everywhere on days of military service remembrance. Nations have different remembrance days, often in early November, the time of signing Armistice ending World War I, on November 11, 1918.[19] The poppy as a symbol is universal. Before there were color ribbons to denote support of causes, there were poppies.

---

[19] In the United States, Memorial Day comes in May, a priority of remembrance for World War II, in addition to November 11, Veterans' Day, remembrance of all veterans of military service.

Although a poppy, as symbol of remembrance is well recognized, few wearing the symbol know from where the poppy came and why. In a culture of marketing tools and fashionable symbols, it is often simply accepted. To those who have given national service, the meaning behind the poppy is as important as solidarity in the showing of respect is appreciated.

Poppies, like other flowers, can be cultivated. They grow wild on recently disturbed soils, where winds distribute seeds to grow randomly on a grassy landscape. Fields of former military action are natural poppy environments. In the aftermath of battles, and the horrors of death, the poppy grows, creating a soft floral mass in contrast to recent events. Poppies are the first memorials of a battlefield. Without regard to names of the fallen, or nationality, they grow in masses.

Major John McCrae was a surgeon attached to the 1st Brigade of Canadian Field Artillery, during some of the bloodiest battles of World War I. Later, historians confirmed in a broad sense the horror he saw from the midst of carnage. Soldiers dying on his operating table had names he knew from home. When his close friend died, McCrae paused just long enough to write a memorial poem. The poem, *In Flanders Fields*, was three short stanzas of pain and remembrance.

McCrae's poem was a call for aid to soldiers in the field. He caught the contrast between horror of battle and poppies growing from the bases of crosses of graves in the field. He immortalized the poppy as the irony of all he saw and felt.

Three years after McCrae's poem was penned, Armistice was signed. A worker for the Overseas Young Men's Christian Association (YMCA) found a small fund to purchase poppies and sell them to be worn in tribute to fallen service personnel. Emotions were strong. Poppies proliferated.

Reflect a few moments on the story of Major McCrea, his poem and the symbol of the poppy. Few symbols of respect are as joined in meaning to the remembrance served. Know your poppy.

A Human Face of War Fatalities

Medical Bunker at Essex Farm

As a young man in Ontario, Canada, John McCrea suffered asthma and chose poetry over sports. Born in 1872, he could not resist volunteering to serve in the royal army in South Africa in 1899, with other young men from Guelph, his home town. He led an artillery battery. By 1904, the horrors of war overcame youthful patriotism and group spirit. He resigned his commission.[20]

Before military service, McCrae studied medicine. He did his residency at Johns Hopkins Hospital in Baltimore, Maryland. To relieve stress of treating terminally ill patients, McCrae wrote poetry. One of his early poems, *A Song of Comfort*, was written in tribute to a first love, who died at age eighteen.[21] McCrae never married.

---

[20] For a detailed biography, see John F. Prescott, In Flanders Fields: The Story of John McCrae, University of Toronto Press, 1985.
[21] Herwig Verlayen, In Flanders Fields: John McCrae, Poem and the Poppy, Deklaproos, Brugge, 2012, at 13.

In the first years of the twentieth century, McCrae immersed himself in medical studies. In Montreal, he was a hospital resident pathologist. In London, McCrea, often speaking and teaching medicine, was admitted to the Royal College of Physicians.[22] Cruise guests on ocean liners from Canada to England and Europe had the company of McCrae, who worked as a ship's physician to enable his enjoyment of cruises. In quiet moments on deck, he could be seen writing poetry and sketching scenes from his travels, or writing sections of several medical texts published by 1912.

In 1914 war was declared. Known as the Great War, or War to End all Wars, now known as World War I, once again young men volunteered for military service. At age forty-two, McCrae was no longer young and enthusiastic. He felt that as a bachelor, and medically trained, he had an obligation to serve. He and his brother John joined with fifty thousand Canadians, headed to Europe.

Demarcation Line of Battle

---

[22] https://www.veterans.gc.ca/eng/remembrance/history/first-world-war/mccrae#mccrae3, last visited June 20, 2020.

Major McCrae was stationed at Ypres with the 1st Brigade Canadian Field Artillery. Working under impossible conditions, in the trenches with troops, he set up a medical triage bunker. During the Second Battle of Ypres, one of the deadliest of the war, McCrae wrote to his mother, that for seventeen days of the battle he never changed clothes, such was the press of casualties coming into his bunker.[23] Today, at the scene of battle, tour guides point out where soldiers shot above the medical bunker, literally rolled down the embankment to the door of McCrae's surgery.[24]

As in his experience as a soldier in South Africa, McCrea knew soldiers from his home town. He allowed himself a pause to stand graveside upon the death of his close friend, Lieutenant Alexis Helmer, where he said a poem. The next day, McCrae wrote the three stanzas, to keep in memory of his friend and as a plea for more support for troops in the field. That poem began, In *Flanders fields*.... It was submitted to the magazine Punch on December 8, 1915.[25]

Lieutenant Helmer was buried in a cemetery next to the field hospital. Where his grave was dug, poppies grew amid crosses recently placed to mark the graves of other soldiers, many of whom McCrea tried to keep alive. McCrae was struck by resilience of the delicate flower amidst carnage.

Soon after the Second Battle of Ypres, McCrae was rotated to the Canadian General Hospital near Boulogne, where he was promoted to Chief of Medical Services. The name of the facility gives it an aura of a fine hospital. In fact, the hospital was a cluster of field tents, without heat, or running water. In the winter, the hospital was moved to the bombed-out ruins of a Jesuit College. It was there that McCrea received casualties of the Third Battle of Ypres, also known as Passchendaele, the infamous bloody engagement, possibly the worst of World War I. For Lieutenant Colonel McCrae, the battles were an endless stream of horrific casualties, in a sea of carnage.

---

[23] Prescott, at 77.
[24] The area of the bunkers and cemetery is known as Essex Farm, a name assigned to the area by English troops to evoke a little bit of home at the front. Verleyen, at 22.
[25] Matthew Leonard, Poppyganda, Uniform Press, London, 2015, at 41-13.

Essex Memorial Cemetery

In Canada, London and other cities where the press sought news of circumstances in the field, hoping for some encouraging word of an end to battle, McCrae's poem was often quoted. Penned in part as personal memorial and in part a plea for battlefield resources, the poem had effect. In Canada alone, where the line of: *In Flanders the poppies blow*, was used in the 1917 Canadian Victory Loan Bonds campaign, $400 million was raised for the war effort.

McCrae wrote one last poem, *Anxious Dead*, before he became critically ill. His suffering from asthma and bronchitis progressed under adverse conditions in Boulogne to pneumonia. He received the funeral of a military hero, when on January 28, 1918, he was buried in Flanders Fields, at the Wimereux Cemetery in Boulogne-Sur-Mer, France. McCrea's horse, Bonfire, which he brought with him to Europe, followed behind the hearse carrying McCrea to his gravesite.

Today in Guelph, Ontario, the McCrea home is a museum to the poet/doctor. Added to the grounds is a Remembrance Garden, with a Cenotaph, a spire of recognition raised in the absence of a grave. Such cenotaphs exist in small towns throughout England and Canada, where war dead lie buried in Flanders Fields. The garden is planted with poppies; the flower that grows naturally and with resilience in fields where death permeates the landscape.

Women Picking Poppies

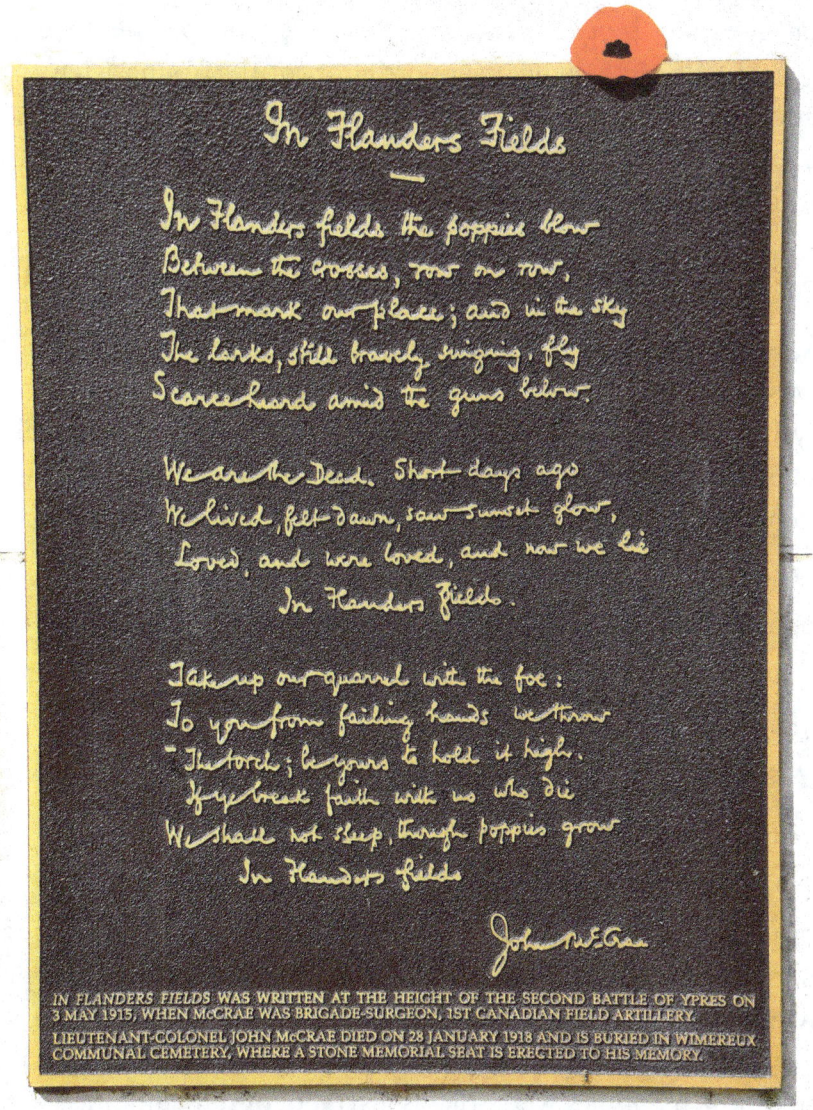

Lieutenant Colonel McCrea gave more than a short poem, easily converted to slogan, to aid the war effort. He gave the effort a symbol: the poppy. Unlike flag waving to raise patriotic spirit to draw volunteers to fight in a war, the poppy is a symbol of the human cost of war. It was invoked by McCrae as a tribute in remembrance of the fallen. Volunteers in response to the call of their nation, gave their lives in service. McCrae saw endless rows of little white crosses. Among them, poppies blew with life. His poem was a tribute to spent lives; the opposite of a call to death in war.

Moina Belle Michael was a few years older than McCrea, when she left teaching in Good Hope, Georgia to become one of the Overseas War Secretaries (OWS) in a civilian support effort of the Young Men's Christian Association (YMCA). An American of French-Flanders ancestry, born in Georgia in 1869, Michael felt called to serve in a civilian capacity in Europe during the war.

Three years after McCrea submitted his poem to an English magazine, Michael saw McCrea's poem imposed over artwork of a battlefield scene with poppies, in an edition of the Ladies Home Journal of November 1918. The poem was familiar to Michael. No doubt, she could recite much of it from memory. In her book, *The Miracle Flower*, published in 1941, Michael credited the moment she opened the magazine with inspiration to focus on the poppy as a sign of remembrance.

In McCrea's poem, he wrote, *To you from falling hands we throw the torch*. Michael wrote her response to McCrea in her poem, where she said,

> *We caught the torch you threw, …*
> *And now the torch and poppy red*
> *Wear in honour of our dead.* (spelling supplied)

Two days before Armistice was signed, Michael collected funds from OWS and went out to buy poppies. Finding no fresh flowers available, she purchased silk flowers. She was pleased when each of her fellow secretaries wore the flowers as symbols of reverence in remembrance of the fallen. This was the first instance in which poppies were sold as a symbol of remembrance.

After the war, Michael was hired by a public relations firm publicizing remembrance events. The poppy symbol promoted by Michael was incorporated into artwork of a torch of a Flanders Memorial flag. Michael found the campaign aggrandizing victory in war, rather than remembrance of the soldiers, whose lives were the cost of war. She soon separated from the firm.

Back home in Georgia, Michael appealed to the Georgia chapter of Veterans of Foreign Wars to wear a poppy every November 11, as tribute to fallen soldiers. They agreed. At the 1920 National Convention of the VFW, the Georgia delegation convinced the national organization to adopt the poppy as a simple symbol of remembrance. Soon, selling poppies was a major VFW program.

To meet demand for the popular poppy, Frenchwoman Anna Guerin, formed a company to produce hundreds of thousands of silk poppies. Guerin envisioned a company staffed by French war survivors, providing jobs in a post-war devastated nation. Profits from her poppy company went to a war-widow fund. The British Legion gave Guerin an order for nine million poppies.[26] She soon had large orders from Canada, Australia and New Zealand.

Neither Michael, Guerin, nor the VFW registered an official poppy. Any form of black-centered red flower might suffice in paper, silk, or felt. Soon factories in Britain and elsewhere produced poppies, reducing the profits that fed the war-widow fund. In Britain, war veterans made flowers.

Remembrance Today

McCrae's poem was immediately popular in the United States. The poppy was slow to become a national symbol, despite support of the VFW. In the US, people wore red, white and blue ribbons to acknowledge the anniversary of armistice every November 11.

---

[26] Leonard at 59.

Poppies at the Tower of London, photo credit Alan Marsden, UK

The VFW did not discourage the ribbons. They added the poppy as reverence to the fallen, separate from a celebration of victory in war. After World War II, ribbons and poppies were worn in May, rather than November, to celebrate Victory in Europe. In Britain, the poppy continued to be worn in November, in reverence to Armistice and those who died on European turf. In France, the poppy never was adopted. The French flower of remembrance was, and is, the blue cornflower, the *bleuet de France*. From the beginning, they were officially made of tissue paper.

In the years of the Vietnam War, anti-war sentiment in the US discouraged wearing any signs associated with war. War memorials were defaced. National flags were burned.

In Britain and English Commonwealth nations, where service in both world wars touched every village, often in direct connection to losses in battles,

November 11 remains a sacred day of remembrance. In 1987, ten thousand poppies were dropped over the battlefield of Ypres in recognition of two hundred and forty-five thousand soldiers who perished in the Battle of Passchendaele. On Remembrance Day, poppies pour from the Tower of London.

In recent years, white poppies were promoted as symbols of peace. Black poppies symbolized world hunger, while purple poppies were worn to display support for Animal Aid. The idea of symbols of solidarity with a cause is neither new, nor monopolized by poppies. However, the poppy is more than a ribbon symbol. The poppies of the battle field in Flanders Fields is a connection to place that rises above marketing tools and random selection of color. To know of McCrea, his experience and his poem, is to understand the meaning of the poppy.

The poppy is not immune to commercialization. Monetizing the poppy has not tarnished its original meaning. McCrae asked that people not *break faith* with those who lie in Flanders Fields. Since the plea of McCrea, there has been another war deposit its dead over Flanders Fields. The poppy, as a sign of ultimate service to country in the military, need not be war-specific to keep faith with troops.

Poppies worn in May or November, or both, signify respect, reverence and remembrance of those who served. Though they did not favor war, they fought. For people of today strident in anti-war sentiment, putting a human cost on war, wearing the poppy, is preserving memory of the past, so that it may not be repeated in the future. A desire for peace is the legacy of the war dead, to those who enjoy life in peace.

Amsterdam Canals

NETHERLANDS

Amsterdam in the Golden Age Of World Commerce

The seventeenth century was the Golden Age of world commerce for Amsterdam. The space of time from fishing hamlet to center, from which there was a dominant position in world trade, actually took less than a century. It was sufficient time to bring abundant capital to the city to finance expansion of canals and develop infrastructure of a world power. When the period of dominance ended, a vibrant commercial center remained.

In 1594, a small group of Amsterdam merchants came together in a bold effort to compete with Portuguese merchant seamen, who held a monopoly on the Far East spice trade. The Dutch planned one venture for their Far Lands Company. The Far Lands fleet had mixed success, proving that the Dutch were capable of replacing Portuguese middlemen, much to the delight of Asian suppliers, who raised prices in response to competing shippers for scarce goods.

Sensing lucrative possibilities, Prince Mauritus, of the United Provinces of the Netherlands, chartered a single overseas company, giving it immense powers, which forced the issue of joiner among several ship-owning Amsterdam merchants. In 1602, Verenigde Oostindische Compagnie, or VOC, known to all as the Dutch East India Company, was given a twenty-year royal charter with which to take command of the most profitable commodities in world trade. The VOC succeeded to the extent of grand dreams of the prince and his new nobles, the merchant class.

By the time war and competition with another small, but powerful emerging world leader, England, clipped profits for the VOC in 1672, and sent it west, in its iteration as the Dutch West India Company; a vast trading network was established. Dutch trading companies had resilient infrastructure, able to withstand diverse conditions of suppliers, from India and Ceylon to the

New World. VOC established outposts, which became cities. They held a monopoly in world trade. VOC directors, shareholders and their homeports became wealthy.

Dutch merchant seamen were more than a group with well-built ships guided by savvy investors. VOC became the first private, world corporation, with a governing board, stockholders, and a multi-national network able to monopolize world trade in the most desirable goods on the European market. Kings still ruled countries, as they did in the past. Private commercial corporations became the future rulers of the world.

This is the story of the Golden Age of commerce in Amsterdam, home of the Dutch East India Company and eventually the Dutch West India Company. When Napoleon entered the Provinces in the early nineteenth century, and put an end to two-hundred years of the vast, private, highly successful, commercial corporation, the little French general could never vanquish the concept of corporate ventures, or traditions well entrenched in the enduring city of Amsterdam.

From Spanish Vassal to World Leader

Great ideas, such as the formation of the concept of a corporation, that would change the impact of government and the form of world trade, do not materialize in a vacuum. Neither do cities become the epicenter of world trade and among the wealthiest on earth, without reasons beyond geography of access to a protected port and raw materials for building ships. In the last years of the sixteenth century, great minds in commercial possibilities came together in Amsterdam, with the bold thought of pooling resources to compete with the greatest commercial sea-power of their time, Portugal. Such audacity was fueled by recent events.

The constellation of events that coincided in late sixteenth century Amsterdam to foster action in city leaders were: the departure of Philip II of Spain from power in the Dutch region; the migration of Protestants to northern provinces of the Spanish Lowlands seeking religious freedom; and greed of Portuguese merchants, who increased cost of spices from the Far East beyond Dutch toleration.

Old Stock Exchange Beginning East India Venture

In 1567, Philip II became king of Spain and ruled what was then known as the Spanish Lowlands. Seven Dutch Provinces comprised the northern section of the Spanish domain, and a divided Flemish and Walloon Belgium were in the south. Luxemburg was also part of Spanish Lowlands. North Lowlands was predominantly Protestant and the south was predominantly, or at least more tolerably, Catholic. Philip inherited Spain, the Lowlands, as well as the Kingdom of Naples, as the south of Italy and all of Sicily was known. Philip was an ardent Catholic. He would not tolerate any religion but Catholicism throughout his domain. For the Dutch, predominantly Calvinists, choice of religion was not the option of a distant monarch.

William the Duke of Orange, also known as William the Silent, though he was anything but, became the champion of the Dutch against the Spanish. In 1572, William led his local bands in revolt. The well-armed and highly disciplined Spanish soldiers put Amsterdam under siege in 1576. Hostilities were resolved for a while, in the 1579 Treaty of Utrecht, in which the north achieved independence from Philip and the ability to be nationally Protestant, while the south remained under the Catholic thumb of Philip. Amsterdam, in the north, prospered under the treaty, overtaking Antwerp in the south, as a leading commercial port in the North Sea. Succeeding Dukes of Orange became governors of a new country.

The Treaty of Utrecht was impetus for wealthy Protestants in Antwerp to quit the city and move to Amsterdam. The resulting cash infusion to ship building in Amsterdam was accompanied by the arrival of talented craftsmen and veterans of employment with Portuguese merchants in the Far East. Migrants brought technical skills, maps and knowledge of sailing to Far East ports, to do business in spices. Capital, skill and experience merged into desire and ability to replace the Portuguese in world trade.

For decades, the Portuguese gave preferential prices for silks, spices and other sought-after items from the Far East to the royals of Portugal and Spain. Prices were higher in Europe and for the Dutch. There was some altruism in the merchants of Amsterdam to lower prices in their city. They also saw a profit potential in becoming the commander of international trade.

Dutch East India Company

Dutch East India Company VOC

In 1595, four ships left Amsterdam loaded with gold and trinkets to be traded for pepper in Java, now known as Indonesian Islands. Prince Mauritus, of the Dutch Provinces, blessed the venture by waiving duties on export of trading capital and import of pepper. Despite being armed with maps for the journey, and experienced captains and crew, it was a naïve endeavor.

Captains of Dutch ships quarreled over the route. Disagreements resulted in a journey of several months becoming a fifteen-month ordeal. One ship was lost at sea and two-thirds of the crews perished from disease. Once in Java there were no diplomatic relations in place to facilitate trade agreements. When the ships returned to port in 1597, pepper profits barely enabled merchants to break even on the venture.

Visions of profits were vivid enough for several Amsterdam merchants capable of outfitting ships to venture forth into competition for the pepper trade. From 1595 to 1601, eight different small investor groups launched sixty-five ships to the Far East. Success upon return varied. They did accomplish one prevailing result. That was, the Javanese pepper sellers realized they had a great demand for their product sufficient to justify a significant increase in price for product at origin.

The stadholder, that is governor, of the United Dutch Provinces, Mauritus, had personally invested in some of the ventures and had given his official blessing to favorable waiver of duties. He realized that royal action was necessary to blend factions into one successful body of merchants. In 1602, Mauritus gave a twenty-year charter to Verenigde Oostindische Compagnie, VOC, which is known widely by its English name, the Dutch East India Company (DEIC).

The DEIC was afforded exclusive, renewable, trade rights in the Far East. It had the power to make treaties on behalf of the Dutch government, enlist soldiers and wage war. The Company would establish trading posts on foreign soil, build forts to protect Dutch interests, including warehouses, and place administrators in foreign ports, who functioned as local government. In exchange, the DEIC owed only an oath of allegiance to the states general of the United Provinces of the Netherlands and its stadholder.

Several independent merchant consortiums were joined under the single DEIC corporate organization. Directors of former companies became directors of the DEIC. Directorships were inherited, so that over time, an unwieldy number of directors became a central board of seventeen major stockholders, above a large inclusive body of directors from the major cities, and at the bottom of the decision-making pyramid, a body of stockholders, with lesser authority. The board directed operations, hired employees, and chose the time and place of trade and auctions of goods from VOC warehouses. Stockholders could band together to veto a voyage, although such militancy rarely occurred.

The first directors each received one percent of DEIC income, from which salaries of employees were paid. As the number of directors settled at a smaller number, income of directors was fixed at three thousand guilders a year, plus travel expenses. Shareholders, which included directors holding large numbers of shares, received lucrative returns above costs.

The number of total shares was fixed and never diluted. If the DEIC required capital for building ships and purchasing gold for minting of foreign coins for trade, they were empowered to commit to loans. Creditors were paid from the proceeds at auction and had first choice to pArcticipate in purchases of incoming goods. In a pinch, the Dutch government provided loans.

Initial investors in the DEIC were wealthy merchants, ordinary wage earners and clergy. All became wealthy on DEIC earnings. Over time, shares were purchased and held by a small group of investors from which the governing board was chosen. Over two hundred years of the DEIC, it is estimated that return on investment was 3600%.[27] There were two-hundred, thirty-million guilders in transactions in a time when the yearly income of a tradesman was three hundred guilders a year. By comparison, Rembrandt charged five hundred guilders for a portrait. The capitalization of the DEIC on Bank of Amsterdam deposit was six and a half million guilders.

---

[27] Els M. Jacobs, In Pursuit of Pepper and Tea, Netherlands Maritime Museum, Amsterdam, 1991, p. 16.

Old Trade Hall & Stock Exchange

The DEIC sailed to Jakarta on the island of Java, to Ceylon and India. Ships returned with pepper and other spices, silk and other textiles, tea and sugar. To facilitate shipping goods and maintaining health of crews on long distance voyages, forts were established in the Cape of Good Hope at Table Bay, near Table Mountain, the present-day city of Cape Town. Stops were made at Cape Verde and St. Helena, off the west coast of Africa and Madagascar.

Ships left Amsterdam at Christmas and Easter. At Easter time there was good weather in the North Sea, although high waves could be encountered in the southern Atlantic. Atlantic seas were more easily traversed in winter sailing, once ships rounded the British Isles. At the equator, Dutch ships traveled a careful route that veered sharply to the east, to avoid being taken by Trade Winds to the coast of Brazil.

The more direct route to the Atlantic was through the English Channel. When the Dutch were at war with the English, as they were during four Anglo-Dutch Wars involving access to commerce on the high seas, the path of least resistance was around the north of Scotland and Ireland, before sailing south to the equator. By the fourth war in 1672, when dominance of the Dutch was less of a factor for the English, the major impact to Dutch ships at sea came from pirates.

VOC employed experienced master seamen. They also hired talented mapmakers and held navigational maps in secret vaults in the East India House in Amsterdam. Maps were never printed on presses. Rather, they were copied on velum to preserve ink and minimize proliferation of proprietary information.

VOC sent envoys to Indonesia, India, Ceylon and Japan to negotiate favored trade status. When local growers refused to give the Dutch preferential treatment, VOC troops landed to enforce trade monopolies. Japan gave the Dutch a monopoly in trade from 1641 to 1853. During this time, Japanese silk kimonos were a popular fashion staple in Amsterdam. In Batavia, present day Jakarta, of the 140,000 inhabitants of the city in 1619, six thousand were European merchants and twelve hundred were VOC soldiers.[28]

---

[28] Jacobs, p. 76.

Golden Age of Amsterdam

Panorama Along the Canal

VOC became the largest employer in Amsterdam, engaging one thousand workers in the city by the beginning of the eighteenth century. Wages were high. Carpenters earned three hundred guilders per year. A master shipwright could be paid one thousand guilders a year, plus free fuel to heat their home, and all the free beer they could consume. Company bookkeepers were paid one to two thousand guilders a year. Warehouse managers were paid three thousand guilders per year, free beer of course, plus a home adjacent to the warehouses. Amsterdam abounded with well-paid residents.

Building three VOC ships in Amsterdam each year, provisioning ships and handling export and import at the city docks, fueled prosperity in the city that was unprecedented. It is estimated that VOC built fifteenth hundred ships over two centuries of its existence, the majority of which were built in the seventeenth century. Launch of a new ship at the Amsterdam dockyard was a major city event.

By the end of the seventeenth century, a merchant ship cost one hundred thousand guilders to build. Toward the end of the eighteenth century a larger, longer, ship, with greater capacity, could be built for two hundred and fifty thousand guilders. Early ships were square-riggers, dependent upon wind direction for travel. Newer ships used several masts of sails to harness wind to control travel direction.

Expanded ring of canals

During the seventeenth century, dikes were reinforced in Amsterdam and three ring canals were added. Homes on new canals were built for wealthy merchants, while side streets were filled with shops. By the end of the Golden Age, Amsterdam achieved much of the streetscape of the modern city. Later, additional reclamation pushed back the Zuider Zee, adding two more provinces to the Netherlands.

During the Golden Age of Amsterdam, talent flocked to the city. Amsterdam became a city of painters, architects and botanists. Rembrandt arrived to stay in 1631. Calvinists resisted any outward display of wealth. With proliferation of tulips available, city dwellers lavished their wealth on country estates, with gardens full of colorful flowers. Landscape architecture came into prominence.

Dutch West India Company

In 1621, the Dutch West India Company was founded by VOC, to colonize the New World, enable commercial monopolies in North and South America, and to pArcticipate in the African slave trade, in order to populate plantations in New World Caribbean colonies. Again, the initial target was competition with the Portuguese. Prior to formalizing colonies in the New World, Dutch privateers targeted Portuguese and Spanish ships returning to Europe with gold.

Waag the City Gate

In 1609, Englishman Henry Hudson was hired by VOC to sail to the Far East by way of a northeast passage. Unable to receive a ship and sufficient backing for his exploration of a northwest passage to India from English financiers, Hudson accepted a contract from the Dutch, knowing that finding a northeast passage was impossible. He left Amsterdam in a VOC ship, and once out of sight of the Netherlands, he turned west and headed for the New

World. Hudson discovered Manhattan, while he spent a month exploring the river named for him.[29]

When Hudson returned to England, the Dutch were satisfied to receive return of their ship, the *Half Moon*. They consoled themselves for Hudson's act of piracy, by sending colonists to Manhattan, where they established a Dutch colony between the French to the north and the Spanish to the south. It was not a profitable venture, so VOC instead concentrated on islands to the south, in the Caribbean Sea.

The Dutch established colonies in Sint Maarten, desired for its natural salt ponds, as the tiny island was not suitable for plantations. Fish caught in Caribbean waters could be salted in Sint Maarten for transport to the Netherlands. Southern Caribbean islands of Aruba, Bonaire and Curaçao became the Netherlands Antilles, a source of salt and fresh water. In 1634, the Dutch built a fort on Curaçao to protect goods brought from Suriname sugar plantations, north of Brazil, and stored on the island prior to transport to Europe. In 1804, the fort fired upon British ships seeking control of the island.

Dutch merchant Peter Stuyvesant was a director of the Dutch West India Company assigned to manage company operations in Curaçao from 1642 to 1644. In 1644, Spain took control of Sint Maarten. Stuyvesant went to the island to oust the Spanish. During the battle he famously lost his leg. Legend has it that he sent the leg to Curaçao for burial, before he went home to Holland to convalesce.

In 1647, Stuyvesant was elevated by VOC to Director-General of New Netherland on the northeast coast of North America, with headquarters in New Amsterdam. Stuyvesant ruled the territory for seventeen years, until English King Charles II granted the land to his brother, the Duke of York, who eventually became King James II. The action prompted a third Anglo-Dutch War.

With a promise of peaceful transfer of control, and with acceptance of current residents, who were tired of war, Stuyvesant capitulated to the English in

---

[29] For more on Henry Hudson and the Half Moon, see Cruise through History, Itinerary VI – East Coast of North America, Port of New York.

transfer of New Amsterdam to England in 1664. The territory became New York. Dutch possessions in the west became limited to Caribbean and Netherlands Antilles islands.

The DWIC suffered a similar fate as the DEIC as a consequence of the Fourth Anglo-Dutch war. By the end of the eighteenth century the DWIC was insolvent. Company assets were liquidated, remaining trade was privatized, and islands became Dutch colonies and eventually independent islands of the Kingdom of the Netherlands.

End of the Golden Age as Foundation for a New Era

Amsterdam Golden Age Palace, Now a Hotel

In the seventeenth and eighteenth centuries, VOC was the largest trading and shipping company in the world. By the end of the eighteenth century, VOC was bankrupt. The Fourth Anglo-Dutch War was a factor. British sea captains were proficient in capturing homeward bound VOC ships, heavy in the water with spices and silk. For two years during the war, trade was suspended. VOC ships were put to use by the Dutch navy. Without the flow of capital from sale of goods, loans could not be repaid and workers could not remain employed. Dutch economy faltered.

In 1795, France invaded the Dutch Republic. When France controlled Dutch government, ability of VOC to access government loans came to an abrupt halt. Napoleon was in shock when he looked at VOC books and saw VOC remained alive on government loans. In 1799, Napoleon nationalized VOC assets, took control of the trade organization, and received all profits from import auctions. By 1800, VOC was officially bankrupt. In 1803, VOC assets were liquidated.

When the Napoleonic era ended, any vacuum in international trade was quickly absorbed by private enterprise. Private Dutch holdings in sugar and coffee plantations in Indonesia and Suriname provided wealth to a few citizens, who banked their assets in Amsterdam. The city did not grow, so much as it repaired and maintained during the private era of Dutch trade.

In 1870, the cycle came back to nationalization of international trade. Armies of nation-states became necessary to maintain sources of trade in distant countries, with unstable governments, long ruled by foreign governments and private companies. The Dutch were among the last of European governments to abolish slavery, doing so in 1863. In 1901, the Dutch instituted an Ethical Policy, aimed at overcoming long-term effects of slavery and expanding education to lands governed as Dutch Overseas Colonies.[30]

Amsterdam Today

Former administrative offices of VOC are now historic buildings in Amsterdam, near the cruise port. Golden Age infrastructure of Amsterdam, including new canals, churches, a town hall and homes of VOC directors remain. Some Amsterdam churches have been restored and are open to the public and some of the homes are now museums.

---

[30] Read more on Dutch East India in Itinerary XIV Ports of the South Pacific and Indonesia, Port of Java.

NEMO Amsterdam Science Museum

Life along the canals today

Amsterdam endured as a vibrant market city, despite loss of VOC. In its wake, VOC left a large, stable and well-capitalized middle class. Today there are numerous corporations in the city with a worldwide reach in commerce.

Amsterdam is a popular cruise destination for beauty of canals that ring the city, which are easily accessed on foot or by bicycle. Imprint of VOC, no longer the major city employer, is an icon of history. Golden Age of VOC in Amsterdam has gone. Golden Age of the city is ongoing.

Walk through Amsterdam with Rembrandt, Keyser & Clusius

Icons of Amsterdam are its canals, tulip fields and windmills that draw water from the lowest of the low lands and pump it back into the Zuider Zee, the inland shallow lake upon which all three are found. Walk next to rings of canals, past rows of houses, with stair-step, or strangely neo-classical pediments, and think of the people who walked these streets, built unique buildings and planted gardens, when the city was still young.

One of the most famous residents of Amsterdam is Rembrandt van Rijn. He came to Amsterdam to visit and to study art in 1625, returning to stay in 1631. He was attracted to the city for its vibrancy, color and darkness, so much of which was reflected on his canvasses and sketchpads.

When Rembrandt achieved financial success, he purchased a grand home on Broad Street near St. Anthony's Cathedral, or St. Anthoniesbreestraat, as it was called in the 1630s. When the street crosses a canal, it becomes Jodenbreestraat, central thoroughfare of the Jewish quarter, as it became increasingly called in the seventeenth century. As wealthy and fashionable residents moved further out to the next rows of canals, Rembrandt walked the streets around his home and sketched those less fashionable and less fortunate. In Rembrandt portraits, sketches and etchings, a human history of Amsterdam is recorded.

The city architect, responsible for so much of the unique style of Amsterdam, was Hendrick de Keyser. Keyser began his career as a sculptor, then came to Amsterdam where he, like Rembrandt, moved away from those who were bound by the Italian style of art and architecture to create a new style, now known as Dutch Renaissance. Towers of Amsterdam, the collection of church steeples and town clock towers, collected in photographs of visitors today, are the work of Keyser. Keyser died a few years prior to the arrival of Rembrandt in Amsterdam. The artist walked the streets, and lived in the shadows, of the architect's city.

Keyser Tower at the Market–Munttoren

The man known as the greatest botanist of the sixteenth century, Carolus Clusius, arrived in Amsterdam before the first tulip. Fortunately for tulips, and for the iconic tulip gardens of Amsterdam's surrounding area, when the tulip first arrived it came to the hands of Clusius, who named it, classified it and propagated it in his garden. Clusius was a true scientist, who was fond of sharing knowledge. Clusius passed in 1609, before more canals and churches were built. His work is seen in gardens, florist shops and fields, that today attract so many visitors to Amsterdam.

The artist, architect and botanist, each endowed Amsterdam with a contribution that is uniquely Dutch and integral to the cultural aura of the city. This is the story of three Amsterdam residents, whose legacies are to be enjoyed on a walk through the city. Their lives overlapped in the seventeenth century. Their creations are timeless.

Artist in His City

Waag where a Rembrandt painting was displayed

The seventeenth century was a wonderful time to be a Dutch artist. The Dutch Golden Age of commerce of that century fostered a large middle class with disposable income. The Dutch enjoyed decorating their homes with Dutch art. Across the channel, the English were great admirers and collectors of Dutch art. Young Dutch artists might travel to Rome to study classical art. They were just as happy to remain home.

Although the Bible was integral to daily life of the Dutch, private commissions of artwork were mostly portraits. Dutch churches did not commission art. Artists were free to paint scenes of daily life, so called genre painting, landscapes, or history paintings, that is, the recording of people and events of the time.

Artists often painted as they so choose, then sold the completed work. It was a novel concept, but then these were times of intellectual freedom in the young Dutch Republic. Rembrandt once said that he painted not so much for honor as for liberty. He was born at the right time, in the right place to be an artist of his temperament.

Rembrandt Harmenszoon van Rijn, son of Harmen, born in Leiden in 1606, was an artist typical of the Dutch Golden Age in art. He looked to, and was influenced to some degree by, Italian masters such as Caravaggio. He was called upon to emulate the Dutch master Rubens. He is recognized as a great artist, not for his ability to replicate the art of others. Rather, Rembrandt is remembered as great among highly accomplished artists of his time, because he took the artistic freedom that financial security and an appreciative public afforded him, to be of his own making.

The van Rijns were a family of millers, living on the banks of the Rhine River, or Rijn, in Dutch. There were sufficient funds in the household to send young Rembrandt to the university at age fourteen, and to allow him to follow his talent into the study of art, rather than to work for the family, or be pushed toward a career in law. He was apprenticed to a master artist from age fifteen to eighteen, which was from 1621 to 1624, becoming acknowledged as a master by the age of nineteen.

In 1625, Rembrandt went to Amsterdam to study with painters, who made a living painting the portraits of wealthy merchants. Still painting on wood, rather than canvass, he painted the *Stoning of St. Stephen*, which garnered instant recognition for the young artist. Constantijn Huygens, private secretary to the stadholder, ruler of the Dutch Republic, became an instant admirer and promoter. He saw in young Rembrandt the ability to paint like Rubens. Several Rembrandt canvasses went into the collection of the monarch. Rembrandt painted the *Blinding of Samson* as a gift to Huygens, in thanks for his royal commissions.

In 1631, Rembrandt came to Amsterdam to live. It was in the vibrant city that so many commissions for portraiture awaited him. His father died in 1630. There was nothing to hold him in Leiden. The Amsterdam that drew in Rembrandt looked then as it does for visitors who arrive today.

In Amsterdam, Rembrandt was as captivated by the praise from his patrons, as he was by the people of the streets, whom he captured in sketches. He quickly became the renowned artist of the city with which he had a bond. Often asked throughout his life, whether he had been to Italy to study its art; Rembrandt demurred. He never had a desire to paint anywhere else but Amsterdam.

Rembrandt's first residence in Amsterdam was behind Zuiderkerk, the church built in 1603. It is notable for its clock tower completed in 1614. On the streets, women sold pancakes from small stoves. Begging was outlawed in Amsterdam. Poor of the streets worked sweeping and performing errands. There were city homes for the elderly poor and orphanages for young children, supported by profits from theaters of the city.

In 1632, Rembrandt painted *The Anatomy Lesson of Dr. Nicolaes Tulp*. The masterpiece was his first major commission, which established his fame. At the time, Rembrandt was living with Hendrick Uylenburgh, also a painter and art dealer. Uylenburgh's cousin, Saskia, became Rembrandt's wife, the mother of his four children, of whom only Titus, born in 1641, survived past infancy.

In the Provinces of the Netherlands, 1639 was a boom-time in the economy. It seemed that with peace and the success of the Dutch East India Company, the expanding economy would continue. Rembrandt and Saskia bought their home at Number 4 Jodenbreestraat that year. A merchant, who favored the step gable so characteristic of Dutch Renaissance architecture, had built the house in 1607. By the time of the van Rijn purchase, the gable had been remodeled to a neo-classical pediment.

Rembrandt House

The elegant home was half-again as large as the other homes in the prestigious neighborhood of publishers and artists. Stone steps led up to the front door. The first floor was full of light from large windows. The second-floor artist studio had windows of clear glass and a row of small leaded windows. Rembrandt could control the flow of light in the room by adjusting the shutters. The family lived on the top floor and several students of their master Rembrandt copied his works in the attic. Life was ideal.

Three years later Saskia died, probably of tuberculosis. Rembrandt was entitled to the income of her inheritance for so long as he did not remarry. He never did. Instead he stayed at home and painted. Saskia's nurse, Geertje became caretaker to Titus and model to Rembrandt. When a younger woman, Hendrickje Stoffels, was employed as a housekeeper, she too modeled for Rembrandt.

Two women competing for the attention of the master was too much for Geertje. She and Rembrandt became entangled in legal action over whether he promised marriage. The matter ended with Geertje in a convent workhouse, Rembrandt ordered to support her for life, and Hendrickje as the woman of the household.

In 1642, despite the emotional upheaval in his life, Rembrandt painted the large canvass for which he is famous. The *Parade of the Civic Guard Led by Captain Frans Banning Cocq*, better known as the *Night Watch*, is even better known to art curators after its cleaning to be the *Day Watch*. He was paid 1600 guilders for the portrait, one hundred guilders contributed by each of those in the painting.[31]

The *Night Watch* was stirring if not disconcerting in its unveiling as subjects were painted in the course of a group activity, rather than as a group in strict portraiture, as paying pArcticipants expected. Some art historians seeking to make conclusions of the thoughts of the artist, or his patrons, claim the artist received much criticism for the painting, by leaving some subjects in lesser view. Rembrandt's independence of style, through groundbreaking, did not

---

[31] Find Rembrandt's self-portrait in the *Night Watch*.

result in the inability to receive portrait commissions. Patrons continued to demand Rembrandt's portraits, including group portraits of notable members in Amsterdam society.

Rembrandt did not often comment on his work. It is known of him that it was his desire to depict in paint the drama of emotion in his subjects. Like the revolutionary Italian painter Caravaggio, Rembrandt used the technique of chiaroscuro, light and dark, for dramatic effect. For Rembrandt, the effect went beyond mood created by chiaroscuro. Light and color were tools to focus the viewer on the emotion of the subject in the painting. In Rembrandt's canvasses, the eye looks to the source of the light. Much of the paintings are in tones of brown, with use of red for emphasis. It is often said of Rembrandt that he is the Shakespeare of painters. His paintings take the viewer to the emotion of the event, where the crescendo moment is highlighted in red.

In the late 1640s and early 1650s Rembrandt had time to paint as he wished and explore etching. The process of etching requires a copper plate to be coated with wax. The artist then uses a needle to remove wax in the areas of

Detail Night Watch

the plate that will be exposed most to an acid wash that eats away the metal. The copper may be recoated and the process repeated several times to achieve the desired effect. When complete, paper is pressed against the inked plate to produce the drawing. Rembrandt experimented with needles that he created to be extremely fine-pointed. An estimated four hundred Rembrandt etchings have survived, attesting to his skill in the medium.[32]

When he wished to clear his mind, Rembrandt often walked along the dikes and on the banks of the Amstel River that winds through Amsterdam. Boats on the river, wooden piers and wharves became subjects in his drawings, as did old Jewish men and women seen in streets of his neighborhood. Nearly two thousand drawings survive of Rembrandt's life in the city.

In 1653, the Dutch boom period abruptly ended. In the Battle of Portland that year, another of the wars over commerce with the English, five thousand-five hundred Dutch soldiers lost their lives. Commerce was interrupted and fewer patrons had disposable income with which to pay five hundred guilders for a portrait. Rembrandt was slow to recognize the shift in fortune. He continued to spend freely and pay high prices at auction for suits of armor and swords used as props in his paintings.

Rembrandt continued to express his dramatic style, whether or not his patron refused a painting, and despite his need for funds. Portraits of the time were popular if they were complimentary. Dramatic, unattractive depictions were not good sellers.

In 1653, Italy came to Rembrandt. A Sicilian noble, Don Antonio Ruffo came to Amsterdam to purchase *Aristotle Contemplating the Bust of Homer*. The painting disappointed the Sicilian connoisseur and was refused, although he later made another purchase. Cosimo de' Medici visited Rembrandt and purchased his work.

By 1660, Rembrandt was adjudicated bankrupt. Household furnishings, completed paintings and expensive props used to set the scene for models, were inventoried by the court bailiff and sold to pay debts. Rembrandt, Hendrickje, their baby Cornelia and Titus moved into rented lodging in the low-rent, Jordaan area of the city. The modest, Bohemian district suited Rembrandt.

---

[32] D.M. Field, Rembrandt, Barnes & Noble Books, New York, 2002, p. 180.

Rembrandt was given an opportunity to redeem his finances in 1661, with a commission to paint a large canvass to be among a collection hung in the city hall. The collection was planned by a popular artist who died before he could execute his designs. Rembrandt's commission, *The Conspiracy of the Batavians under Claudius Civilus* was sixteen square feet of a dramatic depiction of the one-eyed Dutch hero. The work was not popular and was removed the following year.

Last of the major commissions afforded Rembrandt was *Syndics of the Cloth Draper's Guild*, painted in 1662. The painting was very well received for its portrayal of power and prestige of the guild leaders. In his last years, Rembrandt painted *The Return of the Prodigal Son* that now is part of the Hermitage collection, and the painting known as *The Jewish Bride,* although the couple is not Jewish. The painting is part of the Frick Collection in New York, where there is also a Rembrandt self-portrait, one of the self-portraits he painted twice each year to mark his life.

Syndics of the Cloth Draper's Guild

Hendrickje died in 1663. In 1668, Titus married, had a child and died. By 1669, Rembrandt too was dead. He was buried in a rented grave in Westerkerk. In 1877, Van Gogh visited Amsterdam and gave homage to Rembrandt in a visit to his former home on Jodenbreestraat. Van Gogh said of Rembrandt that there was something of the Gospel in Rembrandt and something of Rembrandt in the Gospel. Certainly the same could be said of Rembrandt and Amsterdam.

Dutch Renaissance Architect

Hendrick de Keyser, born in Utrecht in 1565, came to Amsterdam in 1591, as an apprentice artist. By 1595, he was the official city stonemason, responsible for city buildings. Regarded throughout the United Provinces for his sculpture, including the Tomb of William of Orange in Delft, Keyser is known in Amsterdam for his unique Amsterdam Renaissance style.

Keyser's twenty-five years in Amsterdam, before his death in 1621, was time of growth and of the economic capacity to execute great civic structures. As a result, and although other architects contributed much to the appearance of this snugly built, red-brick city, Keyser had the opportunity and the talent to establish the prevailing city style. As new canals were dug and the wealthy moved to outer canal rings, the Amsterdam Renaissance style established by Keyser was ubiquitous in tastes and preferences of residents chosen for their homes and businesses. One of his most notable, and photographed, business buildings was the administrative home of the Dutch East India Company, which stands near the cruise port today.

The first church in Amsterdam built specifically for Protestants was Zuiderkerk, designed by Keyser and built between 1603 and 1611. The bell tower was completed in 1614. It is a display of his iconic square base, with pillars, topped by round towers. Although Keyser windows are typically foursquare pane, the windows here are rectangles. Roof gables are testament to the sculptural background of Keyser. They maintain a truncated outline in fanciful, graceful, rather than stair-step lines, so typical of prior Dutch style. Westerkerk, finished two decades later, has many of the same design elements. Keyser did not design the tower of Westerkerk. It was completed in 1638.

Keyser Westerkerk place of Rembrandt burial

Keyser Zuiderkerk

Keyser designed the red brick city armory, the Bushuis, in 1606, about the same time Rembrandt's house was built. Both buildings have the same square, four-pane windows, with the lower casement windowpanes flanked by painted shutters, and the upper windowpanes set with small leaded glass inserts. Bushuis has stone cornerstones, windowsills and a gable topping that makes it fanciful. Once free of Spanish rule, the Dutch became free-spirited in their lifestyle.

Detail Spires

Keyser's son completed Noorderkerk, two years after the death of the city-defining architect. The base of the church forms an octagon, with four equal sections, as in a Greek cross, and connecting half-height sections diagonally from the outer corners of the base. A later architect placed a bell tower in the center of the cross sections. Massive, yet unique from Catholic churches, which inspired earlier Protestant buildings, Noorderkerk became a model for Dutch Protestant churches.

Greatest Botanist of the Century

Canals, Spires and Boats in Amsterdam

Charles de L'Escluse was born in France in 1526. By the time he obtained his law degree in 1548, he could write in Latin, Greek and Flemish, in addition to French, and could carry on a conversation in nine languages. He had a passion for plants and traveled throughout Europe in search of unique species, which he catalogued. His system of classification predated that of the famous Swedish scientist, Carl Linnaeus. He was so enthralled with Latin classification of plants, that he renamed himself in Latin to be Carolus Clusius.

In the true sense of a scientist, Clusius shared his knowledge. An ardent correspondent, he is known to author four thousand letters to botanists. Royals adored Clusius, although they were not good about funding his work. He discussed gardens with Sir Francis Drake in England and was hired by the Holy Roman Emperor Maximilian II to design a garden in Vienna in 1573. When he came to Hague, the Dutch socialite known as the Princess de Chimay, Marie de Brimeu, called Clusius the father of every beautiful garden.

In need of a job with an income, Clusius accepted a position at the University of Leiden for seven hundred fifty guilders a year and as large a garden as he could desire. Under his direction the university botany department grew in fame.

Tulips were not the focus of his endeavors, although the plant intrigued Clusius. He brought his bulbs to the Netherlands and propagated them in his garden. So beautiful were the results, and so sought after by collectors, that he could fund a huge botany laboratory, if he sold bulbs.

So many tulips were stolen from the university garden, that a frustrated Clusius dug up the ones that remained and gave them to botanists. He is credited with teaching gardeners how to cultivate tulips and use them in the garden. By generously sharing his wealth of tulips with so many local gardeners, intentionally and unintentionally, the flower became synonymous with Holland forever after. Though Clusius died in 1609, his tulip legacy is eternal.

Walking Streets of Amsterdam Today

The home where Rembrandt painted for twenty years became a museum in 1911. The modern addition, which opened in 1999, allows visitors to enter through the adjoining building, which houses a gift shop, maintaining the home's integrity. Museum curators attempt to recreate the ambiance, as it was when Rembrandt painted in his studio and his family lived there. The house façade is preserved from the seventeenth century.

Anne Frank House (now enter through museum)

Broad Street is now a large roadway. After much objection from locals, Jodenbreestraat district was renovated into modern buildings, housing businesses and restaurants. Rembrandt's house is no longer in the context of an historic district. Yet, stepping off the street to the museum, there is still the feeling of old Amsterdam. Near the house are canals filled with boats and lined with cafés.

The Jewish population of Amsterdam, the subject of Rembrandt drawings, was decimated during World War II. Today the Anne Frank House sits on the outer of three canals built at the end of the Golden Age of Amsterdam, near Westerkerk, where Rembrandt was buried. Prinsengracht Boulevard and canal are lovely to walk along today, now that terrors of the Nazi occupation are memories.

The Amsterdam Renaissance style of Hendrick de Keyser is evident in historic buildings, whether they are readily identified as designed by the architect, his son, or those who emulated the Amsterdam style, so popular for a century. Zuiderkerk, restored in 1979, after use during the World War II as a morgue, is now a city administrative office. Noorderkerk is still the home of a Calvinist congregation. Westerkerk Tower, the tallest in the city, is open for visitors willing to undertake a challenging climb for commanding city views. Do not expect to find the grave of Rembrandt, who was interred there, in an unmarked, rented space. Rijksmuseum is the place to see Keyser sculpture in a civic building.

Gardens of Amsterdam today are still thick with tulips, thanks to Clusius. After walking the streets of Amsterdam, visitors can board a bus, hire a taxi, or join a tulip tour. In the outskirts of Amsterdam, wander among fields of tulips in spring and fields of various flowers in summer.

Walking through Amsterdam today, it is easy to be transported back to the seventeenth century and the time of Rembrandt, Keyser and Clusius. Their legacy is visitor enjoyment.

TULIPS, CHOCOLATE AND DIAMONDS

Tulips

Universal symbols of love, celebration and holiday cheer are flowers, such as tulips, chocolate and diamonds. Nowhere in the world are these three symbols brought together more profoundly than in Amsterdam. This Dutch port city was not the origination point for any of the three in development or initial sales. It was arrival in Amsterdam that made each wonderful and desirable, until the trio became synonymous with the city.

Tulips originated in the wild, east of the Black Sea. Ancient traders took bulbs to China. The first sight of cultivated tulips in gardens was in Turkey. Sultans enjoyed a tulip mass of color in flower beds in their palaces each spring.

When tulips came to Amsterdam, in the sixteenth century, excitement over the flower reached a crescendo. The craze became known as *Tulipomania*, a period in which the Dutch deviated from an otherwise cautious lifestyle and gave into a penchant for gambling. Mania has cooled to a simple passion for the flower that remains today. Tulips grown in the fields surrounding Amsterdam are integral to Dutch history, as a major export to the world and a reason for visitors from all over the world to experience tulips in bloom.

Cocoa is grown in seed pods found in tropical areas of the world. Columbus is credited with noticing the plant in his travels to Central America. The Spanish realized that cocoa could be ground and used in a drink, which they observed favored by Aztecs. Unfortunately, the Spanish vanquished Aztecs before they learned the secrets of enjoyment of this new and exotic treat.

Cocoa is also grown in West Africa and the Far East. It was in the early seventeenth century that Dutch sailors for the private commercial venture of the Dutch East India Company, made regular voyages around Africa and to the Far East, enabling the Dutch to monopolize transport of cocoa to Europe. It was the Dutch manufacturers in the eighteenth and nineteenth centuries, who took pale brown, bitter power and turned it into the ubiquitous treat known as Dutch Chocolate. Today, confectioners in Amsterdam take their heritage and raise it to an art form.

Diamonds are found in South Africa. The art of cutting and polishing stones is an ancient skill first practiced in India. Cutting and polishing diamonds as a craft came to Amsterdam, not through commercial efforts, but as a result of Dutch religious toleration, rendering Netherlands beneficiary of religious prosecution in Spain. When Sephardic Jews were cast out of Spain in the sixteenth century, skilled, Jewish, diamond craftsmen came to Amsterdam, where they introduced the city to the diamond cutting industry. Today, Amsterdam is the place to shop for diamonds.

This is a short story of the trio of delights: tulips, chocolate and diamonds, which were brought to their glory in Amsterdam, making the history of each integral to the history of the city. Although Dutch tulips, chocolate and diamonds can be found at home, visitors find it most enjoyable to experience them at the source. There is something so intriguing about the little country that has made such a huge impact on celebrations of life, enjoyed throughout the world.

Tulips

Tulip Festival of Suliman in Istanbul

Tulip bulbs are traced to their earliest known species in the Caucasus area, east of the Black Sea. Grown in the wild, bulbs and flowers are small and not spectacular. Traders brought bulbs to China, where growing bulbs continued, but did not proliferate below the fortieth parallel in the warm climate of southern China.

As Ottoman Turks rode west in the thirteenth century, their tulip bulbs traveled well. When Ottomans conquered Constantinople in 1453, and made it their capital of Istanbul, tulip bulbs were planted prominently in gardens of Topaki Palace. By 1520, Suleiman the Magnificent enjoyed fifteen hundred varieties of cultivated tulips. He favored the long, pointed petals of russet and bright yellow. By 1630, there were eighty flower shops in Istanbul offering tulips.[33]

---

[33] Mike Dash, Tulipomania, Three Rivers Press, New York, 1999, p. 21.

Credit for introducing tulips to Europe goes to a Portuguese envoy to Goa, Lopo Vaz de Sampaio. When called home, Vaz stopped in Ceylon, where he saw tulips. It took Vaz two years to reach Europe, during which time tulip bulbs remained healthy enough to produce flowers, when eventually planted.

It was the goal of all seafaring nations of the fifteenth century to trade with the East. After all, it was an attempt to locate a shorter route to the East by sailing West, that inspired Christopher Columbus to travel unchartered seas. By the sixteenth century, English, European and Dutch trade routes were well established. Earliest of private merchant commerce guilds was that of the Dutch East India Company, chartered by the stadholder, governor of Dutch provinces, in 1602.

Preferred cargo of Amsterdam merchant sailors, was spice and textiles. If considered at all, transport of bulbs was a minor thought, a novelty, or as a strange sort of onion, which might be good to eat. In the second half of the sixteenth century, tulip bulbs were seen popping up yellow flowers in gardens across Europe, as botanists shared bulbs and offshoots of young tulip plants.

In 1559, a tulip was recorded in a Bavarian garden. Tulip blooms were seen in England in 1582, and in France in 1598. Most important for the future of tulips, were bulbs that reached the Netherlands by 1570.

The first bulbs to reach the Netherlands came into hands of Carolus Clusius, the great botanist of the sixteenth century. Clusius, born Charles de L'Escluse in France in 1526, traveled through Spanish Lowlands, as the Netherlands, Belgium and Luxembourg were then known, as well as through Spain and France, always on the lookout for unique plants. When it became expedient for Lutherans to leave France, Clusius changed his name from French to Latin, more appropriate for an eminent scientist, and changed his residence to Amsterdam.

Clusius wrote about four thousand letters to other botanists, while he studied tulip bulbs. The question he pondered in correspondence was, whether this plant should be groomed as a flowering plant or a food item. Fortunately, the verdict ran in favor of flowers.

In 1592, Clusius was given a position at the University of Leiden, where he had an opportunity to build its botany program for study of a range of plants. So often did plant thieves raid his garden for tulips, that Clusius threatened to give away remaining bulbs. He died in 1609, never knowing the legacy of his life's work rose from stolen bulbs, upon which the economy of the young nation of the United Provinces of the Netherlands grew.

In his opus work, *Historia*, Clusius recorded thirty-four tulip species, grouped into early, mid and late-blooming varieties. Dutch botanists soon expanded tulip species to one hundred twenty, building on the work of Clusius. By the 1630s, of the sixteen hundred species of tulips catalogued, five hundred were Dutch.

In the Netherlands, tulips were bred into four colors: yellow, red, pink and white. Variations in color scheme, where red, or pink combined with white, caused excitement among tulip enthusiasts. Soon unicolor yellow, or red tulips were sold in bulk, while connoisseurs prized tulips of varied color and intriguing shape. In 1608, a tulip-crazed miller traded his mill for a specimen tulip.

Standard Color Tulips - photo credit Chris Greinke

Higher prices of variegated color tulips were deemed justified by rarity. Since mother tulips produced few healthy offshoots, variegated tulips were hard to reproduce in great number, fostering scarcity of desired plants. In the early seventeenth century, it was not known that the cause of the condition so prized in bulbs, was the result of a virus, spread bulb-to-bulb by aphids. Merely placing bulbs in a mound of aphids produced a feeding frenzy for bugs, but not always the desired result for bulbs.

An ability of so many citizens in the Netherlands to purchase bulbs and plant gardens was made possible by economic growth of the country. The country enjoyed a rise of a tradesmen class and expansion of the upper class, resulting in availability of discretionary time and disposable wealth. In the 1630s, Amsterdam was the place of economic opportunity. For the Dutch East India Company, Amsterdam was a major port for shipbuilding, departures to the Far East and home base for warehouses for goods imported for sale. Work was plentiful and wages were rising. In 1631, Rembrandt came from Leiden to Amsterdam, to be part of the vibrant city.

Rembrandt did not paint tulips. He painted aficionados of tulips such as Dr. Claes Pietersz, who was so fond of the tulips grown in his garden that he changed his name to Dr. Nicolaes Tulp, tulip in Dutch. *The Anatomy Lesson of Dr. Nicolaes Tulp*, painted by Rembrandt in 1632, established him as a favored artist among Amsterdam society. Lesser-known artists painted tulips.

In 1630, a tradesman in Amsterdam earned about three hundred guilders a year, enough to keep a small family clothed and fed. Tradesmen rarely owned property. In 1636, a weaver made sixty-thousand guilders in four months from astute trading in rare tulips.[34] When word spread through taverns of quick fortune to be made in tulip trade, workingmen sold their tools for tulips and became florists.

Breeding tulips is slow work. A mother-bulb will create two or three baby bulbs in a year, for two or three years. Tulip seeds can be harvested from a flower, which takes skill and patience. Tulips grown from seed do not produce flowering bulbs for several years. Slow growth of tulip inventory fueled demand, until bulbs were auctioned several times in a single year, for increasing prices.

---

[34] Dash, p. 145.

The Dutch government never sanctioned tulip sales at auction. Sales were conducted in taverns after consumption of generous quantities of beer. As the frenzy for tulip selling grew into a mania, tulip connoisseurs of wealth stood back and pArcticipated only in collecting rare bulbs. Tradesmen and laborers, willing to gamble, risked all they had on becoming instantly wealthy from tulips.

Tulipomania, as it became known, would not have been so devastating to so many who had everything to lose, but for instigation of leveraged purchases, conducted with private loans, guaranteed on personal collateral. Enterprising sellers devised sales of futures, purchased with promissory notes, on bulbs not yet bloomed, or for not-yet-produced offshoots. Offshoots were sold, and resold, while still in the ground. Tulip share investments were a gamble, at best.

It is often said of the Dutch, that despite the Calvinist culture of moralism and restraint in personal life, they like to gamble. Tulip auctions preyed on a gambler mentally, with the hope of a life of leisure and otherwise unattainable wealth. In 1633, a house was sold for three tulip bulbs. In 1636, bulb prices doubled in a week. At the height of mania, from December 1636 to February 5, 1637, ten million guilders changed hands in one small Dutch town.

One red and white, highly prized, Semper Augustus, that previously sold for one thousand guilders, resold in January 1637 for ten thousand guilders. On that fateful day in February, a single bulb sold in a tavern auction for five thousand, two hundred guilders. The most Rembrandt received for a painting was two thousand, four hundred guilders.

Within a week of the February 5 auction, there were no buyers in taverns. Slowly word spread of the lack of buyers. Sellers began to panic. Those left holding futures and pieces of syndicates in a single bulb, realized they had nothing of intrinsic value. As end-of-the-chain buyers defaulted on loans, futures, and other creative purchasing schemes, defaults radiated down the paper trail. Holders of actual bulbs had sacks of yellow, or red minimally valued bulbs. Holders of paper and paper obligations were caught in a web of defaults. In 1637 Netherlands, debtors went to prison. Whole households faced liquidating all personal items and work tools to meet obligations.

The Dutch government never sanctioned bulb auctions. Futures Trading was illegal. Despite Dutch law, defaulting Dutch florists looked to their local government to bail them out of possible bankruptcy, or incarceration. Local governments looked to national government in the Hague for a solution. The Hague passed the problem back to cities to hold gamblers accountable. Bankrupt traders blamed Jews and Mennonites, not part of the auctions, as convenient scapegoats.

Reputable tulip collectors and non-gamblers chided amateur florists. Tulips fell from favor as gifts and were uprooted from gardens. Dr. Tulp removed his tulip adorned office sign.

Historic Tulip Market Stalls

In the end, everyone looked to the courts for resolution. Tavern auctions were recorded on chalkboards, leaving no tangible evidence. Finally, cases were settled privately for ten percent of the value of a debt. Along the chain of obligations, financial ruin was averted for most of the florists. Holders of actual bulbs were left to consolidate holdings, which became the beginnings of the new, smaller, restrained and eventually highly successful tulip industry in the Netherlands.

By the eighteenth century, a dozen tulip growers dominated tulip trade in the Netherlands. The dominant province for tulip growing is Holland. Tulip growers learned to breed variegated tulips, not dependent for appearance upon disease. Tulip varieties developed grown year around, making tulips available for gift giving at all holidays.

Chocolate

Dutch Souveniers

In the sixteenth century, when Spanish conquistadors observed Aztecs drinking a foamy liquid made with ground herbs and pulp of a bulbous plant, it did not occur to them the substance would rival gold in value. They brought the curious plant back to Spain. Drinking the greasy, bitter, pale brown powder of the cocoa plant never became popular in Spain.

By the eighteenth century, the Dutch were in control of the world market in cocoa beans. Ships of the Dutch East India Company brought beans from the East Indies along with shipments of spices, and from West Africa, where ships stopped for water, when homeward bound. Ships of the Dutch West India Company returned with cocoa beans from the Dutch colony of Suriname, on the northeast coast of South America, where cocoa plants were grown in plantations.

Chocolate initially produced from cocoa beans was not the delectable chocolate enjoyed today. Blocks of processed chocolate were rich in greasy cocoa butter, from fat left in the process. The bitter, light brown substance was known as Zeeuwse chocolate.

Spice merchant, Frederick Korff, began producing chocolate in Amsterdam in 1811. His initial factory turned out Zeeuwse chocolate until 1871. The factory was known for its iconic windmill, which ground cocoa beans. In 1880, the windmill was demolished and replaced by the Stoom Chocolate Fabriek de Bijenkorf, that is, the Beehive Steam Chocolate Factory of F. Korff and Company. In 1911, the Company celebrated its centennial of Dutch Chocolate.

In 1978, Korff was sold to General Cocoa of Holland and in 1986, it became part of the Cargill conglomerate. The old sign on the roof of the Amstel Train Station, Kenner Kiezen Korff, Connoisseurs Choose Korff, is gone. The tradition of making fine Dutch Chocolate remains.

Coenraad Johannes Van Houten founded his chocolate company in 1815. In 1828, he developed the two-step process, that has become the standard method of making superior Dutch chocolate as it is lovingly consumed today. First, cocoa is heated and pressed, removing more than half of the fat from cocoa beans. Then cocoa is roasted, to enhance flavor and enrich color to the deep brown characteristic of Dutch chocolate. The Van Houten process results in cocoa powder that is tastier, easier to digest, and soluble in milk, or water.

The Van Houten process created the chocolate bar as it is sold today. In 1850, Van Houten began exporting his chocolate to England, France and Germany. Today, chocolate is exported around the world in varied shapes and with varied additives such as flavorings and nuts. Regardless of the final shape of the confection, the process developed almost two centuries ago is still the epitome of Dutch Chocolate.

Diamonds

Portuguese Synagogue Amsterdam

Religious toleration has long been a characteristic of the Dutch. When the Spanish Lowlands of the largely Protestant Netherlands separated from the largely Catholic Belgium, there remained in Dutch provinces a substantial number of Catholics. Rather than resort to civil war, as almost occurred in Belgium, the Dutch allowed for religious diversity, as long as Catholics and eventually Jews prayed at home. As a result, there are hidden Catholic chapels in the attics of Dutch homes, some of which became Synagogues, and some of which became hiding places for Dutch Jews during the Nazi occupation in World War II.

Another benefit to the Dutch, as a result of their religious toleration, was economic. When the merchant class of Jews was forced from Portugal and Spain, a number of Jews settled in Amsterdam. There they often became successful when engaged in trade with former antagonists in Iberia. By 1670, the largest Portuguese synagogue in the world was in Amsterdam.

Portuguese Jews brought to Amsterdam their skills in the diamond cutting and polishing industry, a trade previously unknown to the Dutch. Tradesmen in the Netherlands joined guilds, where skills were learned and jobs were given. Jews were prohibited from joining guilds in the United Provinces of the Netherlands, despite an ability to live freely in the country. Since diamond cutting was not an existing field for Dutch guilds, there were no diamond cutting guilds from which Jews were excluded. Jews formed their own guilds and made Amsterdam the diamond capital of the world in the seventeenth century. Dutch have led the diamond market ever since.

Seeing, Sampling and Shopping in Amsterdam Today

Bulb Market Today

Today, nine billion tulip bulbs are harvested annually in the Netherlands, most in the province of Holland. Holland provides two-thirds of the world supply of tulips to florists. Peak season for viewing tulips in the fields from Haarlem to Leiden is in mid-April. Cruise guests who arrive too early for tulips will be treated to crocus and daffodil blooms and those who arrive late will enjoy fields of lilies. Just south of Amsterdam is the town of Aalsmeer, where billions of cut flowers and plants are sold at the largest flower auction in the world.

Dutch chocolatiers still lead the world in making rich, dark brown, Dutch chocolate, although most of the cocoa grown in the world now comes from Ecuador. Dutch confectioners have raised chocolate to an art form. There are chocolate tours, to take guests to several leading purveyors of Dutch chocolate. Those who visited Amsterdam a decade ago will remember little chocolate windmills and clogs. Today chocolate is laced with spices and molded into delicate shapes that are treats for the eye, as well as the palate.

Shopping Amsterdam Today

Although Amsterdam is no longer the largest diamond capital of the world, it is still a major center for diamond cutting. There are a dozen diamond-cutting factories in the city. Amsterdam diamond sellers pride themselves in the quality of their stones. Coster Diamonds, for example, has been in business since 1840. Tours of diamond factories and of the Diamond Museum will create new enthusiasts for bright stones.

Amsterdam is a popular cruise port for the beauty of its streets and depth of history, so easily accessed from the port. Ride a bicycle through the streets, past chocolate shops and diamond factories, then into low-lying, flower-filled, countryside as the Dutch love to do, or walk, or be driven through the area. This is a gem of a city, in a small country, which has given people of the world the means to celebrate meaningful moments in life with flowers, chocolate and diamonds.

Tulip Garden photo credit Chris Greinke

NORWAY
Viking Ships, Fram & Kon Tiki in Oslo

Viking Tomb Area Overlooking Oslo

It was not by accident that Oslo was founded at the head of a deep and picturesque fjord at the entrance to the Baltic Sea. The Viking chief who chose the site in the eleventh century knew that his future home was impressive to all who sailed past. With a clear view of the approach, the town was defensible, even without protective walls. When years of returning home from profitable raids was at an end, the Viking king would board his funeral ship and be buried in the growing circle of funerary ships used as tombs above the town. From this vantage point, for all eternity, in life and in death, Vikings could look out upon Oslofjord and feel a part of the sea.

Oslo was founded late in the Viking era. It was neither a strategic port, nor a natural site of industry and commerce in early stages of formation of Norway. Other towns founded along Oslofjord became fortified, active ports, closer to maritime traffic passing through the Baltic Sea. Oslo, as the home of a powerful Viking king, bestowed of his resources and attention, became the capital of the territory by 1300. The city never lost its preeminence among cities of Norway, through medieval times to the present day.

Oslo was not merely born of a people, who lived to venture out to sea. Traditions, spirit and psyche of its people continue to be inexorably linked to the sea, as a vehicle to explore the maritime world. Possessed of Viking DNA, to look beyond land, albeit with a calm and peaceful desire for knowledge rather than conquest, Norwegians are drawn to Oslo, from which their dreams are launched.

In the late nineteenth century, explorers of the world were focused upon discovery of the North Pole. Many ships were lost in the effort, as victims of *screw-ice*. This was the terrifying experience of fast enveloping blocks of ice, that would imprison a ship, while ice gyrated, tearing the hull to shreds, leaving sailors drowned, or stranded on ice. Ships of the day were not suited for the ghostly phenomenon.

Undeterred and armed with a life of experiences at sea, an explorer from Oslo pursued his theory into form, until he became captain of the greatest polar exploration vessel ever built. The *Fram* was built to task, like no other ship previously conceived. It remains a marvel of maritime engineering. It is natural that the ship to overcome terrors of the frozen Arctic, was conceived in Oslo.

Early in the twentieth century, a young college student in Oslo questioned all entrenched theories in his texts, of capabilities of man to traverse the sea. Self-professed to have a fear of water, he drew upon his Norwegian heritage to express his curiosity by launching a raft to travel the sea in the manner of early man. In the voyage of the *Kon-Tiki*, Thor Heyerdahl tested his theories by personal experience. He succeeded in adding to the body of scientific knowledge, as much as he continued the legacy of his adventurous ancestors.

In Oslo today, there are monuments to the Vikings, the *Fram* and the *Kon-Tiki*. Their stories make up the story of Oslo more so than events of terrestrial experience. In brief, this is their story.

Beginnings of a Viking Capital

Oseberg Viking Ship

Vikings were great seamen. They were not also great writers. Although archaeologists have determined from human remains of a millennium, that a Viking king founded Oslo in the eleventh century, they are not certain upon whom to bestow the honor. Norse sagas, oral and written tales dating from the twelfth century, attribute beginnings of Oslo to Harald III in 1049. Harald perished in the Battle of Stamford Bridge in 1066, leading up to the Battle of Hastings. In singing praises of one who died in epic battles of its age, attribution for founding a great city is an appropriate honor.

Archaeologists have also determined from excavated burials, that life began in Oslo about a century prior to the arrival of Harald. Oslo seized on the earlier date to celebrate a millennium anniversary in 2000. The earlier date opens possibilities to consideration of several Viking kings of Norway, as possible founding monarchs.

Tune Viking Ship

The Fairhair dynasty of Viking kings of Norway ruled the land from about 872 to 1066, with some interruptions. Founding patriarch, Harald Fairhair united Viking clans of Norway before he died in 932, leaving nine sons to contest his kingdom. Harald's son Eric I, known as Bloody Axe, killed seven of his eight brothers to become heir. The surviving brother, Haakon the Good, vanquished Bloody Axe, to become King of Norway in 954. Haakon was too busy with war to establish a family, so upon his death in a battle in 960, the son of Eric I, Harald Greycloak, became King Harald II. This Fairhair king died in battle in Denmark in 970.

Descendants of Harald Fairhair welcomed his great-great-great-grandson, Olaf Harald, as king of Norway in 1015, when he seized on an opportunity to push Danish kings from control. Danes reasserted themselves in 1028, ousting Olaf. Two years later, Olaf was back leading the famous battle of Norwegian history at Stiklestad, Sweden. In battle, Olaf inspired his men to Fram, Fram, (forward, forward), in the name of Christ. Faith did not protect Olaf, who died in the battle.

Olaf II, as he was known, was a cruel king, well regarded for accomplishing conversion of his flock to Christianity. The year following his death, Olaf was recognized as a saint by a local bishop for giving Norwegians respite from Danish rule and for furthering the church. In 1164, Olaf officially became a Roman Catholic saint; canonized under Pope Alexander III. An axe, seen thereafter in the coat of arms of Norway, symbolizes Saint Olaf.

When Olaf's half-brother Harald died in England in 1066, the Viking era died with him. Two of Harald's sons became kings of Norway in a new age. Turf wars to protect a homeland replaced going to sea to forage for treasure. In 1299, the Duke of Oslo outlived his brothers to become King Haakon V, King of Norway. Over the following year, Oslo replaced Bergen as capital of the land. The city founded by Vikings grew as the capital of Norway, even during long periods when Norway was united with, and controlled by, kings of Denmark.

Akershus Fortress Oslo

King Haakon V protected his capital city from incursions from Swedish kings by erecting Akershus Fortress, in which he built a castle. Continually under military control, and previously used as a prison, the fortress was never breached.[35] The castle was rebuilt in the 1700s, to add a moat, in response to advances in warfare. For centuries Akershus was home to rulers of Norway. Today it is used for state ceremonies and occasionally as a theater.

It is fitting that Akershus castle, built by the first king of modern Norway, is the resting place of the first king of independent Norway, King Haakon VII. Denmark controlled Norway for 434 years, until Frederick VI of Denmark handed the country to Sweden in 1814, retaining the Norwegian province of Greenland for Denmark. In 1905, Sweden and Norway agreed to separate. The son of the Danish king became King Haakon VII of Norway.

It would be fair to the memory of Vikings to note that not all Norse Vikings were drawn to a peaceful life in Oslo. Thorvald Asvaldsson was exiled in 960, by Harald Fairhair for manslaughter, and went back to sea with his young son, Eric the Red. Together they colonized Iceland. Eric was much like his father and was exiled from the Iceland community for violence. Eric went on to colonize Greenland with his son, Leif Erikson. The travels of Eric and Leif are another story.

Today the University of Oslo is home to the Museum of Cultural History and the Viking Ship Museum. Viking ships used as burial tombs, found on farms in Norway, excavated from 1867 to 1904, have been preserved for further study and to delight visitors. In 1904, on Oseberg farm in western Norway, the burial vessel of two noble women, dated to 870, contained burial goods of an advanced, artistic society. Gokstad farm revealed a longship of thirty-two oarsmen, built around 850, and entombed for over a millennium. In the 1880 excavation, sixteen Viking shields of alternating yellow and black were still discernable above the oars. The wealthy man buried in the ship died in battle, his wounds evident in his remains. Gokstad ship has been restored in a display

---

[35] The prison was not escape-proof. In 1835, notorious serial burglar Ole Høiland was imprisoned at Akershus. He escaped after four years of imprisonment, was apprehended and returned to Akershus three years later, where he committed suicide in 1848.

as impressive today as the ship must have been to clansmen and adversaries when it last sailed. Unrestored is the small ship, Tune, excavated in 1867, and dating to 900. Tune had twenty-four oarsmen. In the age before sail, these ships commanded the sea.

The Viking Ship Museum captures a vision of Viking ships rowed into Oslo, where Viking kings established a home that has endured for a millennium, even as Viking culture evolved into peaceful, terrestrial pursuits. In death, as in life, traversing the sea was their realm. Future seafarers of Oslo are their legacy.

How the *Fram* Conquered the Arctic and Antarctic

The *Fram* was a wooden ship that sailed further north and south than any ship had gone before. It safely carried crews under captains, who explored the North and South Poles, as well as mapping the west coast of Greenland. Proven to resist shredding in treacherous *screw-ice* of the Arctic, the *Fram* and its captains put the attention of the world on seafarers of Oslo. The *Fram* quickly became, and still is, a symbol of pride of Norwegians in their mastery of the seas.

The story of the *Fram* begins with polar explorer Fridtjof Nansen. Nansen sailed the Arctic, then he crossed inland ice, in his search for the North Pole. Prior to sailing, he carefully studied tragedies of others, to build on their experience. Notably, Nansen looked for pieces of wrecked ships as they drifted to land. He found bits of wrecked vessels that had attempted Arctic exploration from Siberia and the Bering Strait, washed up on the beaches of Greenland. From all he saw, Nansen developed a theory that an ice-worthy ship, sailing into an Arctic Sea current, could drift across the sea through unknown reaches of the Arctic, farther than any ship had sailed before and return safely.

Nansen's theories were well received in Norway, among people who innately understood the sea. In November 1892, when Nansen presented his plan to the Royal Geographical Society in London, the scholarly explorers were skeptical. They advised Nansen continue to sail near the shore, avoid unknown currents, and prepare to become trapped in ice for years. Renowned polar explorers wished him luck in his bold venture on untested theories.

Another accomplished Norwegian sailor, Otto Sverdrup, was intrigued by the possibility of sailing further north into the Arctic and he had faith in Nansen's ability to do so. Together they approached master ship builder Colin Archer, at his home in England, to build a ship to task, for which there was no prototype. Archer defined his assignment as one to build a ship "so sturdy that it will resist the greatest possible pressure from any direction."[36] It became a test of man, material and the physics of engineering, pushed into another realm.

Collaboration of the three men produced a design for the *Fram*. The greatest polar expedition ship would also be the most expensive to build, rig and equip. With Norwegian King Oscar II as a patron, and with substantial government funds, together with private subscriptions, launching the *Fram* became oversubscribed. Even the Royal Geographic Society invested in the venture.

The *Fram* was built as a three-masted schooner, with a 220-horse power engine, capable of six to seven knots. Electric lights were wired to run from the engine, or a generator, powered from a deck-mounted windmill. The assumption was that the ship would be at sea for years.

Captain Nansen and Master Sverdrup wanted comfort and safety for themselves and ten sailors onboard to be integral to the ship's design. They specified comfortable beds, an exercise area, fresh air below deck and an electrically lighted library and card room. When the ship was provisioned, the best knowledge of the time in nutrition and food preservation informed their commissary. The *Fram* carried eight lifeboats, a motorboat and supplies necessary to live on ice for an extended period.

Unveiling of the *Fram* was a moving experience. The smooth, rounded hull from stem to stern was a sculpture of simplicity. The Fram is 128 feet long, 32.5 feet across the beam, and sits an impressive 114 feet above the water line. There were no protrusions upon which ice could attach. It was evident to all that technology of shipbuilding made a quantum leap in their lifetime. Spirits of long-dead Vikings, from their ship-tombs above Oslo, had to be smiling.

To appreciate the genius of *Fram* design, it is necessary to venture below deck into the maze of struts. The frame of oak and iron is surrounded by a four-

---

[36] FRAM, The Committee for the Preservation of the Polar Ship Fram, Oslo, 1961, p. 12.

feet thick oak bow. Between frame sections, pitch and sawdust was poured to ensure the ship would continue to float should the skin be pierced. Breaching the hull was not likely, given iron plates hung as exterior planking to resist screw-ice. Nansen later wrote in the ship's log, that sailing the *Fram* he felt he was in "an impregnable castle."[37] For so long as it sailed, the *Fram* never disappointed its captains.

Fram

---

[37] FRAM, p. 13.

Archer designed dynamics of the *Fram* in ice to act as a smooth nut pressed between his fingers. The more pressure applied, the more likely the object to move upward. The higher the ship was pushed upward by the press of ice, the more the weight of the ship pushed against the crush of ice. The *Fram* was designed so that under pressure from ice, eventually the ship would sit on top the ice. To avoid tipping over on its keel, as it rested on top of ice, the keel of the *Fram* was flattened.

On June 24, 1893, the *Fram* was launched on its maiden voyage from Oslo harbor. During its three years at sea, the *Fram* engineering was tested in Arctic ice. At one point an ice wall rose above its decks. The port side of the ship was so fully engulfed in ice that the whole ship was rolled to its side. Captain Nansen ordered lifeboats be deployed. At the last critical moment, the *Fram* began to violently shake. Suddenly, without any further action of the crew, the *Fram* began to throw off huge boulders of ice and rise above the threatening tomb. Archer's design was fully vindicated. Nansen was free to sail further north than any captain before him.

Nansen sailed the *Fram* north and east to the New Siberian Islands. From there the *Fram* was allowed to drift toward Greenland in Arctic Sea current. On March 14, 1895, Nansen and one of the sailors, Fredrick Jalmar Johansen, left the ship and trekked across ice, in an attempt to reach the North Pole. Unable to do so, the two men turned south, missed the *Fram* as it floated past, and reached Norway, in an amazing feat of their own, arriving on the coast of Norway within days of the *Fram*. Both expeditions accumulated vast amounts of knowledge of terrain and wildlife of the far north.

Three years later, and with some modifications to the deck of the *Fram* to resist accumulation of ice, Sverdrup borrowed the ship for an expedition to map the west coast of Greenland. In four years at sea, Sverdrup accomplished his goal while he accumulated fifty-three crates of minerals, fifty thousand plants, and two thousand glass jars of biological specimens. Disappointed that Norway demurred to Canada on dominion over the territory he mapped, Sverdrup was pleased to receive a medal from Canada. He sailed back into the harbor at Oslo as a national hero.

In February 1909, Norwegian Roald Amundsen borrowed the *Fram* to enable his quest to outdo Nansen in sailing north to discover the North Pole. Before Amundsen set sail, on April 6, 1909, American Robert E. Peary reached the North Pole on foot. Not to be outdone, Amundsen turned course to the south in an effort to be the first to reach the South Pole. His landing party reached Whale Bay on December 14, 1911, from which point Amundsen trekked to the pole. Victorious, the explorer returned to Whale Bay in January 1912, where he rejoined the *Fram*. The *Fram* added to its record by sailing further south than any ship to that time.

Amundsen wanted the *Fram* to add another first to its pedigree. From October to December 1913, the *Fram* waited for the Panama Canal to open, so that it would be the first ship to traverse the locks on its way to the Pacific, and exploration north of the Bering Strait. The canal did not open for another six months. Frustrated, Amundsen sailed south to Buenos Aires, where he received orders to return to Oslo. The *Fram* was property of the Norwegian Navy, which had other priorities in 1914.

Fram Museum Oslo

During World War I, the *Fram* sat neglected. After the war, the Ministry of Defense wanted to dismantle the historic ship and build a replica for display. Fortunately, Sverdrup and the Committee for Preservation of the *Fram* persevered, until the *Fram* was installed, somewhat refurbished, in its own museum.[38] The museum opened in 1936, in its permanent home in Bygdøy, near Oslo, in the presence of King Haakon VII.

Kon-Tiki Continuing the Legacy

Kon Tiki

Not satisfied with ethnological and linguistic studies that tied people of Easter Island to ancestors in Southeast Asian islands, Thor Heyerdahl sought to prove his theory that the island was first peopled with sailors from South America.

---

[38] Norwegian beer brewers, the Ringness brothers, deserve note for financial commitments to voyages of the *Fram* and to the home for the *Fram*.

He and five friends built a balsa raft, in the manner of early native people, and sailed from Santiago, Chile, in a one hundred and one day, 4,300 nautical mile journey in 1947. His log of the journey became a best-selling book and a documentary film. The film won an Oscar in 1951, and nomination for an Oscar and Golden Globe for a remake of the film in 2012. It was the legacy of his heritage that would not allow Heyerdahl to leave a question of sea exploration unanswered.

While on his honeymoon, ensconced in university study in Polynesia, young Heyerdahl was enthralled by island legends of white-bearded gods the people called Tiki. These peaceful gods taught Inca of South America life-ways and architecture. The gods sailed to Hawaii and then to Samoa, Tonga and New Zealand, building enormous statues in each place. Heyerdahl named his craft Kon-Tiki in honor of these tall, white-bearded gods.

Based on the voyage of the Kon-Tiki, Heyerdahl continued to assert that people from South America reached Polynesia directly, or through Hawaii, in 1100 CE, and that Asians arrived later by an alternate route. Conventional archaeology holds that Malaysians first populated the islands, and that island people engaged in trade with South Americans, who ventured out to sea. Heyerdahl sparked lively debate with his propositions. He later sponsored study on Galapagos, the results of which claimed habitation by early people. It is uncontroverted that Heyerdahl proved a balsa raft was capable of long-distance sea voyages.[39]

The voyage of the Kon-Tiki continues to ride high on waves of popular culture, as a contemporary tale of bravery at sea, not unlike centuries of delight brought to readers by Norse Sagas. The library of Polynesia studies is now part of the Kon-Tiki Museum in Oslo, a monument to the former student, who was inspired to travel far out to sea.

---

[39] Read more on Heyerdahl's theories in the Galapagos in Cruise through History Itinerary IX Ports of South America, Port Galapagos; and Thor Heyerdahl, Kon-Tiki, Simon & Shuster 1973, paperback 2009.

Oslo Today

KonTiki Museum

Today Oslo is a many-faceted cosmopolitan city. It has been home to great artists, athletes and inventors. Edvard Munch donated over a thousand paintings and a version of the Scream to Oslo. Three-time Olympic gold figure skater Sonja Henie founded the Henie-Onstad Cultural Center in 1968, which she endowed with part of her fortune and her art collection. The Nobel Peace Center occupies an ultra-modern renovation of a train station that would have made its native son proud.

Still, it is the connection to the sea, upon which Oslo was founded, that remains central to its identity. That explorers from Oslo completed maps of the world, does not mean that all questions of maritime science have been answered. The Oslo harbor is a vibrant place. Though the last Vikings sailed a millennium ago, their spirit remains alive in Oslo.

Detail Viking Ship

Detail Monolith

Vigeland's Dream for Oslo

In the center of the capital of Norway is a gift from the city of Oslo to its residents. Comprising over ninety acres of carefully designed gardens, the grand gift is the largest sculpture installation in the world by a single artist. Today that gift is shared with visitors from all over the world.

Native Norwegian, Gustov Vigeland came to Oslo at the age of fifteen to learn woodcarving. He returned to his favorite city after being schooled in sculpture by greats of the present and past in Paris, Florence, Copenhagen and Berlin. After establishing himself as a sculptor of merit, Vigeland made an historic agreement with Oslo to rid himself of daily logistics of life and business of art, in exchange for endowing the city with decades of his effort, in a self-imposed monumental task.

The result of the contract in 1921 between Vigeland, then age fifty-two, and Oslo, was two hundred and twelve sculptures, artfully installed in Frogner Park. For the first-time visitor, the park can be overwhelming. When understood as a walk through the cycle of life, it can be a cathArctic experience. This is the story of the man, his monuments, and the artistic experience of life in its simplicity and beauty in Oslo.

Making of the Man and Monument

Gustov Vigeland was only and always a sculptor. As a young man he sculpted tiny designs into knife handles, working among his family of cabinetmakers in a Norwegian town outside of Oslo. Vigeland knew he had talent, so he left home for the city when he was fifteen, to work making woodcuts for sale.

Vigeland Sculputre Garden Frogner Park Oslo

Vigeland was born Adolf Gustov Thorson in 1869. He and his brother, also a talented artist, went to live with their grandparents on Vigeland farm as young boys, upon the death of their father. Vigeland means Viking Land, an appropriate surname for a man destined to become a national icon in Norway.

Vigeland debuted as a sculptor in his early twenties. He then traveled to study from 1891 to 1896 in Europe, Germany and Denmark. When he exhibited in Norway through 1896, he received critical praise.

From 1897 to 1907, Vigeland had steady work in restoration of the cathedral at Trondheim. His work in the grand cathedral comprised forty-four sculptures, including sixteen gargoyles, angels in relief and in full sculpture, as well as seven sculptures in oak above the screen near the altar. His most notable work in the church is that of saints. His job was to restore, not create, so today it takes a practiced eye to distinguish Vigeland's work amid the grandeur of Trondheim.

For thirty-year old Vigeland, regular employment enabled him to support a family. He married Laura Andersen in 1900. They had two children: Elsa and Gustov.

In 1905, Norway became independent of Sweden, unleashing a strong spirit of nationalism through the country. For Vigeland this meant commissions to create busts of famous people in a new nation seeking symbols of Norwegian heritage. He sculpted a bust of well-known playwright Henrik Ibsen, the father of realism and modernism in theater and the author of the frequently performed A Doll's House.

Vigeland was also given a commission to sculpt the bust of Niels Henrik Abel, who lived a short, impoverished life from 1802 to 1829, recognized little during his life as a master mathematician. In a seven-year period, Able created proofs later pondered by mathematicians for a century, solving problems that evaded great minds for two hundred fifty years. Abel died of illness just days before he received an appointment as a university professor. Oslo gave posthumous and lasting recognition to its bright scholar, in whose honor Abel Hill was named. When the original site of the Abel memorial was subsumed within Vigeland's sculpture garden, the statue of Abel was moved to the drive leading to the Royal Palace.

Vigeland Fountain

In 1900, Vigeland drew plans for a fountain to be placed prominently in the road leading to the Royal Palace. Initial plans for a bowl held high by giants grew by 1906 into a fountain surrounded by twenty bronze trees. People living in the trees depicted lives of ordinary people from cradle to grave, in the act of living through normal life emotions of fear and joy. When plans of the fountain were released to the public, leaders in the art world proclaimed from Paris that Oslo would become known for the Vigeland fountain.

A model of the 1906 version of the fountain sparked controversy, when displayed in the Museum of Arts and Crafts in Oslo. Some thought the nude figures provocative and would have a deteriorating impact on morals of viewers.[40] The response, of more than four thousand people viewing the model in a single day, was to donate to the project. The city donated heavily to the project. Swedes sent funds to support the fountain. In a few months the project was fully funded.[41]

For ten years, from 1906 to 1916, Vigeland worked on the fountain in a cold, damp, rudimentary studio in Oslo. In April 1916, he opened the studio for one week for public viewing of his progress. The response was overwhelming. People waited in long lines for hours for an opportunity to view the work, and then returned to the rear of the line to wait for another opportunity.

Instead of being shocked by nude figures, viewers found they could easily relate to the people in the trees. Five tree groups were of children, ten of youths evolving to adults, and five were of people in old age. Bronze children swarmed at play, a young woman had closed eyes, while a man chased away his life. There were men and women intertwined and yet struggling to be free of the branches that held them. In trees of older people, one man clung to the tree of life, while a woman reflected back near her grandchild at play.

Vigeland continued to work on his creations. The project grew from bronze tree groups to include models for granite sculptures of groups of people, also on the theme of stages of life, and reliefs sculpted into sides of fountain pools.

---

[40] All of Vigeland's sculptures are nude. Guides suggest that Vigeland wanted to portray people in a classless state of age and emotion.
[41] Ragna Stang, The Vigeland Sculpture Park in Oslo, 2nd ed., Tanum, 1967, p. 4.

The new models for granite sculptures included figures of people depicted in a rounded, simplified shape. Vigeland's plans for a sculpture installation expanded to a round, several-layered, staircase leading up to major granite works. Clearly a larger site and more funds were necessary to produce the expanded effort.

In 1921, the city of Oslo and Vigeland entered into an historic agreement. At age fifty-two, and shortly about to marry a young woman, Vigeland wanted to concentrate on his art and be relived of concerns of obtaining financial support for his eventual public installations. He agreed that all of his creations would belong to the city without payment. In return, Oslo would furnish a new, fully equipped studio, supplies for works of art, and compensate the artist's assistants, stonecutters and bronze workers. The agreement required the city to supply land for the installation of the full project, within Oslo.

Once the contract was signed, the city demolished Vigeland's old studio to build a city library on the site. The new studio in Frogner Park was not completed until 1924. Vigeland began to live and work in the studio before the building was finished. It became his home for twenty years, to the end of his life. Today the studio, including his residence on the third floor, is a museum.

Amid hardships all Norwegians suffered in World War II, Vigeland died in 1943, at age seventy-four. His ashes were placed in a niche in the belfry of the studio, now the Vigeland Museum in Frogner Park. The museum, containing his studio and residence, as well as plaster models of projects, opened in 1947.

Vigeland Sculpture Arrangement

Wheel of Life

The Vigeland Sculpture Arrangement in Frogner Park, as it is officially known, consists of two hundred and twelve sculptures, some with over one hundred figures of people in stages of life. Vigeland anticipated a wall surrounding the sculptures, so he created eleven gates. The wall was never completed, although there is a main gate and eight smaller gates. The main gates have fanciful, wrought iron dragons. The smaller gates carry forward the theme of life. In one gate there are three girls walking arm-in-arm through clover.

Once inside the gates, there is one main path, along which sculptures are arranged. First, the visitor crosses a three hundred-foot long bridge adorned with fifty-eight bronze figure groups. There is a fetus on its head, children at play, and the famous Hothead statue of a young child stamping his foot, evidently angry. End-posts of the bridge, on each side, have people in a struggle with monsters, the symbol of evil. A monk defeats evil on one post, while a man loses to his demon on the other post.

The fountain surrounded by bronze trees is prominent in the center of the sculpture arrangement. Water flows into ponds with walls, on which reliefs continue the theme of stages of life. Also cast in bronze, is a series of human wheels. In the Wheel of Life, there are seven people intertwined in an eternal circle. The circle, completed in 1933 to 1934, is ten feet in diameter on a pedestal. It sits at the top of a flight of stairs, giving visitors the opportunity to ascend in life.

The crescendo on the Arrangement is in the fifty-foot-high, solid piece of granite, that is the Monolith, set on top of a platform, above three layers of steps. It took six months in 1928, to move the stone into position and then build a scaffold around the stone and next to a plaster model. The Monolith took three stonecutters thirteen years to complete the intertwined one hundred and twenty-one figures. Figures on the Monolith climb, collapse, help others to continue, and are lifted as they seem to strive to the top. On the steps are sculpture groups in a fourth rendition of the cycle of life, in larger, simple figures, carved from their granite bases. Vigeland commented that people could interpret the Monolith, as they liked. Clearly there is a struggle. Viewers supply their own meaning, as they step among the figures, or just sit and contemplate life.

Consumed by Demons

Frogner Park Pedigree

Locals refer to the largest sculpture garden in the world and the largest park in Oslo, as the Vigeland Sculpture Arrangement in Frogner Park. They correct those who refer to the famous garden as Vigeland Park, as they are fiercely proud of the long pedigreed relationship between the city and its historic residents. There is more to Frogner Park than Vigeland, although locals admit that Vigeland has given the park international attention, including continued visitor popularity.[42]

Frogner estate first came to prominence in the 1740s, when purchased by the Danish-born military officer and Royal Chamberlain, Hans Jacob Scheel. He built the original Frogner Manor, since expanded and now a property of the Oslo Museum. Scheel was commander of the Fredriksten Fortress, located further out along the Oslofjord, who enjoyed the serenity of his large forested estate in what is now Oslo. He opened wooded areas to create a romantic park setting in 1750. Scheel died defending the fortress in 1774. When his heirs sold the Frogner Manor estate, it passed to some of the richest and most accomplished men in Norway.

Bernt Anker, a timber merchant, was the wealthiest man in Norway and an accomplished playwright, when he purchased Frogner Manor. He expanded the estate house by 1805. Benjamin Wegner, also a timber merchant, came from Berlin to be part of a large industrial enterprise in the city. He brought the pavilion in Frogner Park from Germany, after he purchased the estate in 1836. It was his wedding present to his wife. Wegner expanded the park and gardens in 1840, before he began to sell parcels to developers.

In 1896, the land was purchased by the city of Christiania, now Oslo, with the plan to use the land for its growing population.[43] Instead, the city kept intact the landscape so enjoyed by its former owners, opening it to the public in 1904, as a city park. Prior to opening the entire grounds to the public, in 1901 Frogner Stadium opened, offering the public a place to play and watch soccer

---

[42] The city trolley has a stop immediately in front of the main Vigeland gates.
[43] Christiania was changed to Kristiania in an effort to make names more Norwegian. It grew as a suburb of Oslo until merged within the capital city.

in the summer and ice skate in the winter. The Jubilee Exhibition celebrating the centennial of the Norwegian Constitution was held in the park in 1914. In 1956, a swimming pool complex opened to the public.

Giving land within Frogner Park to the Vigeland Sculpture Arrangement meant the public lost a substantial part of the romantic, historic, setting to a formal sculpture garden. The decision of the city to engage in the historic contract with Gustav Vigeland was not concluded without public debate. As much as Norwegians appreciated Vigeland, they held dear the natural setting within the city.

Today it is accepted that the national sculptor be well represented in the center of the capital city. Soon, the installation will have a centennial celebration as a great gift to the public. To acknowledge Vigeland Sculpture Arrangement at home in Frogner Park, is to incorporate all of the illustrious history of which Oslo and all of Norway is proud.

The Other Vigeland

Gustov was not the only talented Vigeland. His younger brother, Emanuel, distinguished himself as a painter, sculptor and stained-glass artist. He is widely known and admired in Norway for stained glass installed in churches and the University of Oslo. Emanuel lived from 1875 to 1948, near his more famous brother, without garnering commissions that enabled the older sibling to enjoy international fame. The Emanuel Vigeland Museum is in the Slemdal section of Oslo. His work can be seen throughout the city.

The focal point of the museum is a large barrel-roofed room, completely covered with frescos by Emanuel. The theme of the work, like that of the other Vigeland, is the cycle of life. There are also bronze figures on the wall. Although Emanuel has a style unique to his brother, his figures are also bare. Their emotion is raw.

The museum was established in 1926, as a private foundation. Initially intended as a gallery for Emanuel's work of sculpture, windows were shut and the purpose transitioned to a mausoleum for ashes of the artist. In the *Tomba Emmanuelle,* visitors can sit in the darkened room and be engulfed by the art.

Today in Oslo

Although Rodin impressed Gustov Vigeland, the Norwegian never sought to create the same intense expression in his sculpture as the creator of The Thinker. Vigeland was a social artist. His theme, repeated four times in the sculpture installation in Oslo, is the cycle of life: infancy, youth, adulthood and old age, with all the joys and fears recognizable in each.

No art curator is necessary to accompany a walk through the Vigeland installation to offer understanding of the works. Although the sculptures have titles, no explanations are needed. Each visitor brings their life experiences, for their age, as they walk through the park.

On warm days young people splash in the fountain pond and laugh at the relief showing a young person stick their hand in the mouth of a monster. Sculptures of older people have no meaning for them. An older visitor viewing the reclining old man gesturing to two youths instinctively knows how hard it is to pass along wisdom to the young. Any woman who has been in love or who has had children will immediately understand emotions of the women in bronze and stone.

The Vigeland Sculpture Arrangement remains as Vigeland intended. His gift to Oslo residents was an ability to visit the park numerous times through life and see their most private emotions in art. Long distance visitors need not be Norwegian to have the same empathy for Vigeland's creations. Stroll through the park to enjoy life, at any age.

Oslo City Hall

Nobel at Peace in Oslo

The name Nobel is universally familiar. The man is largely unknown. When he was fifty-five, Nobel was surprised to read his obituary in the newspaper.[44] Although he had been gone from Stockholm for quite some time, he still felt very much alive. Attaining middle age was an accomplishment for the man who had been perennially ill as a child.

Alfred Nobel was a success in bringing several inventions to industrial use. He did not invent nitroglycerin. That discovery belongs to an Italian, when Nobel was fourteen. Nobel invented dynamite from nitroglycerin, in a stable form. He then opened manufacturing plants and held patents for his product around the globe, including: Russia, Germany, Spain, Italy, Portugal and Sweden. France allowed him a patent, so crucial to building the Suez Canal. Nobel left the United States in disgust due to corruption and hurdles to doing business and receiving credit for his patents.

One of four sons of an unsuccessful inventor, Nobel was chastised by his father for being of lesser intelligence. He was later accused by his father of stealing the elder's idea. Ridiculed by his father for being so close to his mother, who nursed him through continuing episodes of illness, Nobel tried to develop relationships with women, that were other than nurturing. He felt responsible for the death of his brother in a lab. Most devastating to Nobel, was transition in the use of dynamite from mining and railroad building, to war. He was a man of principle, deeply concerned over the effects of his actions and inventions on others, be they family, or the public.

---

[44] The obituary was for his older brother Ludvig, born 1831, who died in 1888. Mistakenly identifying Ludvig as the inventor of dynamite, the newspaper called him the merchant of death, who made a fortune through sales of the means for devastation.

Nobel had a rare combination of an ability to solve design problems, others could not see, and a sense of when to capitalize on a market for the invention and when to pass on a questionable opportunity. He attained great wealth, although wealth was not his goal. He changed the ground plan of warfare, which deeply saddened him. He wanted to be known as a man of science, who advanced the quality of life.

One random act of Nobel, hiring a housekeeper from a newspaper advertisement, led to a life-long friendship. Countess Bertha Kinsky von Chinic, later von Suttner, brought Nobel to realize where his principles lie. Bertha introduced Alfred to the movement for world peace. He was impressed by the cause and the organization.

Nobel Prizes are awarded annually at a gala event in the Stockholm City Hall. Honored are accomplishments in physics, chemistry, medicine and literature. The Nobel Peace Prize is awarded separately, in Oslo, Norway, for political reasons recognized by Nobel.

In Stockholm, in the former stock exchange building, on the square of the 1520 Blood Bath of Swedish nobles, is the museum of the Nobel Prize. In Oslo, immediately visible at the cruise port pier is the Nobel Peace Center. This story is a description of the man deserving of the prize that is given to others.

The Nobel Family of Sweden

Alfred Nobel was born in 1833, in Sweden, into a family of inventors, in a time when science was moving from alchemy to chemistry. The Nobel family traced their talents for science back to the mid-seventeenth century physician, Olaf Rudbeck. He discovered the pituitary gland, when he was twenty-two, and later founded a medical school.

Unfortunately for Rudbeck, he became enamored with locating the fabled city of Atlantis. Publication of his opus work on Atlantis cost Rudbeck his position at the medical school and in society. His daughter married a peasant, a man with no family name, whom Rudbeck considered quite a noble man. Thereafter, the family name of Nobel was distinguished in Sweden to an extent that would have gratified the patron physician.

Olaf Rudbeck in Stockholm City Hall Ballroom

Young Nobel was a sickly child. He suffered from skeletal and gastric ills, which often left him bed-bound. His mother was his constant nurse, spending so much time with Alfred, that she was unavailable to her husband, Immanuel, and the other children: Ludwig, Robert and Oscar. When Alfred was nine, his formal education ended when the family moved to St. Petersburg, where Immanuel had a commission from the Russian emperor to manufacture land mines. Immanuel also invented a central home heating system, even more useful in Russia than in Sweden.[45]

In 1850, when he was seventeen, Nobel was sent by his father to New York, to study under a family friend, John Erikson. Erikson was in the midst of developing a steam-powered screw propeller system for an armed ship, the *CSS Monitor*. The *CSS Monitor* went on to defeat the USS *Merrimac* in the American Civil War. By that time, Alfred was in Paris, where he discovered women. In Paris, Alfred wrote poetry.

While living in St. Petersburg, Alfred proposed marriage to a young woman, who refused him. In Paris, he developed a relationship with a lovely young woman, who died during his courtship. Alfred looked back upon his mother with devotion.

While Alfred was maturing, the world around him was erupting into war. Russia gave an ultimatum to Turkey, which brought France, as an ally to Turkey, into the war. This was the Crimean War, in which Britain entered late, and in the winter, in order not to be left out of any agreement negotiated to end hostilities. The Crimea was a bloody affair for all.

Alfred's war duties included working in a chemical factory and traveling to Europe to purchase supplies. The Nobel family was flooded with orders for land mines to protect Russia's borders. Alfred had the opportunity to put his American experience to use building a steamship for Russia from Erikson plans.

The Nobel boys saw the worst of war. They found that corruption in government meant that the Russians had an inventory of non-existent weapons. Over 200,000 lives were lost before the 1855 Treaty of Paris ended the hostilities. The new head of Russia, Alexander II, blamed faulty equipment for the military

---

[45] Late in life, Immanuel invented plywood.

defeat.[46] Contracts with the Nobels were cancelled in mid-production. The family was bankrupted.

In 1858, unable to find financing for the munitions business in France or England, Alfred, his parents and younger brother, Oscar, returned to Sweden. Ludwig stayed in Russia as a manufacturer of small arms and tools. Robert started an oil lamp factory in Finland. Years later, Alfred aided Robert by developing an oil refinery for the lamps. The oil refinery became a lucrative family business.

Alfred Nobel's Explosive World

In 1847, Italian Ascanio Sobrero added glycerol to a mixture of nitric and sulfuric acids, causing the mixture to blow up in his face. For years, chemists experimented with a means to make the compound stable, so that it would explode only on demand. One such chemist was Russian Nikolay Zinin, who was Alfred's tutor, when the Nobel family came to St. Petersburg. Zinin and Immanuel Nobel worked for years to find a means to make the explosive practical for commercial use.

Alfred observed the efforts of his father and tutor and saw a solution to the problem that evaded them. In 1862, Alfred put nitroglycerin into a tube with gunpowder and a fuse. The mixture was stable, until the fuse was lit. When he was thirty years old, Alfred was granted a Swedish patent on his explosive. Patents in his name followed in France, England and Belgium. Alfred gave beneficial interest in a Finnish patent to his brother Robert. France gave Alfred financing to manufacture the explosive, which was so critical to construction of the Suez Canal.

Quick to credit the work of chemists and his father in the prior work that led to his product, Alfred was unable to convince his father that he had not stolen his father's patent. The elder Nobel accused his son of theft. Secretly,

---

[46] See the story of Alexander II in Itinerary 11, Port of St. Petersburg. Alexander II freed the serfs and attempted to bring Russia into a parliamentary monarchy on the British model.

Immanuel had his son Oscar working on an explosive device in Alfred's lab. When the lab exploded, killing Oscar, Alfred felt responsible. Immanuel's statements to the police, boasting of credit for ongoing inventions, cleared Alfred of any fault.

A Swedish investor gave Alfred half the shares in a factory that used his patent. Alfred gave half of his shares to his father. When Immanuel had a stroke, Alfred sold his Norwegian patent to finance his father's residence in a health spa. In 1868, the Swedish Academy of Science gave a shared medal to Immanuel, recognizing him for experimentation in nitroglycerin, and to Alfred for inventing dynamite. The elder Nobel kept the medal. When his father died, four years later, having the medal was of no sentimental interest to Alfred.

Of Business and War

It is not unusual for great ideas to be copied. In the case of dynamite, imitations were often unstable, causing explosions during transportation. Injured parties in the United States brought lawsuits against Nobel. He defended by testifying as to the safety of his product, which was not the cause of any untimely explosion. In Britain, Alfred was forced to bring a lawsuit for patent infringement against the British Royal Patent Commission, for using their inside knowledge obtained in granting Nobel a patent, to create their own explosive. He won on moral grounds, but lost the patent infringement action.

In the United States, Nobel ran afoul of the powerful DuPont Company. DuPont manufactured gun power, which was more volatile and less powerful in building mines and bridges than dynamite. Nobel came to New York in 1866, to respond to American media reports of the dangers of dynamite. Although his testimony impressed the media and the public, Nobel came to face restrictive regulations.

A man whom had sought a partnership with Nobel, in exchange for maneuvering through government regulations on his behalf, then sought to invalidate the contract and retain any beneficial earnings. The US business partner obtained a patent on the only legal container in which to transport dynamite in the United States. In defeat, Alfred formed Giant Powder with DuPont, in exchange for shares in the company. Twenty years later, he sold the shares. He never returned to the United States, nor did he have further business dealings there.

Alfred resided in Paris, prior to France granting him a patent to produce dynamite in the country. In his mansion on Avenue Malakoff, Alfred experimented with making artificial silk and synthetic rubber. He worked on these peace-time projects throughout his life.

While in Paris, Alfred befriended Victor Hugo. Hugo wrote that one day the only battlefields will be in the international marketplace. Alfred thought that the more educated the populace, the less likely the occurrence of war. It was wishful thinking.

Hugo introduced Alfred to Ferdinand de Lesseps, the French diplomat, who in 1869, had successfully completed the Suez Canal. The much more complicated project of building a canal in Panama was proposed to Lesseps. The Frenchman was interested in obtaining dynamite for the Panama project. Alfred obtained his French patent.

All the demand for dynamite caused Alfred to engage a business partner to run the daily operations and leave him free to spend time in his lab. There were factories in Bilbao, Spain; Turin, Italy; Lisbon, Portugal; and Isleton, Sweden. More factories were opened in Africa, Japan, Canada and Australia. Nobel and dynamite were known worldwide. Alfred moved his lab to the quiet village of San Remo in northern, coastal Italy.

While the dynamite side of the business was growing, the Nobel oil refining business remained a family operation. Nobel oil fields in Baku, on the Caspian Sea, required an oil pipeline to bring crude oil to tankers in Batumi, on the Black Sea. From there, oil tanker ships, manufactured by Ludwig, shipped oil up the Volga River to the refinery operation, outside of St. Petersburg, run by Robert.[47] The Nobel brothers built a town to house company employees.

---

[47] Robert Nobel retired from the business in 1879, suffering from tuberculosis. He died in 1896.

A portion of the profits were deposited by their mother, Andrietta, into ten banks, from which she funded several causes to aid people in need.[48]

Alfred remained active in setting up factories for dynamite and in sales. He left daily operations to his partner Paul Barbe. When Barbe died, suddenly Alfred was thrust into the realities of a mismanaged business operation. Barbe made speculative purchases of glycerin before a substantial fall in price. Barbe also trusted a manager, who embezzled funds. Alfred replaced the entire management team.

World Peace

Nobel Peace Center in Oslo

---

[48] Caroline Andrietta Ahlsell Nobel, born in Stockholm in 1805 and died in Stockholm in 1889. She did not trust putting funds in a single bank, where a bank insolvency could eliminate the assets.

Besides his mother, there were two women in the life of Alfred Nobel. One woman pretended to be his wife and made him cautious of developing close relationships. The other woman came in and out of his life, eventually pointing Alfred to a positive purpose.

Sophie Hess was a flower girl at a restaurant where Alfred went for lunch in 1876. His courtship of Sophie included taking her on Sunday drives and establishing a bank account for her to utilize for her education and self-improvement. Sophie's mother had other ideas. She recognized Alfred as a wealthy patron.

While Alfred rented a villa near Vienna for Sophie to live with her sister and arranged for a tutor, the girls went shopping. Alfred eventually realized that Sophie was not someone, who would be acceptable to his mother, nor would the flower girl be comfortable in Sweden. Still, he allowed Sophie to use his name as though they were married. Although not cultured, nor literate, Sophie quickly learned how to exploit the relationship. Alfred, although brilliant and savvy in the commercial arena, was smitten blind with love.

From 1879 to 1884, Alfred was so distracted by Sophie that he filed for no new patents. He was drained physically and emotionally. Sophie blossomed as a princess in appearance. In 1891, she had a child with a Hungarian noble. Alfred established a trust fund for her support and left Sophie to manage her own expenses.[49]

In 1876, when he was forty-three, Alfred ran an advertisement in the newspaper for a housekeeper-secretary-hostess. The woman who received the job was thirty-three-year old Bertha Kinsky von Chinic und Tettau. She was a single woman, who claimed to have been a countess, whose mother gambled their inheritance and lost. She remained with Alfred for a short while, trying to organize his personal life, while he was involved in the destructive relationship with Sophie. Bertha left Alfred to marry a twenty-five-year old man, who promised a bit of excitement in her life.

---

[49] Upon the death of Alfred Nobel, Sophie was the only person who threatened to contest his will, claiming to be his common-law wife. In exchange for handing over love letters written to her by Alfred, the Nobel Institute allowed Sophie an annuity for life, managed by a guardian.

By 1885, Bertha reconnected with Alfred. She was married at the time to a freelance magazine writer, who had encouraged her writing of life for Vienna newspapers. Bertha had also joined the International Peace and Arbitration Association, which she commended to Alfred. He attended the International Peace Congress in 1892, *incognito*, and was impressed with what he saw. Bertha went on to write a best-selling book called *Lay Down Your Arms*.

Nobel was at a low point in his life by 1891. His mother and two brothers were gone. Sophie was a disappointment. He was concerned that another war would occur in which his dynamite would be the instrumentality of death and destruction as indicated in Ludvig's obituary, the one mistakenly describing him.[50] Even the award of a doctorate from the University of Uppsala, failed to raise his spirits.[51] He wanted more of a legacy to represent the value of his life's work, than being known as the inventor of dynamite.

The Nobel Prize

In Paris, in 1895, Alfred Nobel penned out a will. In it, he gave all his assets to a fund, that would give an annual award to honor leaders in science, literature, and to exemplary acts in furtherance of world peace. In an era of nationalism, the awards were open to men and woman of any country, who most materially benefited mankind in the prior year.

Nobel's assets, at the time of his death, from his patents, dynamite production, oil refineries, gold mines in Africa and other holdings, amounted to thirty-three million Kroner. His will required assets, once liquidated and held in interest bearing accounts, to fund five equal prizes, from annual interest. Nobel Prizes in Physics, Chemistry and Literature would be conferred by the Swedish Academy in Stockholm. The Nobel Prize in Medicine would be

---

[50] France and Russia were joined against the Triple Alliance of Austria, Italy and Germany. It was a recurring source of tension in Europe.
[51] Olaf Rudbeck founded the medical school in Uppsala. He also decided that the lost city of Atlantis could be found in earthworks of ancient civilizations in the Uppsala area. More likely ancient rings near the Rudbeck home were Thing Places, the meeting circles of tenth century Vikings.

determined by the Caroline Medical Institute in Stockholm, and the Nobel Peace Prize, would be determined by a committee of five elected committee members in Norway, where the prize would be awarded.

In August 1896, Alfred's remaining sibling, Robert, died of a heart attack. In November, Alfred suffered a cerebral hemorrhage. He could only communicate in his native Swedish. French and Italian doctors at his home in San Remo could not understand him. On December 10, 1896, Alfred Nobel passed away in his quiet, Italian, seaside retreat.

Although Alfred had ensured the wealth of his brothers, his nieces and nephews were surprised to learn that they would receive nothing from his estate. Led by Alfred's nephew Emmanuel, the relatives agreed to the intent of their uncle. The governments of Norway and Sweden quickly agreed. Only Sophie threatened a scandal and demanded compensation.

Nobel Museum on Stockholm Square

Visiting Nobel in Stockholm and in Oslo Today

New Renzo Piano Designed Tjuvholmen Icon Complex

Every year since 1901, Nobel Prizes have been awarded. The Nobel Peace Prize was awarded to Bertha in 1905. Alfred would have been pleased with the committee choice. He would also be pleased to know that his name is connected to the award of prizes for advancement to the benefit of mankind. Somewhat peripherally, there is general knowledge that dynamite funds the prizes. Mankind has found other more destructive means to wage war than dynamite. Dynamite is still the most efficient means to clear rock to build dams, bridges and roadways. Alfred would be pleased to know that as well.

Nobel Peace Prize administration and museum of the award is housed in an unobtrusive historic building at the Oslo docks. Most cruise visitors bypass the low-key structure on their way to other sights in the city. The award is given in the Oslo City Hall, the impressive red-brick complex between the Nobel Peace Center and the historic fort.

Awards given in Stockholm are conferred in the Stockholm City Hall, a stately building on the city waterfront. Inside, the large hall on the first floor is set with banquet tables on award night. After dinner, attendees climb a staircase to the arched and gold-tiled ballroom above, for dancing and after-award congratulations.

In the ballroom of the Stockholm City Hall, in the inner wall of an arched window, is a classic rendition in tile of Olaf Rudbeck. There are dozens of portraits of figures in the history of Sweden lining the inner arches of the several windows, so the figure of Alfred Nobel's ancestor is not conspicuous by its size. There are no great physical monuments to Alfred Nobel either. Both men made contributions to the betterment of mankind through their application of science. The Nobel Prize is a perpetual reminder to all people, of any nation, that beyond the destruction of war, there is a better part of humanity. The highest form of recognition remain the prizes established by Alfred Nobel.

Morning in the Fjords

Oslo Fjords

Between the North Sea and entrance to the Baltic Sea, there is a deviation north through a scenic waterway that ends in Oslo. Called Oslofjord, this is not a fjord in the geological sense. It is a narrow open waterway, which became lined with ancient settlements, as glaciers retreated and exposed land on shore.

A Viking king traveled Oslofjord in 1100, bypassing settlements along the way, until he founded his home estate at the inner most point of the fjord, Oslo of today. Settlements from outer to inner positions on the fjord, became fortified over time, providing protection, as the forward guard to the Viking capital city. None of the towns grew to the prominence of Oslo. They have preserved their individual lengthy history and contribute a serene beauty to cruise ships traveling to Oslo today, as they have for a millennium of Vikings, inhabitant Norwegians and international merchant seamen.

This is a collection of brief stories of towns along Oslofjord, from the entrance to the inner reaches of the protected Oslo harbor. Given that these towns are not usually included in cruise itinerary port stops, this is a floating commentary, to be enjoyed from a deck chair, as the ship slowly glides nautical miles in or out of Oslofjord, passing through time in Norwegian history.

Guardians of the Entrance: Fredrikstad, Tønsberg, and Sandeford

Fredrikstad: On the eastern side of Oslofjord, on the Glomma River, is the oldest fortified town in Norway, dating to 1567, when founded by its namesake the king of Denmark. Fredrikstad was a trading center in days of the

Vikings, known as the Old Town. An even older town was Sarpsborg, burned by the Swedes, leaving half the residents homeless. Danish King Frederick II offered his new town, nine miles to the south and closer to the sea, which some declined, preferring to rebuild amidst the ashes. Today Sarpsborg and Fredrikstad have grown into a combined municipality that is the fifth largest in Norway.

Forested Hamlets

Fredrikstad was an early center of shipbuilding and forestry. In the mid-seventeenth century, the town was fortified to position Danish troops at war with Sweden. Fredriksten Fortress, south of the town, was actually in the hamlet of Halden, a mile from the Swedish border. Halden is remembered as the burning town. In 1659, residents burned their town to drive out the Swedes. In 1716, the few residents burned Halden again, to thwart being taken by Swedes as an outpost in Norwegian territory.

To reinforce Fredriksten Fortress in 1661, Danish King Frederick III employed Dutch craftsmen to build a stone labyrinth, with walls of passages so thick, they could withstand a barrage of cannon balls. The star-shaped fort had capacity for five thousand troops. It included a bakery and brewery within the walls.

In 1718, during yet another siege of the Fredriksten Fortress by Swedes, Swedish King Karl XII was shot and killed. Norwegians do not take credit for the victory that sent Swedes home. Rather, they claim that his own man, one who was tired of war, shot King Karl.

Fifty years later, Swedes were back. This time the commander of the fort was Hans Jacob Scheel, the owner of Frogner Manor in Oslo, today the home of Oslo's largest city park. Scheel died at the fortress in 1774.

Emanuel Vigeland, the famous stained-glass artist, and younger brother of Gustov Vigeland, the Oslo sculptor, completed stained glass windows in the Fredrikstad Cathedral in the early twentieth century. In 2005, Fredrikstad was a port for the Tall Ships Race, a spectacular event. Today the city is an industrial port.

Tønsberg: The oldest town in Norway is Tønsberg, originally a Viking settlement, directly across the fjord from Fredrikstad. The most likely date for founding is 871. A natural site for a fortification, Slottsfjellet, in the center of town, is believed to have been the Castle Mountain of Viking King Harald I. It was here that Harald buried his sons in the tenth century, felled by their half-brother Eric I Bloody Axe.

Swedes destroyed the fort, built in the thirteenth century, in 1503. Local peasants, unhappy with their overload, may have assisted the Swedes. Few remnants survive today. Slottsfjellet Tower, seen in the center of town today, was erected in 1888, in memory of the earlier fortress.

As proof of the early life of Vikings in the area, in 1904 an excavation on a farm in the area, Oseberghaugen, produced a Viking ship. Oseberg vessel, now in the Viking Ship Museum in Oslo, has been dated to 834. The vessel was the burial tomb for two prominent women, one possibly the wife of a Viking king. Silks, carved bedposts and other personal furnishings, are evidence of broad trade and accumulated wealth of Vikings.

Sandefjord: South of Tønsberg, also guarding the mouth of Oslofjord, is Sandefjord. It was here in 1880, that another Viking ship was found. Gokstad was a Viking longship with sixteen oarsmen on each side. The ship was dated to 850. The rich and powerful man who owned this ship died in battle, evident from deep gashes in his leg bones. When afloat, Gokstad was impressive with its alternating black and yellow shields above the oars. Gokstad now rests in the Viking Ship Museum in Oslo. A replica of the ship sailed in 1893, from Bergen, Norway to Chicago for the World's Columbian Exposition.

Gokstad Viking Ship 850, restored 1880

From the mid-nineteenth to the early twentieth centuries, Sandefjord was a spa town. Former spa buildings are now a cultural center. In the early twentieth century, the city was a whaling center from which ships sailed the North Sea. Today a monument and a museum recall whaling history that ended in the 1950s.

Mid-Fjord Foursome

Åsgårdstrand and Horton: Midway between Tønsberg to the south and Horton to the north is the idyllic artist haven of Åsgårdstrand. Now a tourist mecca, with few permanent residents, at the turn of the twentieth century it was a summer home to great Norwegian artists, among them Hans Heyerdahl and Edvard Munch. Heyerdahl, a mentor to Munch, is known for his famous painting, *Girl at the Window,* painted in 1881.

Edvard Munch was not only Norway's greatest known painter, he was also its most colorful. Plagued by inner demons, Munch painted themes of love, death, darkness and anxiety. He came to Åsgårdstrand from Oslo for summers from 1897 to 1904. A very handsome man, Munch was a favorite of local girls.

During affairs in Berlin and Paris, Munch was shot by his lover and lost a finger. Returning to Norway in 1909, Munch again spent his summers in Åsgårdstrand, where he painted another version of *The Scream*. His final years were lived in a sanitarium, where he died in 1944. Munch donated his collection of eleven hundred paintings and forty-five hundred drawings to the city of Oslo. The National Gallery and the Munch Museum in Oslo, each have a version of *The Scream*.

Horton was also a Viking settlement, and the site of a large number of Viking era graves, now protected in Borre National Park. Excavation of the area began in 1852, and continues today. The site of seven burial mounds was discovered during road construction, when a soft hill used for road fill produced artifacts. Many of the items discovered are in the Viking Ship Museum in Oslo.

Moss and Son: Directly across the fjord from Horton is the historic city of Moss. Moss was an occupied site from the Iron Age into the Viking era. Its notable period in Norwegian history really began in the eighteenth century. The location made the town a natural midway point for merchant traffic between Oslo and Copenhagen. The ironworks were in full operation in 1704, servicing ships.

Moss is closely connected to the island of Jeløy, the site of a pleasure palace built in 1767, now the Hotel Refsnes Gods. In Norwegian, Gods means mansion. The hotel was remodeled in 1998, keeping the historic appearance, with twin towers, and adding a collection of modern art. Guests can sleep over the reefs of Oslofjord, amidst the art of Andy Warhol and several Norwegian artists, including Edvard Munch. All of the art in the hotel is edgy; none of it is restful. The rooms look out over the fjord, where Munch walked and wanted to scream. Munch was attracted to Oslofjord to overcome his demons and excise them into paintings. The hotel has been a place to escape life's pressures for two hundred and fifty years. It is a uniquely Norwegian experience.

The nineteenth century was a monumental time for Norway. Critical events began in Moss. In 1814, Denmark found itself on the losing side in the Napoleonic wars that engulfed Europe. By the terms of the Treaty of Kiel in Germany, Denmark ceded Norway to Sweden, although Denmark retained Greenland. Norwegians hoped to become independent, rather than vassal of their long-term combatant, Sweden. Norwegian patriots convened the Convention of Moss, which met in the old ironworks, to craft a constitution independent of Sweden. They anointed as their king Christian Frederik, heir to the united throne of Denmark and Norway. Norwegians were, and are, fond of independence, with retained historic connections.

The Swedish monarch reacted to Norwegian independence declaration with yet another war. Given superior strength, Sweden prevailed in the short, decisive war. It was a war of a new era. Sweden allowed Norway to keep its constitution, minus their new king. Norway was allowed its separate parliament and much of its self-government, up to the point of still being joined with Sweden and recognizing its royal family as their sovereign.

The War of 1814, became the final war between the two nations, and the final war fought by Sweden. In 1905, the two nations agreed to an amicable parting. Son of the Danish king, Haakon VII, became king of Norway. The old ironworks in Moss, where it all began, still stands.

The town of Son was a small medieval timber town, which today is preserved in time. Like a number of small villages, along both sides of the Oslofjord, little white buildings, with red roofs, are set among evergreen trees in a picturesque setting, that belies turbulent history of the area. Oslo and Oslofjord continually rate on lists tabulated of the best places in the world to live. Floating along the Oslofjord, in view of towns along the water's edge, it seems that only severe winter climate has kept the area from a population explosion.

The Inner Fjord

Drøbak: The narrowest point along the Oslofjord, is the short, half-mile wide narrows at the town of Drøbak. During World War II, Drøbak was the centerpiece of a dramatic attempt by Germans to land one thousand troops from an armada, led by the heavy cruiser *Blücher*, as part of a plan to invade Oslo and control Norway. The Germans did not anticipate that the commander of the century old fort, Oscarsborg, could, or would, mount a defensive response to protect the inner fjord.

Passing the Narrows

On April 9, 1940, as the German fleet approached the narrows, Fort Oscarsborg was manned by fresh recruits on a training exercise. They never had the opportunity to complete their training before they responded in battle. Fort commander, Colonel Ericksen, had no battle orders. At the time the German fleet came in range of Oscarsborg, the official position of Norway was neutrality.

Once Commander Ericksen identified the ships as German, he did not wait for orders. He assumed the Germans received warning shots from active forts south of his position on the fjord. He made the now famous statement, that he would either receive a medal, or a court martial, and ordered the recruits to fire their guns.

The month prior, Commander Erikson went on a brief sick leave and a retired World War I veteran, Commander Senior Grade Andreas Anderssen, was recalled from retirement in Drøbak, to watch over the young recruits. Upon seeing German ships, Ericksen recalled Anderssen to instant, active duty. The aging veteran donned the uniform not worn since 1927, to report to the battle station, where he last began service in 1909.

Anderssen knew the three torpedo guns like old acquaintances. Miraculously, nine torpedoes were left stored on site. Eriksen gave the order and Anderssen brought two of the dormant torpedo guns to life.

The Battle of Drøbak Sound resulted in sinking the *Blücher*. The delay of German ships at the narrows, gave the Norwegian Royal family and Parliament officials in Oslo sufficient warning to evacuate, with the Royal Treasury. The remaining ships in the German armada, turned around, assuming the narrows were mined. Although Germans occupied Oslo with ground forces the next day, supported by air fire, they never controlled the government, which was safe in exile in England. Norway remained an ally of Allied Forces throughout the war, despite occupation of Oslo by German troops.

Today Drøbak is a vacation community, with less than fifteen thousand residents. A tunnel beneath the fjord has replaced ferries running from its small port, whenever Oslo was packed in ice. Those ferries are now floating restaurants. Fort Oscarsborg is a protected historic site. The guns have been re-decommissioned.

Ås: In 1502, Leonardo da Vinci designed a bridge over the Golden Horn, to the palace of the sultan of Istanbul. The bridge was never built. In 2001, an enterprising Norwegian artist, Vebjørn Sand, proposed the bridge be built in Ås, from the original design. Today, da Vinci Bridge is a pedestrian bridge over a main highway, and is a point of pride in the small town, on the outskirts of Oslo.

Slemmestad: West of Oslo, on the inner fjord, is the city of Slemmestad. It was a small farming village for centuries, until it became the center of cement manufacture in the nineteenth century. Today, viewing the town from the water, trees are more numerous than houses. The cement plant is most prominent. To collectors of unique museums, in Slemmestad there is a Cement Museum.

Asker: Immediately west of Oslo, on the inner fjord, is the suburb, formerly the town, of Asker. It is in this exclusive area that royals, sports and television personalities, and affluent artists of Oslo reside today. In 1916, *Maud* was launched from its banks. This was the ship built to take Roald Amundsen to make history in his quest to be the first explorer to reach the North Pole. Instead, Amundsen made history in the *Fram* at the South Pole. *Maud* eventually went to Canada, where she sank in 1930. Efforts to raise the ship and return it to Asker as a museum piece, proved to be cost prohibitive.

Islands of the Inner Oslofjord

Off the coast of Oslo, in the inner Oslofjord, there are eight small islands. Most have natural features, although some retain memories of historic events. Little Hovedøya Island was home to a Cistercian Monastery, built in 1147. Today, there are still ruins of the small order. In 1532, officials at Akershus Fortress ordered burning the monastery. Today the island is popular for summer picnics.

Gressholmen and Lindøya islands had airports for seaplanes. Today, their attraction is rabbit hunting. There was a sanitarium on Bleikøya Island for children with communicable diseases. Today, the island is a nature preserve as is Malmøya, known for its fossils. Some of the islands, like Nakholmen, have holiday cottages. Ormøya is home to a nineteenth century church. Infrequent ferries serve all of the islands. For cruise visitors, these islands are best viewed on a boat tour of the inner fjord, or simply from a cabin veranda, on the way in or out of port.

A Visit Along the Oslofjord Today

Today, there are mini-cruises available around the inner harbor and islands of the Oslofjord. There is even a hop-on-hop-off cruise, much like terrestrial tourist bus excursions. Guests can include dinner, a jazz, or opera concert, or dress like a pirate. Public ferries connect visitors to the Viking Ship Museum, the Kon-Tiki Museum, and the Fram Museum, all located on Bygdøy peninsula, across the fjord from Oslo city pier number three; the pier adjoining Oslo City Hall.

Port Oslo

Hotel rooms are scarce in Oslo any time of year. Fortunate are cruise guests, who have the opportunity to float through history from a comfortable deck chair on board their ship. From a ship, take in the entire length of Oslofjord, and all of its history along the shore, in a single day.

Art and Artists of Bergen

Bergen Today–Find the street art mural

Bergen impresses visitors immediately on arrival as a city dedicated to public art. Not immediately apparent is that dedication goes back to the thirteenth century, when King Magnus established a place in Bergen for painters.[52] Bergen

---

[52] Surgeons were considered artisans, trained by barbers. In 1742, a medically trained Scotsman was imprisoned in Bergen for practicing his art without a license. Five years later, a medical school opened in Bergen, headed by a German, trained in France. Such was the desire of Bergenese to emulate their European trading partners.

was founded as a port of world trade. The prosperous locals channeled their discretionary income into art. Churches were initial beneficiaries of the effort of artists. Today the art-as-integral-to-life ethic is seen in statues, gardens, architecture, museums and ongoing display of outdoor art installations.

Bergen Capital of Arts & Monument to Edvard Grieg

Creativity in Bergen was worldly, informed by access to international influences at the docks, and introspective, impressed by Nordic tradition and folkways. Art of Bergen defies classification attempted by art historians. Bergen looked outward to the world of those who traded at the docks, initially largely English and German merchants. Like the unique *Bergensk* language that developed in west Norway, artistic expression did not follow styles seen elsewhere in Norway.

Influences from England outweighed those of Scandinavia, in this Nordic city, politically controlled by Denmark, or Sweden.[53] Artists came from Germany to Bergen in the fourteenth century, after plague decimated the population, to create commissions for English clients. Romanesque and high gothic styles merged with Norse folk art. Unfortunately, much of the pre-eighteenth century works did not survive a series of fires that several times gutted much of Bergen. Few early church alters survive.[54] Beautiful buildings of Bergen today, are the work of eighteenth through twenty-first century architects.

Artists of Bergen have long been renown through England and Europe. Those born in Bergen, such as writer Ludvig Holberg, born in 1684, who traveled to Europe and wrote in Danish, looked to their roots for historic material. In turn, their work preserved the history of Bergen and gave it notoriety. Holberg wrote a novel in tribute to Bergen's ill-fated poet Cille Gad, and Bergen composer Edvard Grieg wrote the Holberg Suite in honor of Norway's prolific author. Fame of artists of Bergen has been inspiring tourism for three hundred years.

This is a brief romp through history of the arts of Bergen. The vibrant legacy continues today in the art school and museums, which ring open space in the old city. In Bergen, outdoor edgy art installations join classic statuary monuments, folk art and the unique Norwegian genre of troll art. Bergen evokes travel memories like no other city. The artists of Bergen are due thanks.

Establishing an Arts Environment

When King Magnus institutionalized a place for artists, in the thirteenth century home base of his reign, he envisioned local art produced to adorn churches, including the cathedral of his eventual internment. What he received for the gesture was art created in Bergen, by Bergen artisans, that looked as if taken from churches of England. English style art, produced in Bergen, pleased him.

---

[53] Until 1384, Bergen used English currency and barter.
[54] Munkeliv Abby, a repository of substantial fifteenth century art, was burned in the Hansa Riot of 1455.

Bryggen Harbor

Today, rare altar pieces of wood produced in Bergen in the fourteenth century, look as though they were produced in England.[55] Many were produced for English clients. When the plague arrived in Bergen, in the late fourteenth century, population was so reduced, that artisans and local commissions were hard to find. German artisans came to Bergen to create works for export.

In 1450, Sister Birgitta Sigusdatter led Bridgettine nuns of Munkeliv Monastery in creating handicrafts for sale in the Bergen market. Birgitta was a talented artist, who spent her time writing and illustrating Psalter for the bishop.[56] After the Hansa Riot of 1455, in which the Monastery was burned, the nuns moved to Stavanger and Trondheim. Life ended at Munkeliv.

---

[55] See fine examples of Bergen's Medieval church art in the University of Bergen Museum permanent collection.
[56] An example of her work is in the collection of the Library of the City of Prague.

Eighteenth Century of Poetry, Plays and Homes for Art and Literature

Holberg on the market square

The eighteenth century began on a sad note in the literary community of Bergen. Cille Gad, educated by her minister father in Greek, Latin and Hebrew, was recognized as a local poet, when she became involved with a Dutch sailor. Never married, the sailor was long gone, when in 1705 Cille gave birth to a still born child. In desperation, she hid her circumstances by tucking the deceased child among stacks of books.

Such secrets do not last for long. Cille was accused of murder of the infant. She went to prison. Records are not clear, for the charges may have been altered to hiding the deceased, rather than murder. Regardless, the king commuted her sentence in 1707. Cille was released from incarceration and banished from Bergen. She promptly went to Copenhagen, where she was welcomed into the University of Copenhagen community as a poet.

Cille wrote poetry, while in prison, and up until her death at age thirty-six, in 1711. Her early work was lost in a fire in Bergen. Her life was cut short when a plague tore through Copenhagen. Gad is best remembered through the impact she had on students and fellow artists of Bergen.

Ludvig Holberg was born in Bergen in 1684.[57] He went to study at the University of Copenhagen, where he was introduced to the poetry of Gad. He was impressed by the Gad legal case, which occurred when he was twenty-one. Gad appears as a character in Holberg's historic fiction. The case also impacted Holberg's view of arrest, trial and incarceration. Destined to become a priest, Holberg chose instead to study law, prior to recognition of law as an academic discipline.[58]

A prolific writer, Holberg began writing history treatises in 1711, the year Gad died. His 1737 novel of Bergen preserved an image of life of people, in a hive of Bergen activity. He also wrote satirical poetry and comedy for the theater. Holberg's plays were produced in the Danish Theater in 1721, where he also served as a creative director.

Active as an instructor, Holberg felt that students should be taught to reason their way through problems, rather than master subjects through memorization. He enjoyed debating Catholics on the concept of original sin. As a culmination of his broad disciplinary talents, he wrote a book on the natural and international law of Norway. His treatise, *Gynaicologia, or a Defense of the Female Sex* argued that women can do anything; just look at his example of Catherine II of Russia.

Great cities need talented architects to give shape and structure to homes of the arts and artists. Johan Joachim Reichborn was born in Germany and came to Bergen, where he spent the remainder of his life. Reichborn gave people of Bergen a substantial city of stone and brick, after the devastating fire of 1756. By 1765, Reichborn was directing construction of all public buildings in the

---

[57] Ludvig Holberg born in Bergen in 1684 and died in 1754. His father was reputed to be one of the Knights of St. John. Knights of the crusades had a presence in Malta, until the arrival of Napoleon in 1805.

[58] There are many in academia who argue that law study is vocational training. Lawyers earn a Juris Doctorate, but are never referred to as "Dr." not even in academia

city. His efforts can be seen in the Bergan streetscape today, even though few of his buildings survive. His characteristic style of long, tall windows can be seen in Nykirken church. Reichborn was buried in St. Mary's in his adopted home city, in 1783.

Early Stone Architecture

This century ends on a patriotic note, literally, with the Bishop of Bergen, Johan Nordahl Brun. Brun was born near Trondheim in 1745, and lived in Bergen, where he died in 1816. Prior to becoming bishop in 1804, Brun wrote hymns, a song for Norway and the anthem of Bergen. Brun is remembered for inspiring religious as well patriotic emotions in Norway, pArcticularly in Bergen.

Nineteenth Century Music and Poetry

Bull Statue on Ole Bull Plas

In the seventeenth century superb violins were produced in Hardanger, a town just inland, along the fjord from Bergen. Fine instruments of mountain ash and pine, in the hands of Bergen violinist Ole Bull, were brought to the world stage. Bull was born in Bergen in 1810. He founded its first national theater in 1850, a presumption of nationalism, since Oslo was the capital of Norway. Among the first theater managers was Henrik Ibsen.

When he was sixty-six, at the pinnacle of his career, Bull played his violin while seated on top of the Cheops Pyramid in Egypt. For a while, Bull contemplated living in the United States, until he was swindled on a land deal in Pennsylvania.[59] He returned to Norway, where he died in 1880.

---

[59] Could Bull have met with land schemes of Ignatius Donnelly, a character in Cruise through History©, Itinerary I London to Rome, Port At Sea, story of Search for Atlantis?

Bull insisted that Edvard Hagerup Grieg attend music school in Leipzig in 1858. Grieg, also born in Bergen, was only fifteen, when Bull recognized his talent. Grieg was a prolific composer, whose body of music is identified as the national music of Norway. Returning the favor shown to him by Bull, Grieg founded a society to promote music of young composers. Often called the Chopin of the north, Grieg spent his final days in Bergen, where he died in 1907.

Johan Sebastian Welhaven was born in Bergen, in 1807, to a family of distinguished clerics.[60] In the university in Christiana, now Oslo, young Welhaven diverged from expectations to remain in academia as an author and poet, who examined and promoted Norwegian literature, rather than scripture. Into the Norwegian tradition of drawing from folklore and natural environment of home, Welhaven combined influences of Europe, to broaden the aesthetic of Norwegian art. He was non-apologetic. Welhaven argued that art transcends boundaries.

Twentieth Century Social Commentary and Troll Art

A relative of composer Grieg and descendant of Johan Nordahl Brun, Johan Nordahl Brun Grieg was a dashing, controversial, poet-war correspondent.[61] Born in Bergen in 1902, educated at Oxford, he spent time as a merchant sailor around the Cape of Good Hope. Recognized as a published poet by age twenty, his volume, *The Ship Sails On*, was a social commentary on the working conditions of sailors.

Grieg saw first-hand the rise of the Communist Worker's Party in China and repression by the Kuomintang. Sympathy for the poor evoked Communist sentiments in Grieg. His views changed, when Russians sided with Germany in the occupation of Norway. Grieg served in the Norwegian army, during the Winter War in Finland, and made a narrow escape to England. As Captain

---

[60] Johan Sebastian Welhaven was born in Bergen in 1807 and died in 1873.
[61] Johan Nordahl Brun Grieg was born in Bergen in 1902, and died while a war correspondent in Germany 1943.

Entrance Garden to Art Museums

Grieg, he made dangerous flights into Germany, one of which ended in his death in a plane crash. Grieg's volume of poetry, *Freedom*, was published posthumously. He is a Norwegian hero today, who is memorialized in a statue in Bergen as a figure representing the best in the human spirit.

Artists Theodor Severin Kittelsen and Nikolai Astrup were contemporaries in the society of painters of Norway, of the late nineteenth and early twentieth century.[62] Although neither artist was born in Bergen, their art is found in galleries, art museums and book shops of Bergen. Kittelsen found a niche in the art world, when he was asked to illustrate a story book of trolls in the late nineteenth century. In his work, the genre of troll art was born.

---

[62] Kittelsen was born in 1857, and died in 1914. Astrup was born in 1880, and died in 1929.

Kittelsen's trolls are painted in muted, earthy tones, in natural landscapes. His trolls seem to grow from the earth. They are ethereal rather than threatening. Kittelsen's subjects include horses and animals of the forest, all of which are dreamlike. It was his trolls that gave form to age-old tales of Norway. After Kittelsen, trolls, in the hands of other artists, became grotesque and sometimes scary. Kittelsen's work has been copied, but not surpassed in technique, or the ability to give a sense of introspection to his creatures.

The work of Astrup is in the permanent collection of Bergen art museums. Like Kittelsen, Astrup drew upon the natural environment and folkways of Norway, while imparting subtle emotional expression in his subjects. His use of bold lines and colors does not distract from a softness in the landscape. There is light and hope in Astrup's works. His death from pneumonia at age forty-seven, left Norwegians grieving the loss.

Twenty-first Century Art in the Streets

Bergen Theatre Corridor on Ole Bull Plas

Bergen has become a street art capital. Striking modern art installations, supported by the city, punctuate views around the city center lake in front of museums. Street art, as graffiti on buildings, began as social commentary, not necessarily with agreement of the property owner.

By 2011, it was apparent that as the street art phenomenon swept through cities of the world, there were some excellent artists in Bergen. These artists inspired by Banksy, have the added touch of Norwegian originality. The city tried to promote street artists and preserve their work.

The most acclaimed of street artists, whose work with stencil and spray paint are found on buildings, **with** the permission of building owners, is Oslo native Dolk, who was raised and began his art endeavors in Bergen.[63] Dolk's work is blunt social commentary, executed in the medium of stencil and spray paint. One of his best-known pieces is of British Prince Charles wearing a Burger King crown. By 2006, Dolk moved from streets to galleries, where his pieces are sold for hefty prices. Expect his work to be among collections of major museums of the world.

In 2008, Dolk became well-known for twenty stencil works applied to abandoned houses in the Norwegian community of Lofoten. In 2010, Dolk was commissioned to paint striking images of inmates in Halden Prison, a railroad station in Oslo and buildings in Trondheim. Dolk sightings are another reason to wander streets of Bergen, among art of several centuries of Bergen's art tradition.

Today in Bergen

Today there are more cruise visitors annually in Bergen, than the city population. Many visitors wander through streets around the harbor, and through the Hansa Museum at the docks, a World Heritage Site, until they come to the beautiful open space, ringed by public art and museums. Those most fortunate will have time to linger in the Bergen Museum and on the art of Bergen in which the history of the city is best preserved. It is in the art, that the soul of the city and the spirit of Gad, Holberg, Grieg and Dolk can be found. It is in the arts that immortality dwells.

---

[63] Dolk Lundgren was born in 1979 and uses the signature: "Dolk."

10th–20th Century Bergen around Art Center

To spend the day among the art museums of Bergen, begin by crossing Christie's Gate, the street dividing the city at the docks, with the center of the old city. Neatly arranged around Lille Lungegårdsvannet, the small lake surrounded by a garden, are the four Bergen Art Museums of KODE. KODE1 was built in 1896, and holds collections of fine craft and Norwegian design. KODE2 was a gift to the city of local businessman, Rolf Stanerson, in 1978. It holds temporary exhibitions. KODE3 was the gift of Rasmus Meyer, in 1916, to house a substantial collection of paintings of Norwegian painter Edvard Munch. KOBE4 is the former power company offices of 1938, repurposed in 2003, to the KunstLab Children's Museum, also the home of an installation of the work of Nikolai Astrup.

Further out of the city are house museums of Bergen's composers, also part of KODE. *Troldhaugen* is the home of composer Edvard Grieg. *Lysøen* is the home of violin master Ole Bull. Still in the old city, and beyond KODE, are the University of Bergen Historical Museum and Museum of Natural History.[64] Look here for early Bergen and artworks rescued from Medieval churches.

---

[64] The Natural History museum first opened in 1867. It closed for renovation to reopen in 2019.

KODE Bergen–Greig Concert Hall in rear

Lysøen home of Ole Bull

Norway chose to honor their most famous scribe by instigating the Holberg Prize in 2003. The prize honors contributions in the arts, humanities and social sciences. An international cadre of distinguished artists and academic humanitarians have been recipients.[65]

National Theatre & Ibsen statue by Nils Aas

When arriving at the pier in Bergen, look up to the tree-covered mountains, which surround the city. The natural landscape of western Norway is never out of sight. Bergen is set within a steep valley from green hills to the docks. Artists of Bergen are a part of their natural and historic heritage, preserved in their poetry, paint and music. Look forward to being in, and returning to, Bergen, city of art.

---

[65] For a full list of Holberg Prize honorees see the Holberg website.

THE SECRET LIFE OF TROLLS

Trolls live in Norway. They would not be happy in any other place. They live in vast forests, amid fjords, where there are few humans to encounter, and more than a few bridges to sleep under. For their part, Norwegians are just as pleased that trolls keep to themselves. A human encounter with a troll is never a positive moment for the human.

Trolls care little how they look. Their long hair hangs down in billows from between oversize ears. Their body proportions, so unlike humans, are cumbersome, with a formless torso and large hands and feet. Finding a wardrobe is hard for trolls. Only a mother troll thinks her sons are so very handsome. Cute, cuddly, collectable trolls are a product of marketing in the 1960s.

Trolls are a product of an active imagination. They are large and ill-formed, like creatures of shadow that form on the wall when scary stories are being told to children, in front of the hearth fire. Do not tell that to a Norwegian. Like leprechauns to the Irish, and ghost dancers to the Navajo, trolls to Norwegians are so integral to cosmology of life, that they are real. They are real in spirit and in form. Instinctively, a Norwegian knows when they have met a troll, even when the troll appears in a very human-like form, and appears outwardly civil. To meet a troll is to know it.

This is a little story of creatures of myth, folklore and life in Norway, going back a thousand years. Trolls existed in the minds of Norwegians long before they were forever captured in ink in the nineteenth century. The history of trolls in inexorably linked to lives of people of Norway beyond the few large cities. Fortunate are those who will travel up the fjords, to land of trolls.

Before a visit to Norway, pArcticularly where the visit will be to small towns in remote fjords, the type accessible to cruise ships, it is good to go armed with a little troll knowledge. Today, most easily visible trolls will be in gift shops. Still, when walking a forest path, or alone past a bridge, a troll encounter may occur. Be ready for a wonderful experience. Expect any trolls you meet to avoid your camera. They are too quick and fleeting to be caught in a selfie. If you are fortunate, trolls will leave only wonderful stories to tell grandchildren.

The Cosmos of Trollology

Troll Welcome

There is at least one indisputable fact of trolls. They are not Christian beings. Trolls exist in the ethereal world of belief systems, yet they are at once pre-Christian and parallel to the Christian world. In Norway, which has had a lengthy legacy of a Norse-Viking experience, in which the Viking kings adopted Christianity in the tenth century, the people retained their folk-beliefs, so integral to their relationship with the land. The people of Norway, long under the powerful bishops of Trondheim, who were more powerful than kings, could look to the lord above and still be mindful of encountering a troll behind a tree, or under a bridge. The lord brought deliverance from a hard life well lived. Trolls brought trouble to otherwise god-fearing people.

Troll energy began with the beginning of time. The earliest written records in Norway include encounters with trolls, so their actual existence goes back further. In the ninth century, Norse poets wrote of Vikings and trolls. Vikings were fierce, warlike and certainly mortal. Trolls were anti-social, troublesome to individuals, although encounters were rarely fatal, and ageless. Both beings were sources of mythology.

Norsemen had names, some of whom became legendary gods in their accomplishments. Trolls have no booty in museums. They are nameless beings of the streams, woods and caves. Trolls, even when revealed in writing, remain in dark places, where humans fear to tread.

In the ninth century, Norse poet Bragi the Old had a conversation with a nameless troll. Bragi sang of the Norse god, Odin, and his heroes, who delivered Norway to the light of summer. Their enemy was the troll, who cursed a village with darkness and evil. Bragi wrote from personal experience. He had his own close encounter with a female troll, when he was crossing through a forest on his sled. She claimed she was able to swallow the sun and throw people into eternal darkness. Such was the fear of all villagers of the northern fjords in depths of winter. Bragi assured all who heard his song, that with a poetic flourish, rather than a sword, he overcame the troll.

Trolls changed shape to confuse villagers they encountered into thinking they would help with chores, or bring luck if the villager shared hospitality. Notably, village men, returning home at night from a pub, might encounter a female troll, who made herself attractive in the dim evening light. Female trolls were notorious in rural Norway for holding men, made weak by drink, and not releasing them until the morning light caused them to flee in the forest darkness. Many Norse men told of such encounters. Few Norse women believed them.

Another generally accepted fact of trolls is their association with magic. Trolls could not only hold back the sun and change shapes, they could interfere with the birth of calves if not treated with hospitality. They distracted people from going to church and invaded dreams with nightmares.

Troll stories, passed among villagers of the fjords, was an effective means to teach children lessons of life. For instance, since trolls could change shape and wield magic, they could appear to be a wealthy and attractive marriage partner. After the wedding, appearances returning to normal and the money all spent, all that was left was a troll spouse. The moral of the story is, that outward appearances are fleeting and happiness in a marriage for money is an illusion.

One of the common and most dreaded acts of a troll was stealing beer. If a keg of beer became light in the night, and it was always during the night, the sure cause was the act of a troll. If confronted by a troll begging a beer, it is no use to lie and say the beer is gone. Trolls know a lie when they hear it and will trick the liar by drinking a great deal of beer, until it is truly gone.

There can be no doubt, that troublesome as they may be, trolls provide a necessary balance to life. Without the fear of evil there can be no appreciation of good. Villagers of Norway have given thanks, in a Christian and secular way, to days without trolls. They enjoy living in the sunlight.

One last caution is due. Do not confuse a troll with a fairy. Fairies can be anywhere, they do not pop in the light. They bring good wishes. Fairies are small and harmless. Forewarned, it is not likely that the chance encounter with a troll will be confused with that of a fairy.

Troll Hunting in Norway

For the fearless, or carless, visitor to Norway, one way to see a troll is to enjoy a quantity of good Norwegian beer. This will work well on a hike into the forest, followed by a nap in the tall grass, near a bridge. In town, trolls can be seen welcoming shoppers into gift shops. They may look wooden and cute. Beware, they are intended to distract frugal shoppers into random purchases.

For a thousand years, the best place, certainly the safest place, to find trolls in Norway has been in Norse literature. The nineteenth century was a pArcticularly good time to find trolls on bookshelves. Forester Peter Christian Asbjørnsen was born in Norway in 1812. He grew up hearing troll stories and admonitions about behavior, certain to draw trouble from trolls. As a woodsman, he had credibility as someone who brushed daily with trolls. He collected troll tales in the 1840s, and collaborated with Jørgen Moe, a Lutheran Bishop, on a book of troll stories. The pair drew verbal pictures, recognizable to Norwegians, of trolls they all knew.

In 1879, an illustrated edition of Asbjørnsen's troll tales was published. Trolls were brought into the daylight, on the pages of a lovely book, where everyone could see the ethereal, which previously had only been imagined. The trolls of Asbjørnsen and Moe were large and lived under bridges. Some had three eyes, or three heads. They were hairy, had long noses and bad posture. Some trolls held clubs, as if they needed an outward gesture of the trouble they could cause.

The man responsible for the prevailing vision of trolls enduring in Norway is Norwegian troll artist, Theodor Severin Kittelsen.[66] He accepted the commission from Asbjørnsen and Moe to illustrate their book and give Norway a genre of fantasy art. Kittelsen's imagery captures the ethereal nature of trolls. His fairy-like white bear and white horse leaving the lake, embody more than a cliché troll art of a cartoon image. In Kittelsen's art there is a softness of the light at dusk, when vision is uncertain. At a time when the art world was tending toward flowery flourishes of Art Nouveau, Kittelsen kept his story illustrations soft, in muted colors. His trolls were neither demons, nor threatening. There is an earthy quality of beings at one with the landscape.

---

[66] Theodor Severin Kittelsen was born in 1857, and died in 1914. He is recognized as a popular artist, who blended serious political imagery into his troll art. It is so troll-like to insert a bit of critical meaning into playful pictures. Kittelsen's trolls terrorized caricatures of leading citizens of Oslo. Henrik Ibsen, whose 1867 play *Peer Gynt* used troll characters, is depicted by Kittelsen as more bored than concerned about trolls.

One of Kittelsen's most famous illustrations shows the back of a simple human figure, walking into the pink mist of a landscape. The man is Halvor, hero of the story of *Soria Moria Castle*, one of Norway's best known and loved stories of Asbjørnsen and Moe. In the story, the hapless hero leaves home and slays a three-eyed troll, to free a maiden, who turns out to be a fairy princess. The princess has two imprisoned sisters, whom he also frees, by additional daring deeds involving larger and larger trolls, with three heads and three eyes.

Returning home as a noble prince, Halvor revels in new-found respect and attention from local ladies. As he sleeps, the princess removes his magic ring, which will bring him back to her castle. Awakening to his loss, the hero must find his way back to the castle and the princess he loves. He proves his devotion by returning to her.

A trip to fjords of Norway, land of trolls, begs the question of whether this is land of Middle Earth, land of Trolls in J.R.R. Tolkien's classic story of dwarfs versus trolls, written in 1937.[67] Read as a young person, Bilbo Baggins and his dwarves battle wits with trolls in a story easily made into a comic adventure. Read as an adult, the not so comic reaction to World War II and evil trolls in society, take on a new and more sinister light. The book is a perfect read for a sea day, when slowly floating through fjords of Norway. It is, however, distantly related to trolls of Norway.

Tolkien was a scholar of Old Norse and the stories of Norway. His Hobbit, Bilbo Baggins, was a dwarf, who outsmarted the large, strong, but not very clever, trolls he encountered. Gandalf of the trilogy, *Lord of the Rings*, published completely by 1955, when Tolkien was sixty-three years old, confuses trolls by imitating their voices, to keep them muddled until daylight, when they turn to stone.

Tolkien's trolls are toeless foils for his commentary on the lower rung of sentiment. They are not magic denizens of the forest, who play tricks on unsuspecting humans. Bilbo does have a magic ring, like the hero Halvor of the Soria Moria Castle. The ring is the essential possession for a *Lord of the Rings* after all. Frodo inherits the ring and the story continues.

---

[67] John Ronald Ruel Tolkien, an Englishman, born in South Africa, was educated in England and was a professor at Oxford. He was born 1892, and died in the U.K. in 1973.

Tolkien saw the horror of war first hand at the Battle of the Somme, in World War I. In his writing, he created his own world of ageless characters, with their own language and rules. A trip to Middle Earth is a delightful escape. However, Gandalf and Bilbo never traveled the fjords. They may have preferred it to Middle Earth.

A Troll Experience Today

Beware of Troll

Today trolls pop up everywhere, and not just in the dark of night, or in deep woods. Troll, so associated with negative experience, was used in Medieval Norway to refer to *others*. *Others* are people not from around the village. Icelanders used troll to describe Greenlanders.[68]

Trolls have slipped their evil magic into computers. Trolls create havoc with hardware, roll through and destroy data. They operate in the dark domain of the hard drive, change shape and cause un-Christian language from unsuspecting data managers.

---

[68] John Lindow, Trolls: An Unnatural History, Reaktion Books, London, 2014, at. 41.

Birchlegs and Baglers Battle for Bergen

This little story of Bergen in its early years of development, in the late twelfth century to the middle of the fourteenth century, is a tale of clash of intransigent personalities. This period of Bergan's history was like a play with universal themes of power struggles, protection and retention of turf, and establishment versus the new and vibrant social shakers, who do not accept the world as it is, or seems to be. This power struggle erupted into civil war, which engulfed western Norway. At its lowest point, the pope stepped in to resolve hostility.

Colorful personalities driving the rift in western Norway, make this a fun tale to tell. This story fills the gap between domestication of the Vikings and founding of Bergen, to dominance of the port of Bergen, in the era of the Hansa League of merchants. This story may never have happened, if leadership of Norway was settled, as it was in Europe at the time. In the often-termed Dark Ages of history, when there were competing contenders in the royal family, matters were settled by fratricide. The last man standing ruled.

In Norway, contentious off-spring of dying kings resolved matters by agreements to co-rule. Partners to such agreements were rarely enthusiastic about their resolve. Often questions of leadership persisted. Problems for Bergen began shortly after it was founded by Olav III. His son Magnus II had so many love children they did not know what to do. So, they fought it out in a lively chapter in the history of Bergen. This is not a chapter for Bergen school books.

In the end, one hundred and sixty-five years of dissention accomplished little. Bergen lost its status as capital of Norway to Oslo in 1299, after a century of fighting. Civil war proved only that Bergen's strength was as a port that looked outward to the mercantile world. Politics meant little.

Old Bergen Gate

Prelude to Rift

Lyse cloister 1146, outside Bergen

The last of the raiding, warring, Viking kings of Norway, Harald Haardraada, died at the battle of Stamford Bridge in 1066. Vanquished with him were his brother Tostig and hundreds of the pride of the Vikings of Norway. That battle was the culminating event in the waning years of the Viking age. Several months later, William the Norman came across the channel to begin a new age in England. In Norway, Harald's son became king Olav III of Norway. He began a new chapter for Norway by founding Bergen as a place for trade. Future battles would be in the marketplace.

Olav's desire for a peaceful kingdom did not last beyond one generation. His son, King Magnus II had so many children he set the stage for a rift. Magnus died in 1103, in a battle in Ulster. Contacts between Ireland and western Norway were frequent, facilitated by the sea; more so than contact between Oslo and Bergen, separated by mountains.

Initially, the death of Magnus II created no problems. His acknowledged sons, Sigurd and Eystein quickly agreed to co-rule Norway. Sigurd had other priorities. In 1107, Sigurd sailed to Jerusalem in a crusade, while Eystein stayed home and built churches, as he ruled Norway as Eystein I.

When Sigurd returned from the crusade, he desired a new wife. His first wife was still living, so the Bishop of Bergen forbid Sigurd his desire. Sigurd left Eystein in Bergen and went to Stavanger to build a church for the Bishop of Stavanger, who was more understanding. Sigurd does not exit the story.

Eystein I passed a peaceful kingdom to his son Magnus III, when he died. Then the place became lively. In 1129, the sheriff of Sunnmøre went to Orkney, probably to collect taxes. There he met Harald Gilchrist, who claimed to be the love child of Magnus II. The sheriff brought Harald home to Bergen. Gilchrist, it turns out, had ambition unimagined by the sheriff.

Gilchrist located Sigurd and subjected him to an ordeal of fire, until Sigurd acknowledged Gilchrist as his long-lost brother. Circumstances of the ordeal are not well known. It likely entailed a near death experience, since extreme negotiation was Gilchrist's style.

Next, Gilchrist went to a monastery and subjected the monks to torture, until they disclosed the location of royal treasure. The existence of any treasure is doubtful. The monastery was a convenient place for Gilchrist to imprison the reigning king, Magnus III.

The reign of Harald Gilchrist of Orkney was brief. Another son of Magnus II, Sigurd Slembe appeared. Sigurd wasted no time in finding Gilchrist, whom he murdered in his bedroom in 1136. There followed four years of civil war, in which Sigurd and Magnus III battled the sons of Harald Gilchrist for control of Norway.[69] Sigurd and Magnus III were killed in battle.

Queen Ingerid enters the story at this time. Ingerid was a Swedish princess, who married a Danish prince. She either had another lover, or was tired of contributing sons to become characters in this story, so she escaped from home disguised as a boy. The prince found her and dragged her back home, where she produced more sons, who will die in this story, until the prince died.

Queen Ingerid married Irish Harald Gilchrist, as her third husband. Their son, Inge succeeded his father, and outlived his cousins Sigurd and Magnus

---

[69] The family of the sheriff who unleashed the evil genie, fought on the side of Magnus.

III, relations once-or twice removed, to become King Inge I. After Harald was murdered, Ingerid had a son with a lover and then married Arne Arnesson. Their home was in Vestland, the western part of Norway, near Bergen.

The son of Ingerid and Arne is a central character. Nicholas Arnesson was born in 1150.[70] He became the Bishop of Bergen. Of importance to this story, Nicholas led the bagler army.

While Ingerid was off delivering more sons to this story, Inge I was left to rule Norway. He too had too many brothers, two of whom wanted to be co-ruler. Eventually, the brothers killed each other, leaving seven-year-old Magnus IV, to be crowned by church leaders in 1164. Magnus was a grandson of Sigurd the Crusader, by his daughter Kristina. Remember this Sigurd?

Magnus IV was off to a good start. He and his brothers were great friends. They supported his rule. However, their father was suspicious of fraternal loyalties and had the brothers killed. Kristina was enraged by his act. She went off to Constantinople with a lover. Magnus was alone.

Sverre vs the Pope

Up in the fjords of Norway, the rebellious Sven Sverre was building a guerilla army, intent on taking Norway from Magnus IV. Sverre had no family legacy of entitlement to the crown. Opposed by aristocrats, merchants and church, Sverre looked for support among farmers and fishermen of the fjords. For the most part, rural people wished to be left alone.

As Sverre sought to gain ground in the fjords north of Bergen, he was often repelled by supporters of Magnus. His little renegade army was so ill funded, that when Sverre was pushed back to the fjord town of Voss in snow, his men fashioned shoes of birch bark. Thereafter, the rebels were known as Birchlegs.

Magnus IV sought aid and protection in Denmark. In a crossing, he was lost at sea. Sverre took control in Bergen, married a Swede, encouraging Swedish alliances, from which he obtained control of the Shetlands for Norway, and

---

[70] Nicholas Arnesson lived to 1225.

opposed the powerful Bishop Absalom, the founder of Copenhagen.[71] Sverre was sufficiently astute to make a respectful public event of the Magnus funeral. Magnus was entombed in Christ Church Cathedral in Bergen, where his ancestors lie. Unfortunately, that edifice did not survive to today.

Sverre and his Birchlegs

Sverre sought to further legitimatize his rule by requiring four bishops for his coronation in Bergen. He included the Bishop of Oslo and Nicolas Arnesson, Bishop of Bergen. Magnus IV was the choice of the church. Sverre forged a papal bull authorizing his investiture. That act aroused the ire of Pope Innocent II, who excommunicated him.

Bishops pArcticipating in the coronation of Sverre had to choose between king and pope. Arnesson sided with the pope. Sverre looked around him and blamed the bishops for all the problems he saw in Bergen. Arnesson led those opposed to Sverre, with the clergy at the head of the line. The bishop's crozier, known as the *baculus*, became their standard, known as Baglers.

---

[71] Norway controlled the Shetland Islands through the thirteenth century.

By 1195, sides were declared. It was the Birchlegs against the Baglers. Sverre faced off with Bishop Arnesson of Bergen, who was a relation to the legitimate aristocracy of Norway.

In 1198, Sverre took his battle to Trondheim, where he thought the bishop might be sympathetic. The Baglers burned Bergen in his absence, and locked his Swedish queen in the castle. Sverre returned to rescue his queen and Arnesson sent a fire ship into the harbor.

The battles left Bergen abandoned. Two years later, Sverre returned to Bergen. Bergen was still the best port for trade in the North Sea. By 1202, Sverre was dead and buried in Christ's Church.

From somewhere unknown, a sister of Magnus IV appeared and swore that Sverre was actually a lost brother living in the Faeroe Islands.[72] His origination had always been mysterious. The probability of royal status enabled Sverre's son to become King Haakon III without a scuffle.

Haakon III worked hard to unify Norway and to make peace with the church. Then one evening he went to dinner at the invitation of his Swedish stepmother. Two days later, after severe stomach pains, Haakon was dead and the Queen mother was off to Sweden. Birchlegs quickly found an heir to the kingdom in Inge II. In 1206, the Baglers renewed their attack.

There is a painting, famous in Norway, of Birchlegs on skis racing from Bergen with the infant Haakon IV, to protect him from Baglers. Bagler leader, Bishop Nicholas Arnesson stepped up to broker a three-way leadership share to satisfy everyone. Unfortunately, by 1217, all three in the triumvirate were dead.

Haakon IV lived to return to Bergen and rule Norway. Pope Innocent IV allowed the Archbishop of Trondheim to officiate at the coronation, for a hefty fee. When Skule, a half-brother to Inge II, appeared and demanded a third of all taxes, Haakon IV married the man's sister. Skule caused problems until his death in 1240.[73] Haakon IV was able to lead Norway into a golden age of peace.

---

[72] All of this material for Grand Opera is actually true.
[73] Skule is depicted favorably in the Icelandic Sagas of Snore Sturluson. They were friends.

Peaceful Postscript

Monument to Founding Bergen

In peaceful times, Haakon IV was able to rebuild Bergen, even though a fire did much damage in 1248. Before he died in 1263, Haakon IV built Haakonshallen Palace Hall, where his successor King Magnus V and Queen Ingeborg celebrated a double coronation. The big contentious issue of the day was the privy placed on a ledge by Franciscan monks, over the garden of Dominican monks.

The city had some excitement after Magnus V died in 1280, and Ingeborg died in 1287, leaving Erick II to rule. Erick II married Margaret, heir to the crown of Scotland in 1281, when she was twenty-one and the groom thirteen. In 1283, as Margaret was crossing the North Sea, her ship was lost. She left a daughter Margaret, Maid of Norway, heir to the crown of Norway and Scotland.

Scotland refused to honor Margaret as its queen. Always the enterprising fellow, Edward I, King of England, recognized Margaret and arranged for her to marry his son Edward II. The marriage would have unified England, Scotland and Norway, avoiding much bloodshed centuries later. However, Margaret died on the sailing to Orkney and her wedding.[74]

In 1300, German merchants, trying to stir some trouble, brought a woman to Bergen, who claimed to be the Maid of Norway. False Margaret was burned at the stake, launching a following of those who believed her claim.[75] At this time Erik II was already buried and his successor Haakon V moved the capital of Norway from Bergen to Oslo.

United Norway

In 1883, a railroad line was extended from Bergen toward Oslo, completed in 1913. In the twentieth century, for the first time, the two major cities of Norway were only hours apart. Norwegian nationalism was founded on such ability to communicate and by neutrality during World Wars. While nations around them, and former trading partners of Bergen, were engulfed in war, neutral Norwegian ships bought prosperity again to Norway, a prosperity shared across the mountains.

Bergen erupted in violence in the street in 1868, due to the Great Potato War. Speculators bought up the staple crop at the docks and held potatoes in storage to cause a steep increase in prices. Residents of Bergen were outraged.

---

[74] Erik II claimed the crown of Scotland, or at least a stipend on behalf of his daughter.
[75] Before she was sacrificed, Margaret prophesized that Haakon V would lapse into insanity three times, which occurred.

Since 1455 and the battle between Olav Nilsson and the Hansa merchants, there had not been such uncontrolled frenzy in the streets. The governor literally read the riot act aloud to the crowds three times, before some folks were impressed to drop their projectiles. It was the last display of violence in Bergen, until 1944.

During World War II, Bergen was occupied by German troops. In April 1944, a Dutch cargo ship, sitting in the Bergen harbor, holding one hundred twenty tons of German dynamite, was ignited, most likely by accident. The blast flattened much of old town Bergen. One hundred and fifty people died in the explosion. Wooden buildings that had withstood fire, or were reconstructed, were destroyed. The 1536 Rosenkrantz Tower, built around Haakonshallen Palace Hall, was heavily damaged.

Center Bergen Today

Birchlegs In and Beyond Bergen Today

In 1939, a ski race was begun to commemorate the rescue of eighteen-month-old Haakon IV in 1206. Twentieth century Birchlegs wear the latest in ski fitting. Birchlegs America is an annual event.

Moving the capital of Norway to Oslo, had no impact on business at the docks in Bergen. Construction of houses increased along the harbor after 1300, commensurate with increased activity at the docks. The lengthy civil war reduced the ranks of contentious folks and left fishermen and farmers to persevere as they had through the Viking era. Norwegians are resilient.

Hills of Bergen at Harbor

Hansa Shop Sign

Saga of Olav Nilsson and the Fall of Hansa

Bergen, Norway was founded in the eleventh century for the purpose of providing a center of commerce in a community dependent upon the sea. It was founded by Olav III, the son of the last Viking king of Norway, at the close of the Viking era. No longer would Norwegians deplete their stock of strong, young men in raids upon neighbors. New wars were fought for access to markets.

For the millennium of its existence, Bergen has been a trade hub for products of Norway sent around the world, and for life-sustaining goods brought into western Norway. Prosperity and position in the network of markets made Bergen desirable for Hansa, the thirteenth century German-based trade consortium, which wrested control of Bergen port from locals. Stronger than the king of Norway, and above the law, Hansa ruled Bergen. Local interests were not its concern.

Bergen became the battle ground of the first war of the new millennium. It was not a war of land, politics, or religion. It was a war for supremacy of law; the international law of self-serving Hansa, versus the civil law of the local jurisdiction in which Hansa did business. It was a test of will.

The combatants in this war were the powerful Hansa, which possessed the trading strength of over one hundred ports and a private army and navy, against the city commissioner for the king. Olav Nilsson was a noble, who fought as a knight on behalf of his king. His battle for Bergen was waged with the support of a bishop and assorted local residents. Hansa met their match in Olav.

This is the short saga, of a brief battle, in the fifteenth century, of critical importance to the emergence of modern Bergen. Olav and his supporters lost the battle, lost their lives and Bergan lost a centuries old monastery. They won the war, leaving a legacy in the development of laws governing international trade, which persist today. The battle marked the beginning of the end for Hansa and the rise of nation states, protecting their domain, profits and people. This is the story of Olav and his battle against the commercial giant of his day.

From Viking Village to Capital of Norway

Hansa Lodges at Bergen Docks

There is evidence of human life in Vestland, the western lands of Norway, of which Bergen is the main town, going back almost four millennia before the current era. Bronze age people of the area produced an axe in 1700 BCE. Imposing cold of the Little Ice Age, ended in 200 CE, enabling bands of people to move north in search of farmland. In the fifth century, Attila the Hun terrorized Europe, making relocation to the north attractive. By 450, Rodulf, the king of Vesterland, is recorded as traveling to Ravenna, in northern Italy, a center of the Christian church.

Small kingdoms proliferated in Norway, with various farming-based settlements, having no unifying cause. Not all Norwegians were Vikings. Even through two centuries of the Viking Era, from the ninth to the eleventh century, most Norwegians lived quiet lives of farmers and fishermen. When Norwegians sailed the twenty-four-hour journey from Vesterland to the east coast of Scotland, they were most often in pursuit of farmland on which to settle. By 872, colonists from Vestland could be found in Ireland, Orkney and the Shetland Islands. A Norwegian king of the time, Olav lived in Dublin, while his brothers headed clans in Limerick and Waterford.[76]

In 792, a ship of Vestlanders landed in Lindisfarne on the English coast, intent on raiding and looting the monastery. The solitary monks were unprepared to protect their valuable vestments and silver. The raid began the notorious Viking Era, when the sighting of their elegant ships threw fear and panic into people of coastal fishing villages. Skilled as sailors and warriors, Vikings preferred raids to farming, or raided annually, between planting and harvesting crops.

Harald Fairhair battled with Olav of Dublin for control of Norway from 872 to 900. Harald was the eventual victor and unifier of Norway, although the battles depleted his strength. He died in 933 near Bergen. Chieftains caught on the wrong side of decades of battles migrated to Iceland. By 930, Iceland and Norway adopted the Viking law code of old Norse Gulathing, portions of which were read aloud each year by Thingmen at chieftain gatherings, known as Things.[77]

Progeny of Harald ruled Norway from settlements near Bergen, when they were not sailing to England and the Baltic, raiding towns from Ireland to Tallinn, at the entrance to the Neva River. There were several pagan kings of Norway, including Harald Bluetooth, who unified Denmark.[78] In 985, Olav I arrived from England to Christianize Norway before he headed off in 990, to battles elsewhere, and died in 1000. Olav's son made the crossing from England in 1016, where his battles did not keep him from establishing churches in Norway, from which he dispensed Olav's Law.

---

[76] This Olav was known as Olav the White, to distinguish him from later Olav kings.
[77] The petition of a Viking Egil Skallagrimson has survived to provide a sense of Gulathing justice. Skallagrimson was born in Iceland and found a wife in Norway. Upon her death he returned to Norway to present his petition for his wife's estate at a Thing. Resolution of his claim is unknown, although it illustrates civil justice of the time. See generally, Frank Noel Stagg, West Norway and Its Fjords, George Allen & Unwin Ltd, 1954. Se also, the Port of Iceland in this Itinerary.
[78] Find the story of Harald Bluetooth in Cruise through History© Itinerary XI Ports of the Baltic Sea -Fredericia, 2018.

Early Church in Bergen

In 1027, Olav II faced Canute, the son of Harald Bluetooth, in a battle for control of Norway. Canute was the king of Denmark by inheritance and king of a large portion of England by his own effort. Canute was acclaimed king of Norway at Trondheim, then known as Øreting. Olav went into exile, from which he emerged at the famous Battle of Stiklestad in 1030, where he died. Olav had the last word on Canute, so to say. He was beatified as St. Olav of Trondheim.

Hansa Church

Progeny of Canute and Olav, Harald Hardrada[79] and Magnus, decided upon joint rule of Norway rather than a battle. Magnus died in a battle in Denmark and Harald went to England in 1066, accompanied by two hundred Vesterland vessels manned by the pride of the Vikings. At the Battle of Stamford Bridge, the future of England and Norway took a step into a new era. Harald and the vestiges of the Viking Age died in that battle. William the Norman Conqueror became King William I of England later that year, after the Battle of Hastings, and the son of Magnus became Olav III of Norway.

Olav III decided that paucity of males fit for battle made it provident to opt for peaceful rule, in harmony with the church. He founded Bergen as a port, to receive fish from the northern fjords, to be traded for goods incoming from England and elsewhere in the North and Baltic Seas. For the next seven hundred and fifty years, Bergen became the largest and wealthiest town in Norway.

Hansa Overtakes Bergen

In the late twelfth century, King Sverre of Norway, ruling from Bergen, called a Thing, the ancient Norse version of an open town council meeting.[80] He gave thanks to the English for sending wheat, honey, flour and cloth to his western Norwegian domain. He was gracious to the people of Orkney, Shetlands, Faroe Islands and Iceland for sending to Bergen's port so many of the necessities of life, upon which his people depended. Of the Germans, King Sverre said that his people would be better off had the Germans never arrived. The undesirable visitors bought Norwegian butter and cod in trade for wine. Until arrival of the plague, centuries later, alcoholism was the scourge of the docks. Sverre's

---

[79] Sometimes the name is spelled Haardraada. Viking names translate variously in Norwegian and English.
[80] Some historians refer to Norse public meetings as tings and others call them pings. The term is a matter of translation pronunciation. Whether called Thingmen, Tingmen, or Pingmen, they led the meetings.

sentiments were repeated by town rulers through the nineteenth century and quoted by the resistance movement during World War II.[81]

In fairness to the German merchants of Lübeck, their enterprise broke the strictures of Medieval society in the twelfth century, with a rise in independent merchants. A vibrant middle class grew each time private vessels reached out across the Baltic and into the North Sea. Treasuries of kings, depleted by repeated turf battles, were unable to impede the progress of the new kings of the sea, who were the merchants with independent ships, interested in profit, not conquest.

Merchants needed places to store their goods until market day, safe harbors for their ships and established trade relationships, upon which to depend over the years. In the twelfth century, strangers were not welcome to stay in towns for more than a few months. Large ships of the day, moving low and slow in the water, obviously filled with cargo, were prey for pirates.

What began as practical arrangement, to carry forward a small market economy, in the absence of omnipresent control of overlords, evolved into an international guild of seamen, merchants and diplomats. At its height, the guild was a voluntary association of one hundred and seventy cities. Cities asserted home-rule with elected councils, the councils sent envoys to guild meetings, and the guild negotiated favorable trade treaties in the thirteenth century with world powers, such as England.

In 1356, the guild convened and gave itself a name, the Hanseatic League. League members pledged mutual support and defense. Instead of war to resolve internal differences, they used consensus and compromise agreements. Rather than empty shops, mills and industrial centers to provide soldiers to nobles, members sent funds to purchase armies. The League hired their own force to protect its interests. The League became larger and stronger than any kingdom.

---

[81] Thomas M. Wilson, Local Option in Norway, John Grieg printer, Bergen, 1890. The local option was a proposal to regulate sale of liquor by issuance of a limited number of licenses, the fees of which would fund the public burden of dealing with health and impoverishing effects of alcoholism. For a history of Bergen read, Inquild Øye ed., Bergen and the German Hansa, Bryggens Museum, Bergen, 1994.

Hansa Sailor & Trades Lodges

Hansa Lodge World Heritage Site

In Bergen, trade agreements entered into by the king and Hansa began in 1250. German merchants, with the means to build homes and warehouses, quickly overcame local fishermen and shopkeepers, with their more sophisticated trade arrangements. Hansa kept negotiating more favorable terms, which by 1270, included the ability for Hansa merchants of Lübeck to own homes in Bergen. By 1300, when Bergen was eclipsed by Oslo as the capital of Norway, German shoemakers had a monopoly on their trade in Bergen. German bakers, barbers, tailors and gold smiths formed guilds in Bergen, which excluded Norwegians. Lutheran Germans in the Catholic town of Bergen used St. Mary's Church as their parish church, which Hansa held until 1766. The church stands today near the harbor.

Hansa merchants in Bergen demanded privileges, without accepting obligations expected of locals, such as night-watch, levy for the king's navy and military service. Norwegian citizens were subject to local laws, breeches of which resulted in incarceration, or execution. Hansa merchants deemed themselves above the local law, and subject only to their own rules. When two Hansa merchants were accused of murder of an Englishman in Bergen, in a trade dispute in 1375, the Hansa took the matter out of local hands and arranged for the accused to leave town.

Night Watch Bergen

Townspeople tried to stand united against Hansa, only to be undermined by further agreements with Hansa settled by their king, in the name of trade deals. Initially, Hansa could only control fish once fishermen brought their catch into port. Fishing and transport north of Bergen was beyond Hansa control. In 1370, a treaty was struck between Hansa and the king of Denmark, who controlled Norway. Hansa was given control of all fisheries in Norway. Locals never recovered.

When the Bishop of Bergen tried to intercede on behalf of his flock, and claim rights to tithes received by the bishopric, Hansa issued a decree that the shoemakers guild would not sell shoes to clerics in Bergen. When any Scandinavian king tried to retake control of the port, Hansa sent its navy to blockade Bergen's harbor. All trade ceased. By 1433, Bergen was a Hansa town.

Olav the Knight Becomes a Pirate

The Olav of this story was no saint. Like many notables of his time, the date of his birth is unknown, although the date of his death in 1455 is certain. He was likely born in Trondheim to a family, with enough of a connection to a royal to deem him a noble. He rode to Jerusalem as a crusading knight, in the company of Eric of Pomerania. By 1430, Olav served his mentor Eric in the Norwegian government and was given command of Bergenhus Fortress, still seen today, a prominent feature at the entrance to the Bergen harbor.

Eric had such influence on the leadership development and career of Olav, that a word on Olav's mentor is due. Eric was born Boguslav, in Pomerania, now part of Poland. As a child, he was taken as a son to his great-aunt Margaret I, Queen of the Kalmar Union, to be raised as her successor. She named him Eric, a suitable name for the future king of the Tre Croner, the three crowns of Denmark, Sweden and Norway. Margaret succeeded her husband to the crown of Sweden, was elected queen of Denmark and conquered Norway. She was truly a great leader, deserving of a story of her own. The Kalmar Union was formed by the three crowns as a competitor to Hansa.

Bergen Fortress

Eric became Eric XIII of Sweden, Eric VII of Denmark and Eric III of Norway.[82] Eric was off to a grand start in his inherited kingdoms. He instituted Sound Dues, which charged Hansa for passage through the narrow passage between Sweden and Denmark, guarded by Kronborg Fortress, a castle built with the tax.[83] The powerful Hansa merchants fought back at Eric by agitating nobles in his domain. Eric was deposed as king of Denmark and Sweden in 1439. He hung on to Norway for two more years. He moved to the Swedish island of Visby, where he built a castle as a home base. Then Eric became a pirate attacking merchant ships of the Hansa League.

Eric's successor, his nephew Christopher, put Olav in charge of a complaint department in Bergen, charged with resolving disputes between locals and Hansa. Olav decided that he would use his military garrison in the Bergenhus to enforce local law. That put Olav in the cross-hairs of Hansa. King Christopher died in 1448, and his successor Christian I of Denmark offered Olav no support. At the urging of Hansa, Christian replaced Olav in Bergen with a Swede. Olav followed the lead of his mentor Eric of Pomerania and became a pirate, who focused his attacks on ships of Hansa merchants.

The height of Olav's pirating accomplishments was the capture in 1455 of the Fortress of Älvsborg, a Swedish town.[84] Olav offered to turn Älvsborg over to King Christian I, if the king would reinstate him as the commander of Bergenhus Fortress. The king agreed. Olav returned to Bergen in a triumphant display, celebrated by the locals. Hansa merchants were not amused.

---

[82] The number of prior Erics in each country is questionable. There have been only two Queen Margarets; Margaret the Great in the fifteenth century and Margaret the present queen of Denmark.

[83] See Cruise through History, Itinerary XI for more on Eric and the history of Denmark, Sweden and Norway.

[84] Also known as Elfsborg or Gothenburg. Olav threatened to turn the fortress over to the Swedes, if the Danes did not meet his demands.

Revenge of Hansa

Olav's Fortress

Hanseatic merchants of Bergen banded together, with their reinforcements, and attacked Olav in Bergenhus. The fortress was not a formidable garrison at this time. Since it was first erected by King Olav III in the tenth century, the fortress had not been much changed. In 1455, Olav had few soldiers in residence. Leif Thor Olafsson, the Bishop of Bergen, came to Olav's aide, with dozens of local supporters. They fought the well-armed Hansa through the streets of Bergen, until they found refuge in Munkeliv Abby, on the bluff overlooking the Vågen, the Bergen harbor.

Munkeliv Abby was built in 1110 by Olav III's grandson King Eystein I of Norway. A statue of Eystein previously ensconced in the Abby is today in the University of Bergen Museum. The head of Eystein is all that remains of the Abby. The Hansa horde went after Olav with a boundless rage. They set fire to the Abby. In the melee, Olav, one of his sons, the Bishop of Bergen and sixty of their supporters died.

Commeration of Eystein I

After they left the bloody scene at the Abby, the Hansa horde paraded through Bergen, still in a mood for revenge. They went to Olav's home and tore through his possessions as his widow, Elitza, huddled with four-year old son Axel. When tempers cooled, Hansa merchants returned to business as usual in Bergen.

No More Monastery on the Hill

Olav's wife, son and daughter never overcame the trauma of the day. As soon as he was old enough to captain a ship, Axel Olavsson became a pirate. Olav's wife captained her own vessel, as did a daughter. The son captured Hansa cargo until he felt he had achieved reparations for the damage to his family. Olav's daughter went on to be an irritant in Hansa shipping for years.

Bergen Today

The brazen melee in which Olav perished, marked the beginning of a decline in the power of Hansa. King Christian I of Denmark, head of the Kalmar Union, died in 1483. Norway had its king Hans, who gave trade advantages to the Dutch over Hansa. Hans entered into trade deals with King Henry II of England and Tsar Ivan in Russia. Bergen, Amsterdam and Brugge were joined by Copenhagen in preferring trade with the Dutch over Hansa.

Street in Old Bergen where Hansa pursued Olav's family

Trade relations between Bergen and Denmark were much improved in 1507, when King Christian II of Denmark spotted Dyveke, the little dove, working with her mother, Sigbrit Willums in a cake shop near the port in Bergen.[85] The mother and daughter were among those relocated from Amsterdam. Dyveke became mistress to the king from 1507, until her death in 1517, possibly from a ruptured appendix. Sigbrit became a financial advisor to the king, serving as royal treasurer.

---

[85] Sigbrit Willums is also spelled Willoms or Villums, depending on the source. Her daughter was Dyveke Sigbritdatter. Mr. Willums is unknown.

Upon the death of her daughter, Sigbrit was made part of the queen's household staff. Possessing a keen sense of public health and avoidance of plague, Sigbrit was also put in charge of hygiene in Copenhagen. She impressed the king to issue a law that people clean house weekly. In the sixteenth century the display of talents in service to the king by a woman left Sigbrit open to charges of being a witch. In 1522, a woman matching Sigbrit's description was executed for being a witch. King Christian II left Denmark at that time and Sigbrit was never heard of again.[86]

While in Bergen, Sigbrit convinced Christian II to appoint Jørgen Hansson to be town administrator. Hansson renovated Bergenhus into a proper fortress. He picked up where Olav left off in invoking local law for all in Bergen, including the German merchants of Hansa.

There were two additional town administrators of note, responsible for the appearance of the Bergen docks experienced by visitors today. In 1556, Kristofer Valkendorf, a Dane, reinforced Bergenhus and pushed the red-light district out of town. He invited German shoemakers to become Norwegian or leave town. His memorial can be seen today in the city hall.

City governor Erik Rosenkrantz came from Denmark in 1560, to put the death stamp on Hansa control of Bergen. The new wealth of Bergen was created in timber exports from inland Norway to the Dutch, through the docks at Bergen. Hansa had no control over timbermen. Rosenkrantz is best remembered in Bergen for what he did not do. He was ordered by King Frederik of Denmark to tear down the tower of Haakon IV, that had stood since 1260, and to tear down the chapel of King Magnus built in 1273. This he declined to do. Instead he built Rosenkrantz Tower in 1536, a structure that protected the older buildings until 1944.

Buildings in Bergen were initially built of wood. Periodic fire, the result of accidents, or civic strife, left Bergen devastated several times in its history. The city seen today was largely built after the fire of 1702, when townspeople refused to fight fires threatening homes of wealthy merchants and aristocrats. When Governor Frederik von Gabel reorganized city government with thirty-two elected councilmen, Hansa was a minor presence.

---

[86] The last known witch trial in Norway was in 1734.

Fire Survivor

The city arrangement of today is little changed from the twelfth century. As ships sail into Vågen, the Bergen harbor, rebuilt buildings of the Hansa era, the Bryggen that was designated a World Heritage Site in 1981, appear on the port side, just inside the Bergenhus Fortress at the entrance. On the starboard side are eighteenth century and later buildings of the wealthy of Bergen. At the head of the harbor is the market area and beyond streets lead through shopping areas, where the Olav Nilsson family walked almost six hundred years ago.

Once in the harbor, look up to the bluff, where the site of the Munkeliv Abby is now open space. In the center of the old town there is a lovely lake, ringed by museums and display of public art. The open space helped the city to manage control of fires, which lessened with buildings of brick and stone. Take in the whole view today from the top of Mount Floyen, reached by cable car.

Monument to Olav Street now a coffee shop sign

Bergen is still an import shipping port for western Norway. The industrial docks have simply moved down the bay, leaving Olav III's port of Bergen intact for visitors. The city has never ceased being a lively place since its inception. It is, as it has always been, a hub for international travelers.

Saint Olav in Trondheim

Trondheim: Nidaros Cathedral – The Power of Place

King vs Bishop in Nidaros - The Power of Place

The Norse Sagas tell of brave Norse king Olav, who fell at a great battle in 1030. It was a pivotal time in the history of Norway, when the Viking king was leading his people into Christianity. The coming end of the Viking Era was marked by the establishment of settlements and people rooted to place, rather than looking to raid far-away places over the sea. King Olav became a symbol of the new era of Norwegian nation-building. His grave site became a shrine.

The local bishop declared miracles to occur at the grave of Olav. A chapel was built there, then a church. A spring of healing water came forth at the shrine and was incorporated into the church by a well, from which pilgrims retrieved healing water. Through Medieval times, when plague devastated ports such as Oslo, people sought a healing spirit, by walking the Way of St. Olav.

The Way of St. Olav

Nidaros was the name of the little town in the bend of the Nidelva River, so close to the fjord leading into the North Sea. From the docks, ships came and went to the reaches of the Norse empire: north into the White and Baltic Seas, across to Iceland, Greenland and Vinland, south to England, Ireland and Spain. An enterprising bishop recognized the power of the place could be enhanced by elevation to the seat of an archbishop. Archbishops served in lofty cathedrals. Nidaros would have a cathedral. Such a notable place needed a more substantial name. It was anointed Trondheim. The cathedral retained the Medieval name of the place by the river Nidelva.

The archbishop, who began building Nidaros Cathedral in the twelfth century, knew how to capitalize on the power of place. He returned from exile in England where Gothic cathedrals were popular. A cathedral is distinguished from a mere church by the presence of relics of a saint. Nidaros had not just relics, but the entire burial of the patron saint of Norway. The axe of St. Olav features prominently in the national emblem. As a pilgrimage destination worthy of the saint, Trondheim experienced economic prosperity. The archbishop built a palace. Over the centuries, leading citizens built fine homes on the street from the harbor on the fjord, to the cathedral.

The emblem of Trondheim has an archbishop facing a king. In the twelfth century, the church vied for power with the crown. Trondheim lost political power in the twelfth century, when the archbishop backed the losing contender for the crown. The victor made Bergen his capital. The archbishop regained prestige by building a cathedral so wondrous, that it was the place for coronations and burials of kings. Through the cathedral, Trondheim remained the cultural heart of the country. The mystique endures. This is the story of the power of place that is Trondheim.

Saga of St. Olav

Quiet repose of Olav on Nidelva River

The often-cited author of Norse Sagas, Snorri Sturluson, made a visit to the shrine of St. Olav in Trondheim from 1219 to 1220. He described the newly unveiled second shrine of Olav as covered in gold and silver plate. It was coffin-length, with a hinged lid, to enable viewing on feast days. The gilded reliquary sat on a brick pillar, with an arcade of gothic arches, in the chapel center.

Snorri described Olav as stout with a moustache. Since all other accounts describe the full beard of Olav, which grew even after death, Snorri may have been recording current assumptions. The Bishop of Bremen described Olav in 1300 as tall. The Bishop also complained that King Harald Hardrada (Hard ruler) confiscated gifts left by pilgrims at the shrine to pay his own soldiers.[87]

Olav of this story was Norway's king Olav II.[88] Olav was a descendant of Viking king Harald Fairhair, who united Norway. Olav, desirous of continuing the legacy, never shied from battle in defending, or reclaiming lands of Norway. In his travels, he befriended Duke Richard II of Normandy, the grandfather of William the Conqueror. The Normans were Christian. Richard introduced Olav to Christianity, which Olav embraced upon his Baptism in Rouen, France.

Whether or not Olav brought Christianity to his Norsemen during his lifetime, he is credited posthumously with the feat. Olav was defeated in his fatal battle of Stiklestad in 1030, by the great Viking king of Denmark, England and Norway, Canute, who wrested Norway from Olav in 1027. Canute takes some credit for bringing Christianity to Vikings. It was Olav, who was canonized.

Canonization of Olav was due to the effort of an English missionary in Olav's company, a man named Grimkell.[89] Grimkell was made an English bishop for his work with Olav. Olav was known in his lifetime for brutality. Grimkell

---

[87] Harald Hardrada met his fate in the Battle of Stamford Bridge in 1066, failing to take the crown of England and weakening defenders, who were overcome later that year by the upstart king William of Normandy.

[88] Olav Haraldsson was born 995, in Norway and died on July 29, 1030. He was canonized in 1031.

[89] Also spelled Grimketel or Grimkjel. He lived to 1047, and is buried in Canterbury.

authored a softer side of the man, in what became known throughout Norway as Olav's Law. At the death of Olav, Grimkell became the first bishop of Nidaros. Olav was buried on the sandy shore of the river Nidelva. Upon canonization, remains were moved to the more appropriate Church of St. Olav, the new seat of Bishop Grimkell.

Olav traveled several times, after his first burial in the warrior's repose next to the peaceful river. Once Grimkell raised his stature, but before the new church was complete, Olav resided in St. Clement's Church on the north edge of town. In 1040, St. Olav's was ready to occupy. In 1060, Olav was moved to St. Mary's, then the central church of Medieval Nidaros, just off the market square.[90] That church still sits off Market Square, under the shadow of Olav on a pillar. St. Olav's is now the foundation for Trondheim Library, which has Olav-era exposed burials in the floor.

St. Mary's Church Trondheim

---

[90] St. Mary's is also known as The Church of Our Lady, or Vår Frue Kirke.

The mythology surrounding St. Olav includes a chapter about King Olav III, the son of Harald Hardrada.[91] According to the legends, in 1070, Olav III came to Nidaros to build a church on the site of the original burial of St. Olav. Despite extensive archaeology, there is no evidence of such an effort. There is evidence of the beginnings of what became Nidaros Cathedral later, in 1100.

By 1153, Trondheim merited an Archbishop See. The simple English-Romanesque style church was transformed in mid-construction to the larger, modern, technology of the times in a Gothic church, worthy of a great English city, or the home of a new Archbishop in Norway. Archbishop Eystein was the agent of change. He was exiled to England in 1180, for backing the Trondheim contender, who lost to Sverre, the next king of Norway. Sverre made Bergen his capital.

Archbishops More Powerful than Kings

Archbishop Eystein with St. Olav and the Saintly Graces

---

[91] To keep the Olavs and Haralds straight, Olav III is known as Olav Haraldsson Kyrre, born in 1050, and died in 1093. He is also known as Olav the Peaceful.

Archbishop Eystein learned a great deal about church building during his three years of exile. He was also enterprising and shrewd enough to realize that a shrine to St. Olav in the cathedral could elevate its importance, not only in the ethereal eyes of the church, but also in the worldly lives of pilgrims. Pilgrims were good for business. Until his death in 1188, Eystein promoted the Cathedral of Nidaros as a pilgrimage destination and the venue of royal ceremony from coronation and marriage, to burial of kings. If Bergen was home to business and armies, Trondheim was home to history, culture and leadership of the hearts and souls of Norwegians.

In the early Medieval era, in which Eystein lived, governments were unstable. Nations as they exist today were still in formative stages. Norway was tossed between control of Denmark and Sweden until the twentieth century. For Norwegians, the church was a rod of stability in their lives. A display of strength and majesty by the church was reassuring to people. Eystein appreciated the value of the church for the people, as well as a means to retain power over kings.

Since archbishops did not lead armies, their mortality rate was lower than kings. Archbishops received rents from land and donations from the faithful. They spent the money at home, not on armies in faraway places. While monarchs of Europe generally found themselves short of funds, church leaders were flush with cash to lavish on monuments, to their god, or patron saint.

To promote St. Olav as the patron saint of Norway, Eystein included a shrine in the cathedral. The shrine in the center of the Octagon, behind the choir in the east end chapel, became St. Olav's home for the next four hundred years. Only the end of Catholicism in Norway dislodged him. The long-trod road of kings and armies between Oslo and Trondheim evolved from the King's Road to the Way of St. Olav.[92] Pilgrims flooded Trondheim, making it wealthy.

---

[92] There is some historic symmetry to the Way of St. Olav. Olav II escaped from Canute in 1027, when he fled on the King's Road to safety in the fjords of west Norway. The road has also been known as Trollstigen Road, the place where trolls hide. Frank Noel Stagg, West Norway and Its Fjords, George Allen & Unwih Ltd., 1954, at 233.

Shrine Box of St. Olav

Politically compromised, Archbishop Eystein no longer had the ear of the king. That did not keep him from orchestrating the selection of kings and hosting their coronation in the cathedral. The ancient Norse leadership selection conference, known as Øyraping, or Thing, seated the lead man on the King's Chair, a stone of antiquity. For decades, the King's Chair was ensconced in the cathedral garden in Trondheim. The new king passed through the garden and across the threshold of Nidaros Cathedral to receive his crown.

In the fifteenth century, when Norway was part of the Kalmar Union with Denmark and Sweden, Kalmar monarchs chose Nidaros Cathedral for their coronation. Reformation and the expulsion of Catholic clerics in the sixteenth century, did not end Nidaros tradition. The cathedral became a Lutheran cathedral. Coronations continued unimpeded by religious politics. The tradition of Nidaros Cathedral as the choice venue of coronation ceremonies for kings and queens of Norway continues today. The most recent was the 1991 coronation of King Harald V and Queen Sonja.

Nidaros Cathedral place of anointing kings

Celebration of marriage and internment in the hereafter are religious events. The most popular venue for the marriage and funeral of kings of Norway was Nidaros Cathedral. Up until the exile of Archbishop Eystein, kings were buried in Nidaros. In the thirteenth century, Nidaros Cathedral became once again the chosen venue. Kings appreciated the power of place.

The most powerful person in Norway, if not the wealthiest, could command a large palace. The Archbishop of Trondheim built a palace compound next to the cathedral. It remains today a monument to the prestige of ecclesiastical leadership. In this place, the worldly home of majesty of the divine was manufactured into art objects of enduring beauty, Eystein's other legacy.

Archbishops of Trondheim were known to enjoy collecting carved ivory, pArcticularly a carved ivory crozier and chess pieces. Such a chess piece of a bishop is in the collection of the British Museum.[93] Ivory harvested from

---

[93] The ivory chessmen have their own story in this Itinerary.

Archbishop's Palace

walrus tusk in Greenland, was carved into chess pieces in the bishopric of Iceland, and sent to the Archbishop of Trondheim as a gift. Archbishops of Trondheim had not only funds, they also had the artistic resources of the northern Norse empire upon which to draw to create objects for ecclesiastical ceremony worthy of an archbishop.

In the early decades of the sixteenth century, Reformation spread through Europe to Scandinavia. Vatican control of ecclesiastical needs of the people was greatly reduced or eliminated. In 1537, King Christian III of Denmark, then in control of Norway, began to arrest Catholic bishops. The Archbishop in Trondheim prepared to protect the icon saint of Norway.

The last Archbishop of Nidaros Cathedral, Olav Engelbrektsson, escaped to the protection of Catholic king Charles V of the Netherlands. He took with him St. Olav's axe, two tall crowns and an image of St. Olav. The body of St. Olav was taken from Nidaros Cathedral, in anticipation of the coming religious storm, and locked away in Steinvikholm Castle, the Archbishop's fortress.

Mythology of the period spread fear that relics of the saint and treasure of Nidaros were on the way to the Royal Treasury in Copenhagen, when all was lost at sea. In fact, the coffin of St. Olav was in what was left of its outer cover in the Archbishop's fortress castle, where it was slowly denuded by occupying soldiers, of its silver coffin nails. The soldiers, sent to arrest priests, had no idea of what was in the fancy box. In 1543, Dutch privateers captured a ship holding Norwegian church treasures. The story of traveling relics of St. Olav was not yet finished.

Nidaros Cathedral of Trondheim - Icon of Norway

Nidaros Cathedral Entrance

Nidaros Cathedral became the largest church in Norway for one hundred years. Today it is one of the largest Medieval stone structures in Scandinavia. Completed in 1280, over the centuries it suffered effects of plague and fire. Olav III is credited with bringing remains of St. Olav full circle to the place of the original warrior's burial in the south of Trondheim, in the quiet bend in the river. It was the highest point in the landscape. The earliest construction on this site is in 1100.

The first walls were long and narrow, running east from the shrine to the main façade in the west end. A transept, the hall forming a cross, was begun in 1130, and was made more lavish after 1153, to become the seat of the Archbishop. Archbishop Eystein oversaw construction, including the Octagon around the shrine, high walls of the transept, and completed Chapter House, accessed from the Octagon on the north side. In 1188, Eystein was buried in the Chapter House.

Although St. Olav had one home for four hundred years, relics of the saint had four coffins. Description of the first shrine has not survived. The second shrine was described by Snorri as something suitable to lift from the supportive structure and carry in a procession on important days, including St. Olav's Day.[94] Sometime between 1220, and the rising power of Lutherans in Scandinavia in 1530, the first two shrines were encased in a third shrine. The wooden coffin with the silver overlay was situated below a canopy.

When Archbishop Olav placed the coffin in his castle fortress on the outskirts of Trondheim, upon his hasty departure from soldiers arresting priests, it was the misfortune of St. Olav to be housed with the conquering army. Soldiers picked away at valuable metal on the coffin, leaving only lead nails keeping it secure. That coffin was returned to Nidaros Cathedral in 1564, secured in a fourth outer coffin, and placed in a masonry-lined grave.[95]

Although the Danish king could decree the Nidaros Cathedral to be the Royal Lutheran Cathedral, he could not quell enthusiasm of pilgrims, throughout the Catholic world, who visited the patron saint of Norway in a church, that had become an icon of Norwegian people. In an act of cultural/political dominance, in 1568, the Danish king ordered that the gravesite be filled with soil and all traces of its existence removed. For the next four hundred and fifty years, St. Olav rested hidden in peace.

---

[94] Since 1930, the 900th anniversary of the Battle of Stiklestad, St. Olav's Day has been celebrated on July 29.

[95] Margrete Syrstad Andäs, Øystein Ekroll, Andreas Haug, Nils Holger, eds., The Medieval Cathedral of Trondheim, Brepols Pub., Belgium, 2007, at 200. The inner coffin was 500 years old at this time.

The story of Nidaros Cathedral continued. After plagues of the fourteenth century, intermittent fires, and religious wars of the sixteenth century, Nidaros Cathedral was in sad shape. In recognition of its powerful status as a national icon of a people struggling to assert independence from other countries, restoration of the cathedral became a national imperative.

Over a thirty-year period, from 1871 to 1901, the Chapter House, Octagon, chancel, transept and central tower were restored. In 1905, Norway achieved independence from Sweden. In 1906, the king and queen of Norway were crowned following an elegant procession in the restored nave.

In 1930, a Steinmeyer organ, at the time the largest one in Scandinavia, was installed under the Rose Window; the window having been restored through donations from women of Norway. The restored 1741 organ, by the German builder Jürgen Ahrend, sits in front of the massive new organ.[96]

Golden Age of the Powerful City

In 1681, a fire swept through the city of Trondheim, devastating the market center filled with wooden buildings. Danish King Christian V took the opportunity to bring Trondheim from a Medieval town to the glory of a major commercial center. He hired Luxembourg architect Major General Johan Caspar von Cicignon to create a new city. It is the wide, straight, grid in the street plan of Cicignon that greets visitors to Trondheim today.

The main street running from the cruise ship harbor inward from the fjord, at the point of the fish market, Ravnkloa, to Nidaros Cathedral, is cut in the center by Market Square, which is actually a circle. The circle acts as a sundial, with the center pillar supporting a statue of Olav.

---

[96] Tusen År ved Nidelven, Trondheim, Aune, Trondheim, 1997, at 60; see generally Aug Albertsen, A Guide to the Cathedral of Nidaros, published by Nidaros Restoration, Trondheim, 1960.

Olav On a Spire Town Center Trondheim

Along the main street, mansions were built in the eighteenth century by merchants of Trondheim. The largest private home was that of Cecile Christine Schøller,[97] who built the palace on land held by her family for generations. That home now serves as the Norwegian Royal Residence in the city.

On the hills surrounding Trondheim, the wealthy built estate homes in an area known as Lade. One of the homes is now Ringve Manor Museum of Music. On the island beyond the harbor, Munkholmen, Cicignon built the king a fortress. In peaceful times, it is a favorite picnic spot. On the hill overlooking the city from the east, Cicignon built Kristiansten Fortress. It was instrumental in defense of the city from Swedes in 1718. The German army occupied the fortress during World War II. Today it is a museum dedicated to Norwegian freedom fighters.

Built by Cecile Scholler and used as a Royal Residence

---

[97] Cecile Christine Schøller, born 1720 and died 1786. She was appointed Privy Counselor in 1777. The palace name was first given in 1840, when the home was state property and residence of the governor.

Today in Trondheim – Where is Olav?

Looking for St. Olav

Norwegians, never lacking a sense of humor, have their own version of the popular game; Where is Waldo? They have never stopped looking for St. Olav beneath the floor of Nidaros Cathedral. By 1897, the 900th anniversary of the founding of the city, the search went into high gear, presenting a headache to the controlling Swedish government. Eight years later, Sweden proclaimed itself parted from Norway. Norwegians continued the search in anticipation of the 900th anniversary of the Battle of Stiklestad in 1930, the mortal moment for the saint. The search accumulated a popular following for the Holy Grail of Norwegian history.

Extensive archaeology in the Octagon and adjoining chapel areas, disclosed Lutheran era burials commingled with earlier Catholic burials. A couple burials were candidates for the era of Olav. Excavations located the well of healing water, which legend recalled as springing forth at the burial place of warrior Olav, contributing to miracles necessary for candidacy for sainthood.

In 2014, Olav scholars and Nidaros Cathedral Restoration Workshop experts enlisted the technology of geo-radar from nearby Norwegian University of Science and Technology (NTNU). The technique located sub-floor burials. One burial may be that of a king, a generation following St. Olav, that of Magnus the Good.

If a likely burial of St. Olav is excavated, it can be authenticated by a known relic of St. Olav, that of his leg bone, which is in the Danish National Museum in Copenhagen. The bone was a gift to King Christian II, after his coronation in 1514. Among other attributes of the royal relic, including an age range of 1030, the bone shows evidence of injury in battle consistent with those sustained by Olav. A specimen of DNA was taken from the bone and stored to verify future finds.

As the millennium anniversary of the death of St. Olav approaches in 2030, the Norwegian government has appropriated funds to find St. Olav. The effort has yielded the location of the Church of St. Clements, begun by Olav in 1015, and one of his posthumous homes. The Nidaros Cathedral Restoration Workshop continues their scholarly pArcticipation in the search, while they continue to restore the cathedral. Trondheim is a leading center of Medieval art restoration.

Across the Nidelva River on the Gamle Bybrn, the Old City Bridge, built in 1861, is the Bakklandet district. Saved from the Urban Renewal movement of the 1990s, the neighborhood is now a favorite of visitors and photographers. Homes of timber and dock workers of the nineteenth century are preserved on meandering streets. The 1856, Erichsen Konditori café sits in the midst of the Dronningens Gate shopping district, with postcard perfect views of river warehouses.

Across to Bakklandet Fishing Town

On July 29 each year, Trondheim is transformed into a Medieval playground. Visitors might see St. Olav on a horse, with, or without a beard, tall, or stout. At any time of year, the city is a treasure of Norwegian history, home to the icon of power in Medieval Norway, the Nidaros Cathedral, quite possibly still the final resting place of the patron saint of Norway, St. Olav.

Warehouses of Trondheim

Fjords of Norway

Flåm and the Fjords

Fjords of western Norway are part of the psyche of people of the area. There is a special relationship between environment and people, who live among glacially carved crags. Certainly, western Norway is not the only land blessed with glacial fjords splayed against calm blue water. In this place, lives were built to incorporate landscape. Sailing from Oslo and the Oslofjord, then up the entire west coast of Norway, stunning landscape is seen in abundance. This is Norway.

From ancient times to recent times, Norwegians have incorporated fjords into their lives. The maze of fjords is a network of inlets that have names as familiar to locals as a street system to dry land dwellers. Norse legends fill the landscape. Gods, trolls and little people lived in fjords and under waterfalls, fed by glacial streams that ran through valleys and across farms, as water ran to the sea. For believers, trolls exist here.

Norsemen were seamen. Boats, not roads, connected villages and towns from ancient times into the twentieth century. Vikings came from Norway. Traversing narrow fjords in all-weather made them expert navigators. Returning from raids, fjords offered protection and seclusion to tenth century Vikings and twentieth century resistance fighters, returning from raids on German supply ships docked in Bergen, during World War II.

Western Norway has a history apart from politics and cultural development of the big cities of Trondheim, Bergen and Oslo. Fjord dwellers were mostly fishermen and farmers, whose product was brought to market in commercial centers. Outside of the cities, population is sparse.

One of the tiny communities within the fjords, Flåm, was made prominent by connection of the Flåm Railway to the rail line connecting Oslo and Bergen. Flåm has not grown to a population of more than four hundred, despite cruise lines that come to dock, one at a time. Walk the main road of Flåm, passing farms and the Flåm parish church, with all the Flåm headstones, to experience life within fjords, under glacial waterfalls that feed streams through Flåmsdalen Valley.

Flåm Railway has a part of this story of its own. It was an achievement of the nation, local business and workers, to finance, lay track and operate the railway. Norwegians from throughout the country are as awed as first-time visitors when traveling Flåm Railway. The trip is all about the journey, not the destination. Few train rides in the world offer such a view.

This is a short story meant to intrigue visitors to the fjords and Flåm, as they float slowly through a natural landscape that has been home to a history, not apparent in the green cliffs. Those who choose to ride Flåm Railway will sit comfortably through part of that history. Western Norway is a place to experience in person. No single picture can capture the depth and color of the fjords.

A Little History of Vesterland Fjords

Fishing Cottages on a Fjord

Vesterland is western Norway, a thin strip of mountainous land, bounded on the west by the sea. From ancient times to the twentieth century, connecting with neighbors in adjoining fjords meant sailing, or rowing through main fjords, into a network of small fjords; a maze known only by locals. Norwegians sailed into the North Sea to populate Ireland, the Shetlands and Orkneys by 872, just as Scots sailed east to populate some Norwegian fjords. The blended people shared a dialect different from the rest of Norway. They shared an expert ability to sail the fjords.

Not all Vesterlanders were Vikings. Fjords were dotted with small kingdoms before the first raiders went 'a-viking,' across the North Sea to Lindisfarne monastery in 793. It was only a twenty-four-hour journey. Raiding was more profitable than farming. Thus began a connection to foreign commerce from the fjords, in which people became accustomed to looking outward.

The Viking era lasted little more than two centuries. In the beginning, Vesterland was thickly populated with an excess of exuberant males, who were not in line to be king. Raiding England and Ireland provided an outlet for establishing new kingdoms. A Norwegian Viking was king in Dublin.

Olav II, before he achieved sainthood, was in England at the beginning of the eleventh century. He returned in 1016, to capture the son of the king of Norway and install himself as king. His acts touched off a battle with King Canute, the Viking king of England. The cross-sea battle between Canute and Olav II went on until Canute prevailed in 1027. Canute was acclaimed king of Norway at a Viking Øreting ceremony and made Trondheim his Norwegian center of power.[98]

By 1066, the population of Vesterland was so reduced by loss of young men in Viking endeavors, that the area lost its contentious spirit. The Viking era ended. Families farmed and fished the fjords. Their excess product was rowed, or sailed into Bergen, for sale on market days.

---

[98] Call them tings, things, or pings, the system of government and pronouncement of law was Norse tradition. For simplicity this democratic governing council is referred to as Things. Things have their own story in Iceland.

Among fjords during Medieval times, several hamlets supplied men to the kings' armies, built Catholic churches and supported their families selling fish to Hansa merchants of Bergen. The town of Voss, inland from Bergen, on the Oslo to Bergen train line today, populated since Viking times and Christianized by Olav II, supported Archbishop Eystein in resisting Sverre in his battle for control of Norway.[99] The enduring Voss church was built in 1277. The last Catholic Bishop of Bergen came to Voss to retire in 1535, as the country went through Reformation to Lutheran.

Cruise through Fjords

On Hardangerfjord, south of Bergen, are Medieval timber logging towns of Hardanger and Eidfjord. Continuing the tradition of Things, regional governing councils, throughout the thirteenth and fourteenth centuries, Hardanger was also an agricultural center, known for its fruit. Its heathen temple became a Gothic church in 1300. Violins made in Hardanger of mountain ash and pine from 1669 to 1766, were world famous. During

---

[99] Local histories of the fjords were compiled by Frank Noel Stagg, in *West Norway and Its Fjords*, George Allen & Unwih Ltd., 1954.

World War II, resistance fighters from Hardanger so angered the Nazis, that the town was leveled by gunboats.

Eidfjord, at the fjord's end, also fiercely independent, distanced itself from Bergen to become part of the diocese of Stavanger to the south. Its oldest church dates to the thirteenth century. Eidfjord survived the war and endures today.

Eidfjord was the center of Scottish expatriates to Norway in the sixteenth century. Fleeing from rule of the British, expatriate Scots became wealthy on the timber trade. In exchange for timber sold in England, Scottish families of the fjords brought the spinning wheel to Norway and supplied locals with wheat flour, sugar, tobacco, spice, soap, raisins and hardware. Their ships bypassed Bergen and slipped into Hardangerfjord, avoiding powerful Hansa merchants of Bergen.

Most notorious of Eidfjord Scotsmen was the Rustung family, which arrived in Norway from Orkney in 1490. The notable patriarch of the family was Kristofer Trondson, a Norwegian born in 1500, whose three daughters married Scotsmen.[100] The eldest, Anna, was the fiancée, who was jilted and left pregnant by the Earl of Bothwell, who went on to abduct and marry Queen Mary of Scots.[101] Middle daughter Dorthea married James Stewart of the Shetland Stewarts, an illegitimate son of King James V of Scotland. The youngest, Else, married as her third husband Anders Movat, a half-brother to Mary Queen of Scots. She became one of the wealthiest women in Norway.

Kristofer Trondson was a land baron, admiral for Norway-Denmark and sometime privateer, pirating Danish ships. When King Christian III of Denmark sought to annex Norway, Trondson was part of the group of conspirators, which in 1537 murdered the Danish king's envoy to Norway.

---

[100] Kristofer and Karen Trondson had eight children. The eldest son was hanged for highway robbery. The name Rustung is the name by which the family is recorded in Danish history of Norway. Origin of the name is unknown.

[101] The 4th Earl of Bothwell, James Hepburn, fled to Bergen, where he crossed paths with Anna again. He was arrested in Norway and sent to prison in Denmark, where his gravesite was a pilgrimage location for hundreds of women until it was discovered that he was not the person buried in that grave. Spelling is taken from Stagg, 1954.

The episode is part of Norwegian patriotic history and made immortal in a scene in the opera *Olav Engelbrektsson*, the last Archbishop of Trondheim when Reformation came to Norway.[102]

North of Bergen is the one hundred miles long Sognefjord, which branches into Aurlandsfjord, the home of Flåm and the Flåm Railway. At the entrance to this fjord was the Viking center of Gulen, venue of the earliest Thing, a Gulathing, or the Thing at Gulen. It was along this fjord that Sverre mustered his troops in 1184, as he made his assault on Bergen to become king of Norway. Sognefjord is a place to look for restored stave churches, survivors of Protestant Reformation.

Stave Church

---

[102] The opera is set in Trondheim and is performed annually in Archbishop Olav's castle near Trondheim.

Going north along the coast, the town of Kristiansund is attributed some of the oldest settlements of ancient Norway.[103] Fjords are lower in the sea at this point and the town area is comprised of islands, today joined by a highway. The largest of the islands is Grip, once a fishing village and today a favorite of visitors. So popular were fish from the area in Spain and Portugal in the seventeenth century, that traders from Iberia came to the area to establish direct links.

Klippfisk Woman of Kristiansund

Klippfisk of Kristiansund was a robust industry, mostly worked by women, who dried heavily salted cod in the sun, stacked the thin dried fish layers and sold them to Iberian traders into the twentieth century. Klippfisk are best eaten after soaking in a stew. It is a local delicacy. At the pier in Kristiansund is a monument to Klippfisk women.

---

[103] Not to be confused with the large metropolitan city of Kristiansand on the southern coast of Norway.

Northern fjords, or Nordfjord, is the home of people more related to ancient tribes of Finns than to Norwegians of fjords below the Arctic Circle. Olav II came through the area in his effort to Christianize locals, who reverted to old ways once he departed. Twenty-five years later, Olav returned to renew the effort. In this place people herded reindeer rather than cattle.

At the entrance to Geirangerfjord, now a natural World Heritage Site noted for the majesty of its northern fjords, is the ancient fishing village of Ålesund. The town was a regional capital until it was decimated by a fire in 1905. Ålesund was rebuilt with charming castle-like, Art Nouveau gems that make the town a storybook stage set among fjords. Magic in Norway is found in fjords.

Alesund at the Top of Fjords

Floating through the Fjords

Fishermen of the fjords sailed into Medieval Bergen to sell their catch at the large market, still held on weekends at the head of the Vågen, the cruise harbor today. With the introduction of steamships, the journey was made faster. Several families joined in loading their produce, fish and herd animals on small ships. Throughout the eighteenth and nineteenth century, people of the fjords made the six-hour journey to Bergen on steamships. The length of the journey, together with loading times, and sufficient time to shop, took a minimum of three days.

Skyss Transit Today

People of the fjords were expected to provide skyss, that is the requirement to transport through fjords, and to Bergen or Trondheim, state officials and members of the clergy free of charge upon demand. From the seventeenth century, the government organized *tilseiingskyss*, which were relay teams of locals required to row officials to their destination. They were obligated to use their own boats and were not compensated for the service. Farmers and fishermen were expected to leave their fields and nets to provide transport through the fjords.[104] The system persisted through 1860, the time of commercial steamships in the fjords. People were still expected to provide *skyss*, although the government compensated them for their service.

By 1854, there were single ship-owning entrepreneurs with paddle steamers competing for passengers. They crowded major harbors with ships of larger companies until the government regulated traffic. Ship owners were given contracts to carry mail and newspapers.

---

[104] Mike Bent, Steamers of the Fjords, Conway, London, 1989, at 21.

Monument to fishing in Alesund inner harbor

Some steamships installed first class passenger cabins and a tourism industry in the fjords was born. From 1854, until World War I interrupted discretionary travel, tourism bloomed in fjords. Quaint hotels were built in the late nineteenth century. In 1885, the Thomas Cook travel company offered ten-day excursions through fjords, combining steamship, rowboat and horse-cart transit.

Flåm of the Fjords

Nils Kjaer, a writer of the fjords and Norway, wanted Norwegians to sell pictures of Flåmsdalen Valley in 1900, giving it fame beyond Norway.[105] The theater critic/political essayist, who dressed all in black and promoted all cultural facets of Norway, including its language, was distraught over failure of his homeland to be free of foreign control; Danish or Swedish. He was fond

---

[105] Nils Kjaer born 1870, and died 1924.

of writing that birds travel free and wide, while Norwegians are not free. He was known as a Vestlandsfanden, or west Norway devil, for being outspoken. Independence came to Norway in 1905. Flåmsdalen Valley was by that time famous for its beauty.

Flam Valley Fishing Stream

Also promoting the area was Norwegian poet Per Sivle, born in Flåm in 1857.[106] He pleased locals by saying that all his good qualities came from his birthplace. There is a stone monument to Sivle along one of the trails in the valley.

---

[106] Sivle died in 1904.

Monument to Flam Poet Per Sivle

History of Flåm is emblematic of people of the fjords. It was a small village, blessed with a beautiful, large valley, where the Flåm family farmed. The little wooden church has been the family parish church since 1670. To locals, this is the new church, that replaced the stave church, few of which still exist in Norway. Outer walls of the church are tarred against winter weather. Inside, pews and walls are little changed over time. The storage building has a sod roof, like buildings in Faroe Islands, a Danish territory still. The church cemetery reflects tenacity of people, many named Flåm, who stayed with the land under Danish, Swedish and German rule. Politics made little difference in fjords of Vesterland.

Interior Flam Family Church

Sod Roof Shed of Flam

Family Flam Valley Church

Flam Kyrkje 1667

The Flåm Railway

The Flåm Railway is a short line running from Flåm to Myrdal, at the top of the gorge that defines Flåmsdalen Valley. On this line, there are only the two stops. At Myrdal, passengers transfer to the Oslo-Bergen line. When the spur rail line was begun in 1936,[107] it was envisioned as a means for locals to travel up and down the valley, as an alternative to steep hairpin turns on the road.

Such an expense to serve so few people was not politically popular in Oslo. Building the line was not only a feat of manual labor and engineering, it required repeated political victories to bring the line to completion in 1940. Since then, tourism, Norwegians and non-nationals, keep seats on the Flåm Railway filled to the extent of the warm season. It is a success that justifies the effort.

---

[107] Flåm Railway is 20k or 12.5 miles long.

Flam Historic Railway

Flåm Railway boasts of being the steepest standard gauge rail line in northern Europe. The gradient is 5.5%, although from inside the car passengers experience only a gentle ascent, distracted by the view. Rail lines of Sognefjord and Flåm, that connect to the Oslo-Bergen line, are repeatedly acclaimed in travel journals as the most attractive adventure tickets in Europe.[108]

The first railcars on the Flåm line were powered by steam. Upon completion of the hydroelectric generating station, powered by the force of glacial water pouring down the valley, through Kjosfossen waterfall, the rail line became all electric powered. There is no exhaust haze in Flåmsdalen Valley.

---

[108] Norwegian State Railways owns the track and trains, operated by Flåm Development Ltd.; a local group based in Aurland, that is dedicated to continuation of the railway.

Flam Railway through Fjords

The Flåm watercourse from Omnsbreen glacier to Aurlandsfjord, at the village of Fretheim, is thirty miles of dramatic water falls, placid mountain lakes and narrow streams. The waterfall that seems to hang over Flåm church is the Kjosfossen. It feeds streams that run across Flåmsdalen Valley, a spot for salmon and trout fishing.

Waterfall at the Top

Along the Flåm Railway route, travelers are treated to views of Rjoandefossen, the highest waterfall by vertical drop in Norway. Sharp turns are traversed in tunnels, including a full circle in the Vendetunnelen, so the ride is not an amusement park thrill. Scenery is enough excitement. Absent are railway bridges cutting views of fjords. Flåm Railway has none.

Above glacial Lake Reinungavatn sits Vatnahalsen Hotel. Built in 1896, the hotel had a fairytale-like appearance until it was destroyed by fire during World War II. The hotel seen today was built in 1954. It is a favorite ski destination in winter.

New Hotel

From the railcar, travelers can see winding trails of the roadway, replaced for traffic by the railway. From Flåm to Myrdal, the trip is 857 meters going up.[109] Today the road is a favorite of hikers and mountain bikers. Locals call the road the *raller road*, for the railway workers who used the road to lay track for the railway. The line and tunnels, which protect the train from snow, were all the work of manual labor with shovel and ax. There are few cars in Flåm, traveling the single road through the valley, or running guests from the ship landing to Fretheim Hotel.

---

[109] That is 2,800 feet in height of the gorge going up from Flåm to Myrdal.

Flamsbana Travel

For railway history aficionados, there is a Flåm Railway History Museum behind the station. The old locomotive sits for pictures on a side track. There are few attractions in Flåm. Scenery is the draw.

A Port Stop in Flåm and the Fjords Today

Although cruise ships are a constant in Vesterland fjords during summer season, they do not crowd the view. Standing on the deck, there is nothing but natural vista, until a little town comes into view. The occasional local ferry is likely named for a waterfall, like *Viringen*, or *Fjordtroll*.

When people of fjords replaced pony carts with automobiles, there were few roads and none connecting fjords until the mid-1960s. Car ferries were launched to accommodate traffic. In a fjord hamlet connected to Bergen by road, the trip to market and home was reduced to a day. Hotels built for Norwegians became tourist hotels and their business never diminished.

View of Valley from Flam Railway

Flam Farm

In Flåm, there is only one hotel of the nineteenth century tourism era, remodeled for tourists of today. For cruise ship guests, entrance into Aurlandsfjord is as peaceful and scenic as it has been for centuries. At the Flåm pier, the most difficult choice for travelers will be whether to take the train and enjoy majestic scenery from the top, as do almost a million visitors annually, many taking roundtrips from Bergen or Oslo, or walk the single road through Flåmsdalen Valley, along streams fed by the waterfall above. There is no rush to decide. Floating through fjords is a chance to float into a slower pace and enjoy flowers, the calm and the view.

Locals fear that popularity of a port stop in Flåm will cause the natural beauty of Flåmsdalen to suffer, with over one hundred and fifty cruise ships entering Aurlandsfjord each year. There is a new fjord viewing tower at Aurland, and a quaint reconstructed village up the road from Flåm along the fjord at Otternes, both designed to draw visitors from the local road of residents living privately in Flåmsdalen Valley. No doubt Norway, or Flåmsdalen Valley residents, will enact some regulation to keep serenity of Flåm as part of its historic character.

North Cape Visitor Center Today

AT SEA
SEARCH FOR A NORTHEAST PASSAGE

The Age of Discovery that launched ships across the globe was prompted by a search for profits. Monarchs of the fifteenth through eighteenth centuries financed sailing ventures, not motivated by some altruistic ethic, with the understanding that only large treasuries and powerful domains could back missions in the greater interest of mankind. It is a very twentieth century notion that nations such as the United States and Russia flex political muscle in a space race, rather than on the battlefield. New ports, colonized or not, opened new venues for trade for founding monarchs.

Up until the eighteenth century, nations were still forming identity and national boundaries. Individual nobles and church leaders often possessed more wealth than their sovereign. Only a sovereign could license discovery and make claim to new lands. The successful explorer of new lands, financed by private wealth of the monarch, and/or other investors, could profit by receiving a share of profits from exported, or expropriated wealth of claimed territory, and be appointed a noble by their monarch, with all the benefits of inherited wealth for their progeny. Mortality of explorers was high. Benefits made the risk attractive.

Up until 1453, the sea of consequence was the Mediterranean. Venice, Genoa, Spain and Portugal were in turn lords of the sea. England brought tin from ancient times, and later cloth, to Mediterranean ports in exchange for the riches of the Far East, brought overland from Persia, India and China to Constantinople and the Eastern Mediterranean. In 1453, the world changed.

In 1453, the Ottoman Turks, in their conquest of Asia, took Constantinople, the center of the Byzantine Christian church, and made it Istanbul. Christian nations dependent upon trade from the Far East were cut off from their supply route. That Ottoman Turks adopted Islam as their religion, did not render their action some sort of jihad. There was no religious issue involved. The Ottomans were tolerant of other religions in areas of their conquest. Their priority was collection of taxes to support their burgeoning realm. Call it trade, or tax, some desires are universal.

Christopher Columbus was born at the time the Mediterranean became an Ottoman Lake. As an adult he sought to find a new means to the Far East by going west across the Atlantic Ocean. Columbus did more than locate a New World. He began the era of the Atlantic as the waterway of consequence. Following the voyages of Columbus, Vasco de Gama went south and east in 1498, to reach India. Ferdinand Magellan went south and west in 1511, to accomplish that which eluded Columbus. A century later, Henry Hudson perished searching for a Northwest passage from the Atlantic over Canada, after he determined that a Northeast passage from the Atlantic over Russia was impossible.

Columbus launched four centuries in which European sovereigns sought a Northeast or Northwest passage to the riches of the Far East. Profit from trade was the motivator. Captains often had botanists onboard to *botanize* the bays, where they surveyed the landscape for routes to accomplish their mission. Science was coincidental. Often, traders made use of botanists' reports in capitalizing on new mining, fishing, or hunting harvesting opportunities.

England and Northern Europe are closer to the Arctic than the Antarctic. Enterprising merchants calculated that they could cut sea transit time in half, if they could go northeast, or northwest from the Atlantic to the Pacific. The Arctic was a place of myth and mystery. Captains knew as much about what they would encounter as Columbus knew, when he first launched from Spain.

This is the story of the search for the Northeast Passage to the Far East. It is a story of optimism and driving financial interests. It is also a tale of endurance and challenge. Some names are not well known out of home countries of captains of Arctic voyages. Their stories are inspiring. Although the route across the top of Russia, from the North Sea to the Pacific Ocean, is not likely to soon become a regular cruise itinerary, it is a wonderful story for a day at sea.[110]

---

[110] The route Northeast from Alaskan Arctic waters, across Canada, is a Northeast Passage of the Pacific. As ice fields melt, and explorer ship technology improves, Northeast and Northwest passages are cruise itineraries.

England Enters the Age of Discovery

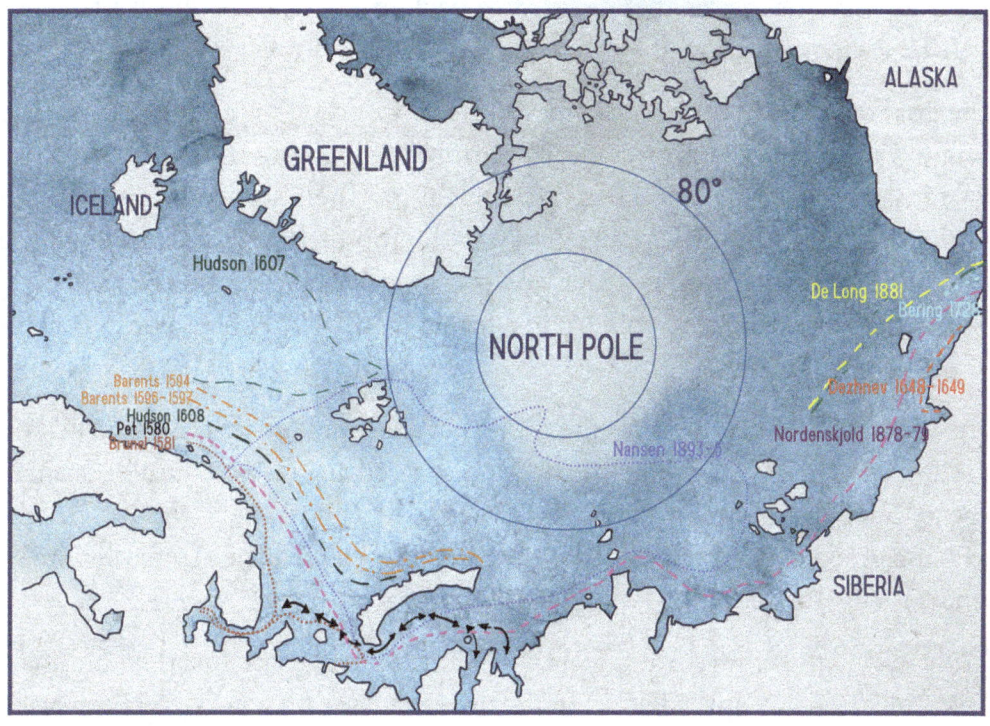

Columbus was a Genoan sailing for Spain. John Cabot was a Venetian sailing for Spain, when prior to 1492, he was consulted by England to test novel ideas of Columbus. Sebastian Cabot advised English King Henry VIII that winds did not allow such travel. Henry Hudson was an Englishman who sailed for Holland, when he went looking for a Northeast and then Northwest passage.

Actually, Hudson was in breach of his Dutch contract when he turned his ship west. He discovered the Hudson River and gave the Dutch New Amsterdam, so he was forgiven for his act of piracy. Portuguese Prince Henry the Navigator went nowhere. He is remembered for his school of navigation that trained captains to sail wherever they might increase Portuguese wealth.

England was late to the Age of Discovery. Easily recognized English sea captains, Sir Francis Drake, Sir Walter Raleigh, John Davis, Thomas Cavendish and James Cook came in a subsequent wave of exploration. Up until the mid-sixteenth century, Spain, Portugal and Holland controlled transport over the seas of spices and silks from the Far East to Western Europe and England.

England did not lack sailing talent. English sailors for centuries transported tin from England in exchange for goods from Mediterranean ports. When a group of London merchants decided to back exploration in the Arctic, they were ready to venture, where others had not gone before.

The goal of almost two hundred investors in London, including two former London mayors, was to form a joint venture company, that would own ships to transact business with Cathay, the Far East. Their ships intended to sail across the North Sea to the Pacific, over the top of Russia, in half the time it took to sail south around the Cape of Good Hope and return with trade goods. It was an ambitious plan, considering in 1551, no one possessed maps of the Arctic Ocean.

The Merchant Adventurers, as the joint venture company was called, relied on the advice of Sebastian Cabot, the most respected and knowledgeable seaman at the time. He compiled existing knowledge of sailing above the North Sea; real, imagined and mythical. Sub-arctic people believed the Arctic Sea was a land of vengeful gods and strange beasts. They were not far wrong.

In the eleventh century, Vikings raided along Murmansk Nos, the land mass north of Finnish Lapland and the northwest corner of Siberia. Vikings were not known to keep sailing logs. Danes sailed above the Arctic Circle in 1496, where they met Russians. Danes were looking for fur traders, not a route to the Pacific. Germans made inroads to northern Russia, actually sleigh tracks, also interested in furs.

Spaniard Estevan Gomez sailed in 1524, from A Coruña, Spain to find a Northeast Passage to the Spice Islands. He was an experienced sailor, who had sailed with Magellan around the world. He sailed into the Arctic Ocean and into oblivion.[111]

In 1553, three ships left London commanded by Sir Hugh Willoughby, sailing for the London consortium of Merchant Adventurers.[112] They had no need of cold weather gear. The assumed ships would pass the wintry coast of Norway

---

[111] John Barrow, A Chronological History of Voyages into the Arctic Regions, London, 1818, at 52.
[112] Read more of the Marvelous Merchant Adventurers in their own story in the Port of Archangel.

and Russia and enter the warm water of the Pacific. The ships were coated with metal to protect against borer worms prevalent in the Indian Ocean.

The three ships planned a rendezvous on the coast of Murmansk Nos, the arm of land that reaches into the Arctic. Their landmark was North Cape. Separated in a storm, Willoughby, and the ship that followed his, sailed east until they went south and west in search of land. They were hopelessly lost. By the time they reached land, native fishermen and Russian fur trappers had all headed inland for the winter. In September, Willoughby settled in for an Arctic winter.

Sixty sailors and nine merchants with Willoughby stayed alive until January, seeking driftwood and local game. All perished before they were discovered and rescued. Their position was on the coast of Murmansk Nos not far from Vardhus, known as Wardhouse to the English, present day Vardø. In high season, the area had intermittent travelers. Cause of death is still a matter of question. Certainly, all of the party suffered from scurvy. When their haven was discovered by Russian fishermen, it was apparent that coal heat asphyxiation may have been a factor.

The third ship, captained by experienced sailor Richard Chancellor, with able navigator Stephen Burrough as second in command, followed land in the storm and found an opening to the White Sea. Chancellor spent the winter with his ship moored in the Dvina River delta. He made friends among the locals and was invited to Moscow, to meet Tsar Ivan IV. Chancellor was drawn into his fate as the man who negotiated the first trade opportunity for England with Russia. He begins a story of that relationship and the city of Archangel, at the place his ship found safety.

Burrough returned to the Arctic in 1556, on the *Searchthrift*, with the intent of going further east than Novaya Zemlya and into the Kara Sea. He befriended Russian fishermen, who gave him basic maps of Novaya Zemlya and guided him to the delta of the Pechora River, just to the east. Burrough sailed to the strait between Novaya Zemlya and Vaigach Island, before ice and a close encounter with a whale convinced him to try the next year. Although he did not enter the Kara Sea, Burrough went further to the northeast than any prior European Arctic sea explorer.

When Burrough returned to London, he found that the Merchant Adventurers had evolved into the Muscovy Company. The focus was changed from locating the Northeast Passage to exploiting trade with Russia through the White Sea. Sebastian Cabot passed away during Burrough's absence at sea. It was a new era in England for trade with Russia through the White Sea.

Explorers in England, such as Martin Frobisher, lobbied for interest in a Northwest Passage. Frobisher eventually made three attempts to sail across the north of Canada. In 1580, English captains Charles Jackman and Arthur Pet convinced the Muscovy Company to back one more convoy to the Northeast. Their voyage took them into the Kara Sea. They succeeded in moving the line of the known Arctic to the east, although Jackman perished with his ship on his return.

At the beginning of the seventeenth century, Henry Hudson brought the English Arctic exploration era to a close. In 1607, he sailed north from Greenland in an attempt to reach the North Pole. He failed to reach the pole, although he sailed 80° north, farther than any recorded sailor. In 1608, Hudson returned to the Arctic and attempted to find a Northeast Passage. His voyage ended on the west coast of Novaya Zemlya, leaving him with the opinion that ships could not go further. He lived to sail west again in 1611; this time to make Northwest Passage history.

A cursory description of sailors in the Arctic, English and those who followed, does not begin to describe terrors of Arctic sailing. Winds are fierce. There are days of no visibility, critical to sailors whose instruments measure distance using the sun and moon. Ice can penetrate a ship at any moment. There were times that captains ordered their ships lashed to ice floes, to keep from being slammed by polar ice. On land, there were polar bears, which could crawl from ice floe to the deck of a ship. Impervious to gun-shot, bears were vanquished in close combat by hand axe.

If these early explorers were able to sail home, warmer seas held bevies of pirates. Once, when Burrough was headed back to London, sailing low with cargo, he was attacked by six pirate vessels. By the end of the encounter, Burrough had sunk one pirate vessel and captured four others. These were days of explorer-merchants, who were also able soldier-sailors.

When technology of ships moved into the steam engine era, captains thought they would overcome environment with steam power. In 1676, Englishmen John Wood and William Flawes sailed as far east as Novaya Zemlya, before they pronounced a Northeast Passage impossible. Other captains followed with greater horse power, but none could transit the ice.

European Explorers in the Arctic Challenge

English sailors seeking a Northeast Passage were not the only activity in the Arctic. Russian fur trappers and fishermen traveled up the Ob River, about halfway across Siberia, and from there east to the Yenesey River and west to the Pechora River. Belgian outdoorsman and goods dealer, Oliver Brunel, accumulated a great deal of expertise living on the Arctic landscape, in the late 1550s to 1570s. He made regular runs between Vardhus to Archangel and the Pechora River Delta, collecting furs from trappers. A legend during his life, Brunel spent time in a Russian prison, accused of being a spy, before he was hired by the Stroganoff family, who ran Siberian operations for Tsar Ivan IV. Records on pursuits of Brunel are sketchy, or he would have his own story.

The last great contribution to knowledge of sailing in the Arctic of the sixteenth century, was that of Dutchman Willem Barents. In 1594, Barents was constrained by his superiors in how he might approach the search for a Northeast Passage. He diverted from his companion ships to sail north over the northern tip of Novaya Zemlya, in search of open water. His travels took him to 77° north, further than his compatriots, who thought they sailed slightly east of him to the Ob River. In fact, they followed the route of Pet, going no further than the Pechora River to the west.

Fellow captains of Barents, who sold their Dutch backers on their much publicized, although overstated, accomplishment, succeeded in obtaining ships for a 1595 return to the Arctic. This time voyagers left later and made progress no further than the Kara Sea. Barents was able to return in 1597, with Cornelius Rijp, funded by Dutch merchants. He returned to Novaya Zemlya until ice forced him to over winter. He was never able to cross the Kara Sea, as he received orders to spend his time looking for lost company ships of the boastful captains.

When missing Dutch ships were found to be safe in port, Barents completed a detailed, accurate survey of Novaya Zemlya. He missed charting Matochkin Shar, the strait into Kara Sea, which Hudson also failed to find. Barents' personal sacrifice of duty over ambition, that kept him at Novaya Zemlya, earned recognition by assigning his name to the adjacent sea. Barents died of scurvy on the return trip.[113]

Before Barents left his winter encampment in 1597, he wrote a detailed letter of his experience and placed it in a powder horn, which he hung near the chimney. In 1876, an English yachtsman stumbled upon the ruins of Behouden Huis, the Barents safe haven. Artifacts retrieved from the site of the Barents expedition are in the collection of The Hague Museum.[114]

Russians Complete the Map

Russia had an interest in Arctic exploration for the purpose of defining a northern boundary. In 1725, shortly prior to his death, Emperor Peter I of Russia launched the Great Northern Expedition, to map the northern reaches of Siberia. Peter sent the Danish sea captain Vitus Bering, a senior captain in the Russian navy, on a mission to determine whether Russia and North America were a joined land mass.[115] For the explorer to traverse the landscape of Russia to begin his voyage was a feat. He spent a winter in Kamchatka, before the sea journey through the strait that bears his name. Bering confirmed that the two great land masses were separate, although his patron died before news reached St. Petersburg, four thousand miles from the east Siberian port of Vladivostok.

---

[113] Men who survived the voyage ate bear liver, which caused a temporary toxic reaction to concentrated vitamin A. Ironically, though the men thought they would die, they recovered and survived scurvy.

[114] Barents's voyages were famous in England. Barents is memorialized by Shakespeare in *Twelfth Night* by Fabian, "You are now sail'd into the north of my lady's opinion where you will hang like an icicle on a Dutchman's beard."

[115] Part of the greatness of Peter I was his inclusive view toward employment on the basis of demonstrated ability.

Bering sailed west into the Arctic Ocean, as far as Chukchi Peninsula, before turning back. He was able to confirm open water to the east, which established that there was no land bridge to Alaska. He was content to map the northern Atlantic Ocean, the area of the sea now named for him.

Bering noted the big island of the Diomede Islands, duly recorded as land of Russia. He missed the little island of Diomede, due to fog. Little Diomede is United States territory. The two islands leave the two nations separated by less than six sea miles; and the international dateline.

Peter's daughter, Empress Anne, sent Bering back to sea in 1733, to confirm there was no land bridge, establish a new city and build light houses for future Arctic voyagers. She also sent explorers over land and sea, to map unchartered areas of Siberia. Dmitri Laptev and Semion Chelyuskin reported they could not sail east of the mouth of the Lena River due to ice. By dog sled they mapped the most northern point of Russia in 1742, now known as Cape Chelyuskin.

In 1741, Bering set sail on an exploration of his own choosing. He had exhausted support of his loyalists in Moscow. He went on to map northern reaches of the Pacific, becoming part of the lore of the seas when he became shipwrecked on the Aleutian Islands and died of scurvy.[116]

The Name of Success: Nordenskjöld

After three hundred and twenty-six years, a dynamic sailor achieved success in navigating a Northeast Passage. He did so in 1878, with a sixty horse-power motor on his sailing vessel, the *Vega*. He almost cleared the entire passage in a single season, but for his desire to linger along the route for scientific data collection. The sailor was Adolf Erik Nordenskjöld, a Finnish-Swedish academic, who became an ironic Russian hero.

Nordenskjöld was the third generation of distinguished Swedish academics, transplanted from Sweden to Finland, where he was born. Adolf Erik

---

[116] Vitus Bering is worthy of his own story in Cruise through History – Itinerary XV North Pacific.

published his first paper in a German chemistry journal in 1855, when he was twenty-two. Destined for a career at the university, the controlling Russian administration in Finland denied Nordenskjöld an academic position in the University at Helsinki due to his outspoken political views. Never reticent about his opinions or abilities, Nordenskjöld staged efforts to return to Finland from Sweden. Russia would not relent.

Swedes were quick to appreciate Nordenskjöld. At age twenty-six he was appointed head of mineralogy at the Swedish National Museum of Natural History, a post he held for forty-three years. While in Sweden, Nordenskjöld met and later married the sister of another of Swedish-noble in Finland, known from his college student days, Anna Mannerheim.[117] Nordenskjöld regretted that his modest academic lodgings were well below Anna's home at the Mannerheim estate. Still, he was driven by scholarly opportunities to explore unknown landscapes, not by monetary ambitions.[118]

Nordenskjöld made seven trips into the Arctic on scientific expeditions, which garnered a medal in 1870, bestowed by the Paris Geographical Society. In 1872, he joined an expedition over the Polar Ice Cap. Despite rigorous planning, the company encountered an early winter and loss of reindeer to pull sledges of supplies. The group trudged seven weeks, going two hundred and fifty miles over ice to reach their basecamp. Meanwhile, captains of steam-powered vessels reported that it was possible to transit the Arctic Ocean from the Barents Sea to the Bering Strait, inspiring Nordenskjöld to try.

Always the scientist, Nordenskjöld collected data from local Siberian fishermen. His trip was financed by Oscar Dickenson, a supporter of the Swedish Academy of Sciences, and by the Swedish king. At the helm of a whaling vessel, adapted for the trip, was Louis Pelander, who had trekked with Nordenskjöld across polar ice. The endeavor was a collegial scientific effort of veteran Arctic explorers. Meticulous planning and a talented crew did not guarantee success.

---

[117] Anna Mannerheim was the aunt of Finland's first president, Carl Gustaf Mannerheim. See Cruise through History©, Itinerary XI – Ports of the Baltic Sea, Port of Helsinki, In Defense of Helsinki, 2018.
[118] See generally: George Kish, North-east Passage, Nico Israel Publications, Amsterdam, 1973.

On board the *Vega* were three Navy harpooners, a Finnish linguist, fluent in Russian, and scientists. Expertise added a range of coverage to Nordenskjöld's interests in the natural landscape. Accompanying the *Vega* was a merchant vessel of Russian financier Alexander Sibiriakoff, literally testing the waters for a commercial trade route.[119]

This was an age of steam-power assisted sailing vessels. The *Vega* was equipped with a sixty horse-power engine for smooth sailing in calm seas. *Vega*, as a civilian ship, could not fly the flag of the Swedish navy, so Nordenskjöld chose the flag of the Royal Swedish Sailing Society, a flag with Swedish colors and the royal insignia. The king of Sweden, also an investor, was pleased.

The *Vega* sailed from Tromsö, Norway to the Kara Sea in ten days, from July 31, 1878. Ahead of the *Vega* was uncharted territory. The ship advanced slowly, close to land, hampered by fog. Frequent soundings were taken to measure ocean depth. Along the way, cans were placed on shore, leaving a record of the *Vega's* journey.[120] On August 19, the *Vega* reached the previously declared impassable Cape Chelyuskin. The moment was celebrated with a five-gun salute.

On August 22, the *Vega* reached Lena River delta, where Sibiriakoff's vessel departed down the river to Yakutsk.[121] Local merchants were awaiting trade goods. All aboard the *Vega* had an opportunity to send letters and telegrams, advising everyone in Sweden of their rapid progress.

Confident of an ability to reach the Bearing Strait by the beginning of October, when ice would impede progress, beginning on September 11, Nordenskjöld lingered ten days on shore to study life of native people in Chukchi villages.[122] As a scientist, he never regretted that decision. As a sailor, he lost the opportunity to transit the Northeast Passage in a single season. On September 28, the *Vega* was marooned in ice, fifty miles from warm, open water of the Bering Strait.

---

[119] Alexander Sibiriakoff (1849 – 1933), was a Siberian explorer who gained his wealth in mining endeavors.
[120] In 1971, one of the cans was located and the Russian ambassador to Sweden presented it to Swedish King Gustov VI Adolf. Kish at p. 160.
[121] Yakutsk was the outpost established by Bering at the insistence of Empress Anne in 1733.
[122] Items collected on the voyage are in the Stockholm Museum of Ethnography.

From September 1878 to July 1879, the *Vega* was an ice prisoner. Unable to send messages assuring family and supporters of their well-being, the biggest worry of crew of the Vega was that people back home would think the worst. Nordenskjöld was not concerned. His Arctic experience was an asset during the ten months on ice. He used the time for scientific study.

Nordenskjöld planned ahead for the possibility of over-wintering in the Arctic. He had daily newspapers from the prior year delivered to the crew each day, with dates altered to the current year. He brought along a thousand books for the lending library. On Christmas, there was a party and gifts for everyone. For those sailors whose families had not sent along gifts, Nordenskjöld personally made advance purchases so that no one was left without a holiday treat.

In the world beyond Siberia, a relief mission was launched by Sibiriakoff and James Gordon Bennett, publisher of the New York Herald. They need not have worried. On July 18, 1879, the *Vega* was free of ice. On July 20, the ship passed through the Bering Strait. The *Vega* was undamaged. No lives were lost on the expedition. On September 5, the Swedish king received a telegram from Nordenskjöld announcing their success. As the *Vega* sailed south from the Bering Strait, a stop was made to rescue the shipwrecked crew of Sibiriakoff's relief vessel.

Along the route to Stockholm, the *Vega's* journey was celebrated in regal style by welcoming ports. Nordenskjöld, always shy of personal honor, allowed his king to bestow a medal in the largest ceremony of the trip. Even Russia acknowledged their banished academic as a hero.

The feat of the Northeast Passage transit in a single season was not accomplished until 1932, by a Russian icebreaker. In 1896, a Norwegian ship, the purpose-built Arctic exploration vessel, the *Fram*, made Arctic exploration history in sailing toward the North Pole and back in safety.[123] Today, there are polar stations, for safety and guidance, along a route suggested by Nordenskjöld.

---

[123] The Fram has its own story in this Itinerary, Port of Oslo.

Twentieth Century Across the Arctic

A passage across the Arctic became a priority for Russia at the beginning of the twentieth century. Russia was at war with Japan in 1905. In the Battle of Tsushima Strait, every Russian ship in the engagement was lost. The Trans-Siberian Railway was proven an insufficient means to send troops and supplies to the western frontier. For the next eighty-six years, until dissolution of the Soviet Union, there was a constant Russian focus upon a viable northern transit of the Arctic.

The last Russian monarch, Nicholas II, capitalized on advances in ice-breaker technology to support two ships sailing from Murmansk in 1909, which reached the Bering Strait in 1910. The feat was repeated in 1914, leaving from the Pechora River Delta into the Kara Sea and arriving in the Pacific in 1914. Although plausible, the route was not sufficiently reliable for regular use.

Stalin made mastery of a Northeast Passage a priority. In 1932, he created the Central Administration of a North Sea Route. That year, the first single season voyage for any vessel, from any country, was the Soviet ice-breaker *Sibirakov*. The following year the super-ship *Chelyuskin*, captained by Vlad Voronin tried to repeat the feat. The ship encountered a light ice year, was surprised by a sudden onset of ice at the Barents Sea, and then trapped in ice, floated to the Bering Strait. The current dragged the ship back north, where the ship sunk. Captain Voronin had planned ahead. All crew and officers evacuated successfully. They were sufficiently provisioned for a stay on the ice, until all were rescued by plane.

During the Soviet Era, the Arctic was closed to traffic of other countries. An exception was the German ship *Komet*, which in 1940 made the journey across the top of Russia short of twenty-two days. Of that, seven days were spent detained by Soviet ships, checking for suspicious activities. Soviets were able to master the route in ten days from Murmansk to the Bering Strait, sometimes two, or three times in a single season, over several years. Weather along the passage was always so difficult to gauge, that the voyage never became routine.

In 1965, the United States Coast Guard icebreaker, the *Northwind*, made an audacious voyage across the Arctic passage. At the time, the United States and Russia were adversaries in the Viet Nam War. Soviet Russia closed access to the route, while it perfected its own ability to cross icy seas in a single season. The USCG mission was reported as a scientific pursuit, while its route left no doubt the voyage was an attempt to traverse Siberia at sea. When the *Northwind* reached Cape Chelyuskin, it was stopped and turned back by Soviet military ships.[124]

Future of Arctic Travel Along the Northeast Passage

In 2010, China sent four ships across the northern route. Two years later, the number of Chinese merchant vessels, avoiding a route through the turbulent Suez Canal area, increased to forty-six ships traversing the Northeast Passage. China had plans to employ the route on a regular basis for about fifteen percent of cargo by 2020.[125]

Small luxury cruise ships, of an expedition class, began competing with Spartan ice-breakers for guest travel in 2016. Staterooms are pricy as the season is limited. Views are amazing and the bragging rights unique among world travelers. Shore excursions are limited.

Travel across the Northeast Passage, from Norway to Japan and China, remained an obsession of adventurous travelers for five hundred years. Successful transit of the route is no longer unique. Among earthly pursuits, such a voyage is still rare and exciting.

---

[124] See: Helen Orlob, The Northeast Passage, Thomas Nelson, Inc., Nashville, 1977; and Richard Petrow, Across the Top of Russia, David McKay Company, Inc., New York, 1967. Petrow, a journalist, traveled on the *Northwind*.
[125] South China Morning Post, August 11, 2013.

Vikings Playing Chess

Vikings, so often symbols of destruction, are contenders for the honor of bringing the highly civilized game of chess to its modern form. Origins of chess are credited to India twenty-five centuries ago. In the first millennium of the Christian era, Northern Europeans played a simple game of strategy, utilizing few, non-descript pieces, until Vikings added dimension to the game.

Chess has been called the mirror of life.[126] Early forms of the board game *tafl*, the word for table, required using strategy as if in war, where game pieces representing opposing warriors surround their king. In a bloodless battle of king versus king, where warriors were sacrificed in game pieces, to protect the king, disputes could be settled armed with a crock of ale instead of a sword.

In tenth century Norway, Vikings added a queen to the game board. Knights, Bishops and Castles came later, long after Vikings domesticated as farmers. Chess as the game is played today, was established by the fifteenth century. Real knights of the fifteenth century perfected skills as Masters of the Seven Arts, which included chess in addition to brewing beer, metal working, justice and cannon law, scripture, medicine and war. Playing chess was included as a critical skill for strategic thinking, as a form of social literacy. Chess sets were ubiquitous in homes.

---

[126] Indrek Hargla, Apothecary Melchior and the Mystery of St. Olaf's Church, Peter Owens Publisher, London, English translation Adam Cullen 2015. In the murder mystery set in Tallinn in 1409, among Teutonic Knights, Guild's Men and monks, a murder is rehearsed on a chessboard, then solved by the sleuth who masters an understanding of chess.

Vikings Playing Chess in Waterford, Republic Ireland

The history of chess, and its integration into social structure of early Medieval life, is seen in chess pieces viewed as works of historical art. The most famous chess pieces in history are Lewis Chessmen, so-called for their discovery on the isle of Lewis in the Scottish Hebrides, early in the nineteenth century. Not only do these pieces speak to the present, with a bit of humor preserved from the twelfth century, their creation, loss, discovery and final placement in either the British Museum or Scottish National Museum in Edinburgh is an engaging mystery.

This is a little story of the history of chess, the fascination of Vikings with the intellectual side of their recreation, and the mystery of the Lewis Chessmen. Although the famous Chessmen reside in museums of the British Isles, their story begins in the land of Vikings. This is a story that runs from Iceland and Greenland to Norway and beyond. Solving the mystery is a fun romp through lives of people of the North Sea centuries ago.

Simple History of a Complex Game

Vikings as Chessmen

Modern chess, as the game is known today, developed from the twelfth century, becoming standardized by the fifteenth century. Like knights, Medieval noblemen were considered civilized if they mastered the Seven Arts of: riding, swimming, archery, boxing, falconry, poetry and chess.[127] Knights Templar

---

[127] Michael Schulte, Board Games of the Vikings – From *hnefatafl* to chess, Maal OG Minne2, 2017, University of Agder, Kristiansand, Norway. The Vikings played *tafl*, here referred to as *hnefatafl* in Nordic translation of the Orkney Sagas. Mastery of the Seven Arts varied over time and are not to be confused with the emerging seven free arts, of a liberal arts education: Rhetoric, Latin grammar, dialect, music, astronomy, arithmetic, geometry.

were restricted from playing chess, as well as falconry and hunting. This is odd, since bishops enjoyed chess, priests made chess references in sermons, and chess is the ultimate game of strategy. Perhaps the Grand Master of the knights did not want his legions to out-think him and check-mate the master.

The beginning of the game of chess has been traced to the great Gupta Empire of northern India in the sixth century CE. The Gupta Empire stretched westward from the Ganges to Delhi. Golden Age of the Gupta Empire was the third to the sixth century, when great Hindu temples were built, and Sanskrit literature flourished. This was when *Kama Sutra*, a lover's manual was written.

Chess in India was a game of military strategy. Game pieces represented military divisions of infantry, elephantry, charioteers and cavalry. Centuries later, in Europe, rooks were the infantry and knights replaced the cavalry. Chariots and elephants fell from fashion in time and in Europe.

Chess spread from India to Persia, which put the game at the center of empires of world trade. Muslim traders of the tenth century, whose trading domain stretched from the Mediterranean to the Indian Ocean, and whose tastes spanned every form of art, brought chess to the ports in their world. Uncouth sailors gambled with dice. Intellectual connoisseurs played chess. Iconoclast Muslims replaced human figures with an elephant, camel and horse game pieces.

Vikings are credited with bringing chess to old Russia in the tenth century. By the sixteenth century, even tsars played the game at the royal court. Ivan IV, otherwise known as The Terrible, died in 1584, while playing chess.

Ivan may have played chess with his English visitors, who opened trade with Russia in 1553. Back in England, Queen Margaret, wife of Henry VI, had a chess set made of crystal in 1450. Kings of England had been playing chess since sons of William the Conquer displaced Viking kings. There is no mention of William I playing chess. He was too busy in live conquest on the fields of England, while he maintained his domain in France. His game would require two boards at once.

In the Christian world, the development of chess pieces took human shape. In the eleventh to twelfth century, the king and his warriors, which were the first rooks, were joined by a queen, whose moves to protect the king were more varied. Bishops stood next to the king and queen, an overt political statement of the power of the church. Bishops were given a diagonal move. Next came deft knights, who approached at an angle. Rooks, the infantry soldiers, completed the lineup. Pawns were left as elliptical topped pieces, without faces, although some were carved with designs. By the fifteenth century, the rook became a castle. Infantrymen became pawns.

Vikings Playing Chess

Chess Family

Celtic influence on Vikings is evident in Viking lifestyle. Vikings admired Celtic jewelry with a passion. Twisted strands of silver metal known as the Celtic torc are found in mass quantity in Viking hordes of loot. Vikings wore torc bracelets, several at a time, as a display of accomplishment and wealth gathered from forays through towns and monasteries. Viking kings gave bracelets to their warriors as tokens of loyalty and valor in battle. Jewelry was not the only contribution the ancient Celtic culture imparted to Vikings.

Celts played a board game known as *hnefatafl*, a variant of *tafl* board games popular in Germany in the first Christian millennium. Vikings appreciated Germans for their skill in metallurgy, notably sword blades. While visiting among Germans, sword shopping, or raiding towns in Ireland, where eventually Celts and Vikings settled the hamlet now known as Dublin, Vikings had opportunities to adopt *hnefatafl* as a relaxing pastime.

In the ninth to eleventh centuries, while Celts settled throughout Ireland and Wales, and as Germans moved from roving herders to farmers, Vikings continued to travel the ocean and across Europe. Vikings traveled with their board games. Always appreciative of craftsmanship, notably seen in Viking rune carvings in stone, Vikings assimilated smooth game pieces of *hnefatafl* into figures finely carved in bone, stone, or wood. Modern chess pieces began to take shape.

Rules of Viking chess are known thanks to the great Swedish botanist, Carl Linnaeus. Linnaeus sat down early in the eighteenth century to make an exhaustive encyclopedia of all plant and animal families, now known as Linnaeus Taxonomy of Species. When Linnaeus traveled to northern Finland in 1732, in an effort to categorize life in Lapland, he observed people playing a game. Unable to understand their language, he relied on his detailed observations to record rules of the game. Long after his death, the travel diary of Linnaeus was published in 1811.[128] His was a bequest of more than taxonomy of species. Linnaeus was a bit of a Viking ethnographer of gamesmanship.

It is not difficult to see how *tafl* games evolved into chess. *Tafl* games are played on a square board, marked in a grid, with opposing black and white game pieces. The objective is to protect a king, while seizing the opponent king. In early forms of the game there was only one king, captured by the winning army. In the two-king version, the king that moves to the end of the board, and escapes, is the winner. An opposing game piece caught between two of the opposition is taken from the board. Pieces could move vertically, or horizontally. Bishops, with the ability to move diagonally, were not part of *tafl*. *Tafl* and *hnefatafl* were games of kings and warriors.

---

[128] Carl Linnaeus, Lachesis Lapponica: A Tour in Lapland, 1811, translated from Swedish by James Edward Smith BiblioLife, LLC for BiblioBazaar, Swagen Press, 2015.

Among academics, some argue that Vikings played forms of *tafl*. Others assert that Vikings, as great travelers and innovators, quickly adapted to chess. The prolific chronicler of Viking events in the Viking Sagas, written centuries after the fact, was Snorri Sturluson. When Snorri wrote of Vikings playing chess in 1220, he did not distinguish the game as *tafl*. Either Snorri wrote what he knew in his time, then assumed the same game was played earlier, or Vikings had moved their game forward to chess. Vikings assimilated new ideas quickly in boat building, why not in chess.

Canute the Great, tenth century King of Norway, Denmark and part of England, often enjoyed a game of chess to relax between conquests. He took the game seriously. Known to be a poor loser, and a bit self-serving when applying the rules, Canute adopted new rules as it pleased him.

To Canute, chess was another form of battle of wits. As king, never wishing to lose a battle, he was competitor and rules judge. Snorri recorded a great chess game, which took place at Canute's fortress home in Denmark, in 1027, in which Canute played chess with one of his captains, Earl Ulf. Ulf responded to a move by Canute that held Canute in check. When Canute moved his piece back, to try a different tact, Ulf upset the board in disgust and muttered something about cheating, as he left the area. The next day, Ulf was dead. His was a fatal move.

Historical records are dotted with references of Viking kings and chess. Canute is credited with donating a chess set to the Abby at Winchester, where his remains found their final resting place.

Given destruction of the church in intervening history, to the point that human remains dislodged from crypts were swept up, comingled and repositioned, any chess piece now found in the collection may be datable, with a non-verifiable donor. One fact is certain, successors to Canute enjoyed chess. Gunnar, Viking king of Greenland, played chess, as did the final Viking king of England, Harald.

Though the Viking era ended with King Harald at the Battle of Hastings in 1066, and though his army included the best Viking warriors, not all Vikings ceased to exist on that fateful day. Vikings continued to raid and trade into the thirteenth century, with less raiding and more trading. Vikings traveled the globe to Constantinople, where they left graffiti in the Hagia Sofia, and to Baltic coasts of Russia, as they traveled with amber traders and hired out as mercenaries.

A colony of Vikings that came to Greenland with Eric the Red, who was banished from Iceland for his violent ways in 985, continued to thrive on walrus hunting until the 1400s. The connection of Greenland and Iceland to walrus ivory, popular for carving, is one of the pieces that fits into the Lewis Chessman story. The reputed last of the classic Viking warriors is Svein Asleifarson, whose exploits in Orkney, until his death in 1171, are included in the *Orkney Saga*.[129] The last chapter in Viking Sagas place Asleifarson in the Outer Hebrides, in the area of Lewis.

Viking progeny constitute eighty percent of people of Lewis today. Strong Viking presence in Lewis is attributed to trade in walrus ivory from Greenland to Iceland, then Norway, where Lewis was a port along the route. This fact of history put tiny, quiet Lewis on the front page of newspapers in the 1830s, when Lewis Chessmen were a sensation. The spot on the beach of Lewis, where the chessmen were found, became a pilgrimage point for chess scholars ever after.

Most Famous Chess Pieces

The British Museum in London and Scottish National Museum in Edinburgh represent their most popular exhibit to be Lewis Chessmen. In the British Isles, Lewis Chessmen have fame comparable to that of the Parthenon Marbles in Greece. The Parthenon marbles have their own room in the British Museum. The Lewis Chessmen have only a small exhibition stand in the English gallery.

These adorable, two to three-inch-high characters, draw crowds because they are endearing. Refrigerator magnets of Berserkers,[130] the Viking shield bearers of the Rook chess pieces, and replica Lewis Chessman sets are among most purchased museum souvenirs. To chess historians, Lewis Chessmen are notable as the earliest known modern European chess pieces, dated to 1150.

---

[129] Asleifarson was the bad boy cohort of Rögnvald, saint of the Orkneys.
[130] Nordic spelling is Berserkr. The pieces are sometimes identified as Warder or Rook.

Lewis Chessmen in Edinburgh

Lewis Chessmen are carved from walrus ivory, which tells part of their story. Ivory is difficult to date. Dating Chessmen to the mid to late twelfth century has been established by the characters portrayed, their dress and held objects. Similar pieces to Lewis Chessmen have been unearthed in Bergen and Trondheim cathedrals and in an abbey in Sweden. Experts in the field of Medieval carving agree, the pieces were carved by the same person. The mystery begins here.

In 1831, a stunning discovery was made on the Isle of Lewis in the Outer Hebrides, of a hoard of ninety-three pieces, found in a sack, which included chess pieces, other game pieces and a belt buckle. The find was made near remains of a long-abandoned nunnery, near the Bay of Uig. People of the area had long held legends of shipwrecks and buried treasure. Still, the find was amazing.

Berserker

One of the local legends held that a shipwreck occurred at Uig in the early 1600s. A man killed the first survivor to the beach and buried his bag of precious possessions. Locals aided the remaining survivors. When the killer was on the gallows for murder, he confessed that his motive was theft. He went to his death without disclosing, where on the beach he buried his loot.

The finder of the bag buried for two centuries offered the items to the Society of Antiquities in Edinburgh, which did not have funds with which to purchase the entire lot. Sir Walter Scott, celebrated Scottish historian, author and dedicated preservation enthusiast for all things Scottish, was in agony over his inability to buy the items, found in Scotland, for the Scottish National Museum. Scott was caught at the moment in bankruptcy, in a gallant move to bail out debts of his publisher. Instead, a private Scottish antiquarian dealer purchased eleven chess pieces and the remainder was purchased for eighty-four pounds, by the British Museum, for display in London.

In 1888, the Society of Antiquaries of Scotland was able to purchase the privately held eleven pieces in an estate sale of the antiquities dealer. By that time the price increased to one hundred pounds, which was paid. These pieces comprise the exhibit in the Scottish National Museum.

Of the hoard brought to the British Museum, the chessmen were determined to be centuries old and of design similar to pieces in possession of Nidaros Cathedral of Trondheim, Norway. A preliminary determination was made that the pieces were manufactured in Trondheim. The twelfth century bishop of Nidaros Cathedral was wealthy, had a large palace where items were manufactured and he was known to appreciate delicately carved ivory. Croziers and other ivory pieces are in the Nidaros collection of the same craftsperson and of the same era as the Lewis Chessmen. The pieces were all initially attributed by experts to manufacture in Trondheim.

Since the discovery in 1831, scholars of early Medieval art have debated location of manufacture and identity of the craftsman of the Lewis Chessmen. In addition to Trondheim, other nominees were Bergen, Lewis and somewhere in Iceland. Clues were sought as to the artist, which would lead to the place of manufacture and complete the story.

Bishop

Queen

Rook

King

Lewis Treasure Knight

According to Nancy Marie Brown, mystery has persisted due to the reluctance of scholars to accept that the craftsman was a craftswoman.[131] In her exhaustive research, begun with the open mind of a scholar, Brown put a name on the

---

[131] See Nancy Marie Brown, Ivory Vikings, St. Martin's Griffin, New York, 2015. The bibliography is extensive.

artist: Margret the Adroit. Margret was a twelfth century housekeeper and carver for the powerful Bishop Pall Jonsson of Iceland. Pall was bishop of Skalholt in Iceland from 1195 to 1211. Margret worked for him as a carver the entire time.

A Norse Saga of Pall's tenure in Skalholt was written shortly after his death in 1211.[132] In the saga, Margret is given credit for her work. In 1954, when excavating around the old cathedral, to build a new church, a stone coffin and crozier were unearthed, identified as those of Bishop Pall. In 2012, carbon dating of remains inside revealed an age to 1220, confirming his identity. The crozier, carved by Margret for Pall, is now a prized item on display in the Iceland Museum in Reykjavik.

Bishop Pall was educated in England and was ordained as a priest by the most powerful bishop of the Scandinavian world in that time, Bishop Absalon of Denmark, the founder of Copenhagen. Pall was married, had four children and refused to annul his marriage. He was sent to Iceland.

Pall enjoyed being extravagant. He loved to hold banquets and sing. He had a lovely voice. In Skalholt, he made the best of life in a remote location by adding a bell tower and glass windows to his modest wooden cathedral. He filled his world with beautiful objects, crafted by Margret.

The Archbishop of Trondheim possessed a prized crozier, much like that of Bishop Pall. Pall reported to the Archbishop of Trondheim, the most powerful bishop of Norway. It is logical that Pall sent gifts to Trondheim. Over the time of his tenure as bishop, with Margret working away with her carving tools, gifts were sent to clerics in Denmark, Norway, Scotland and Greenland. She received her ample supply of walrus ivory from Greenland. Walrus were depleted in Iceland.

Not only was Margret skillful, she had a sense of humor. The rooks of her chess pieces have long front teeth, biting the top of their shields. In fact, Viking berserkers, the front-line warriors, were known to line up before battle and bite their shields in acts of nervous tension. A deft opposition maneuver was

---

[132] The Norse Saga is *Bishop Palls Saga*. He is typically referred to as Bishop Pall, rather than Bishop Jonsson.

for a running warrior to quickly approach a berserker and push up the shield into his upper palate, instantly killing him.

Margret's chess sets were the first known to put bishops and queens on the board and use Viking berserkers for rooks. She did such an accurate job of clothing her chess pieces in fashionable clothing of the day, that dating the pieces was made possible seven hundred years later. Margret put bishops on the board next to the royal couple; the ultimate power position. She knew chess pieces were headed to the Archbishop of Trondheim, who once told his minions: obey god, St. Peter and me.[133] The bishop holds a crozier and wears a hat, in approved Vatican style of the day.

Seated Bishop

---

[133] Brown, at p. 63.

Margret made her king stout and unhappy. Bishops had more power than a king. Her king holds a sword, reminiscent of Viking swords described in Viking Sagas. By putting a queen on the board, Margret trumpeted the power of a queen. Her model was Gunnhild, the legendary mother of kings, wise and strong, wife of King Erick of Norway in the tenth century.

Queen detail

Margret's queen holds her face in her hand, as though she is pondering a decision. The queen knows something the king does not. On the chess board, a queen moves in many directions. The king is a figurehead. Margret is no longer a mystery. She has given posterity hours of diversion.

Looking for Chess Where Vikings Sailed

Bishop in Play

Near to the home of Margret and her modern chess pieces, Reykjavik was the ideal location for the great chess match of 1972, between Bobby Fischer and Boris Spassky. The Roman Catholic bishopric lost power when Iceland became Lutheran. The diocese was dissolved in 1801. The 1950s archaeological excavation gave Icelanders national pride in chess history, regardless of religion.

Iceland, long known for its Vikings, is also known as the home of modern chess. The chess tradition is also strong in Denmark and Norway, places of strong Viking history.

Bishop Pall's tomb now sits in the basement of the 1954 Skalholt Church. His crozier is in the National Museum of Iceland in Reykjavik. In Trondheim palace are more pieces of Margret's work on display. The Trondheim Cathedral, in all its majesty, is testament to the power of twelfth century bishops. Margret would no doubt be pleased to see her work still being appreciated, even if there is not universal consensus on her identity as the artist. She was a woman with a sense of humor.

Alyosha Overlooking the Bay

RUSSIA

Murmansk: The First 100 Years

Murmansk has the distinction of being the last Russian city begun in the Romanov era. It was founded in 1915, as a port to receive supplies critical to Russian defense of its territory in World War I. The fishing village grew very little between wars, until Murmansk rose again to be the critical recipient of war-time supplies in the resurgence of the Russian Front in World War II.

The story of Murmansk is a story of strategic response to military needs. It is the largest city within the Arctic Circle, yet it is well positioned to receive warm North Sea currents, rendering the port ice-free throughout the winter. During World War II, Murmansk was Stalin's lifeline.

There are three phases to the story of Murmansk. The first phase is Murmansk as an Allied military base up until the Armistice of November 11, 1918. There was also a contingent of White Russians in Murmansk during the Russian Civil War, which coincided with World War I. The revolutionary Red Army capitalized on war-weary Russia to overthrow the monarchy, dangling the country into an anarchical abyss. Post Armistice Allied occupation of Russia is the story of 1918: Part II, which takes place in Archangel. Murmansk holds the story of 1918: Part I.

The second phase in the history of Murmansk, is as the destination point for merchant marine convoys, escorted to port by American and Russian military vessels and planes. There are numerous stories of daring and heroism in the saga of the Murmansk Convoys, only a few of which can be recalled in a short story. The convoys launched from New York harbor on Winston Churchill's promise to Stalin of supplies and war machinery with which to keep the Nazis from obtaining control of Murmansk. Murmansk was critical to Hitler's plan to secure a northern ice-free port and access to Russian raw material resources. For United States President Franklin Roosevelt, the convoys were a means to assist the Allies without joining the war.

Murmansk was heavily bombed during World War II. Prior to the war, there was little of consequence in the city beyond direct service at the docks and the railroad, which linked the harbor to Moscow and the Transiberian Railway. Part three of this story is development of Murmansk after World War II. After the war, Murmansk was rebuilt as a modern harbor, and a provincial political, commercial and educational hub in the Murmansk Oblast, the northern land mass of Russia. Today Murmansk is finding additional purpose as a cruise port and a center for Siberian and Arctic exploration. The short history of Murmansk has been full of excitement.

1918: Part I

Murmansk Customs House (blue) & Lenin Icebreaker,
Train Station (green) overlooking the Bay

Russia was drawn into the European turf battle that became World War I in 1914, the Great War. To Russian people, conscription by Tsar Nicholas II for yet another military action was so unpopular, that migration of Russians to the west was more popular than fighting at home. In the midst of fighting the war in France and defending the borders of Russia, the country devolved into civil war. Tsar Nicholas abdicated and took his family to Tsarskoe Selo, the palace built by a daughter of Peter the Great to honor her mother, Catherine I of Russia.

In October 1917, actually November on the new Russian calendar,[134] the Bolshevik Red Army, led by Vladimir Lenin, overthrew the provisional government, still in its infancy and ineffectual in creating a republican Russian government. On March 3, 1918, Soviet Russia entered into a treaty with the Axis powers of Germany, Austria-Hungary, Bulgaria and remnants of the Ottoman Empire, known as the Brest-Litovsk Treaty, which ended Russia's pArcticipation in World War I.

Lenin was concerned that he could not create a government in a civil war and fight an international war. By securing the western border of Russia, despite retreating from the Baltic countries of Lithuania, Latvia and Estonia, Lenin conserved his resources. His reliance on the good faith of Germany was unrewarded. Very soon he found Germans entering his country.

It served the purpose of Lenin in the first months of 1918, to allow Czech fighters to retain their weapons and to have the Allies enter from Murmansk, to keep the Germans from taking the northern, warm-water port. The Allies had a mutual desire to keep Germans from securing a commanding position, from which to control transport of Russian mineral resources. The Allies also desired to reestablish the Eastern Front of the war, to draw German forces from France.

The Allies did not consider entry of the North Russia Expeditionary Force into Murmansk as an accommodation to the Soviets, whom the Allies did not recognize. In the civil war, the Allies backed the White Russian provisional government and the few remaining Imperial Russian leaders, who dreamed of return of the Romanov monarchy. Although keeping the Germans at bay was the publicly stated mission, the Allies had a secondary purpose of arousing a groundswell of support from anti-Bolsheviks within Russia. The Allies were ready to feed, train and arm an anti-Bolshevik army, to encourage Russians, by Allied presence, to come forward to arms.

---

[134] The west referred to the revolution as Red October. Soviets and Russians today refer to Four Days in November.

By the fall of 1918, two facts became clear to the Allies. First, Axis forces were faltering. By November 11, 1918, an Armistice was signed, ending combat in the field and sending representatives to Paris peace talks. Second, there was no appreciable showing of enthusiasm from anti-Bolsheviks in villages of Russia, willing to continue a fight and join the White army.

The British sent then Colonel Edmund Ironside to Murmansk, to lead forces from Murmansk to Archangel, the stronghold of the White army. Murmansk remained in the control of the Allies until October 1919, when Allied forces withdrew from Russia. The story of World War I in northern Russia continues in Archangel. When the Allies embarked in Murmansk to return home, White Russian and Royalist stalwarts went with them, as well as a few Russian brides of servicemen and a number of Russian orphans.[135]

Murmansk Convoys and Defense of the Russian Front in World War II

New and Traditional Church of Our Savior Murmansk

---

[135] For an eyewitness account of 1918: Part I, see, Major-General Sir Charles C. Maynard, The Murmansk Venture, Arno Press, 1928; Albion Press edition 2016.

It is often said that World War I set the stage for World War II. It is hard to believe that nationalistic Germans in the first decades of the twentieth century could imagine the terror wrought by Nazi forces. There are parallels seen in war strategy in northern Russia.

Once again Germany moved into western Russian territory. Finland and Baltic states of Lithuania, Latvia and Estonia were caught in the middle of superpowers. France, occupied by Germany, was experiencing the brunt of devastation in war. Stalin signed a nonaggression pact with Hitler. The so-called deal with the devil did not net Russia absolution from war.

Lenin inherited a financially bereft country. Decades later, Russia's economy was not improved by its experiment with Marxism. Stalin, like Lenin before him, was open to allowing the Allies to fight the Germans on behalf of Russia and to supply the war materials. Winston Churchill assured Stalin he could count on the Allies to supply the means to defeat Hitler.

As in World War I, the Allies wanted to keep Hitler from reaching Murmansk and having access to a northern warm-water port. Hitler wanted Murmansk as a military port and submarine base, from which to control the North Sea and reaches of the Arctic. By reestablishing an Eastern Front for the Germans, the Allied strategy was to take pressure from France, before a concerted push of the Allies to liberate France. United States gave support to the Allies, through supplies delivered by civilian merchant ships. Not until December 11, 1941, was the United States officially in the war.

There is a bit of Franklin Roosevelt lore that has him tearing a page from a National Geographic magazine and drawing a line in pencil north to south across the Atlantic. This was the demarcation line for the U.S. Navy to escort civilian convoys of war materials to Russia, before Russian and British navy vessels assumed protection duty. Envoy Harry Hopkins was the one to take the map to Churchill, upon which Churchill gave assurances to Stalin.[136] On the basis of that map, an estimated sixteen tons of machinery and raw materials was sent to Russia, on what became known as the Murmansk Convoys.

---

[136] Robert Carse, A Cold Corner of Hell, Doubleday and Co, Inc., Garden City, 1969, at 2. Carse writes that the word "skivvies" comes from sailors going to Yokohama. Yokohama #10 was soldier code for a brothel in the city that issued rice-paper prophylactics, known as skivvy papers. At page 28.

At the docks in New York City, sailors were encouraged to sign on to merchant cargo ships paying $1,000 for the run. This was about ten times the monthly pay of the average seaman. A sober sailor should have been suspicious. Fortunately for Stalin, sailors were rarely sober until they boarded ship. Sometime in the middle of the Atlantic, when US Navy craft peeled away, leaving the civilian vessels to continue northeast into the North Sea, sailors realized their peril. The veteran sailor's code for the Murmansk Run was: a "long, long run to a cold, cold place."

Murmansk is 4427 nautical miles from New York. If ships could not reach the harbor in Murmansk through an ocean of mines and German submarines, they continued four hundred miles further into the White Sea, also thick with German U-boats. Often ships over-ran the entrance to the White Sea, to find safety in coves of Arctic islands of Novaya Zemlya, just as Arctic explorers had done three hundred years before.

If merchant vessels were fortunate not to engage with Germans, they had the weather as an enemy. The course from New York ran to Iceland and then east to the Murmansk peninsula. At times, storms off the coast of Iceland were an insurmountable demon. One convoy of one hundred ships left New York and only fifteen arrived in Murmansk, due to a storm. In April 1941, of twenty-four ships that left from Iceland, ice floes were the cause of loss of all but seven ships.[137]

As the merchant marine became more sophisticated about travel through the seas during war, German forces became technologically advanced in the use of radar from ship to plane and communications from planes to U-boats. The US Navy assigned two radio signalmen to ships with each crew of merchant marine. Crews rarely slept when approaching the North Sea.

German Heinkel aircraft, manufactured in Finland, refueled in Norway on short flights in search of Allied convoys. Merchant vessels carried guns, but often had insufficient ammunition in the onslaught of German fighter planes. Survivors from sunken vessels, if not strafed by gunfire, could only hope to be picked up by straggler vessels, those most vulnerable to attack, riding low and slow in the water.

---

[137] Weather planning leaves a short cruise season in the Arctic from late June to August.

The merchant marine entering the Murmansk harbor passed by hulks of disabled, although not entirely submerged vessels. The city was heavily bombed. There were few civilians in the streets, mostly elderly and young boys, who were selling contraband garnered from the supply depot.

The city center of Murmansk ran from Stalin Avenue to the Statue of Lenin, as it does today.[138] The Arctica Hotel had potted palms and stuffed brown bears in the lobby. To one side of the hotel dance floor there was a gilded shell for the orchestra. Down the street was the House of Rest and Culture, a movie theatre. Edging the town center were endless blocks of white concrete apartment buildings. At its height, the population reached one hundred and thirty thousand residents. By 1942, the population was greatly reduced to military personnel. The German Luftwaffe had bases fifty miles from the city. The existence of Murmansk was based on its use as a harbor to receive supplies and load trains to Moscow.

Former Arctica Hotel

---

[138] The city center boulevard has not changed. The name of the street changed in 1961 from Stalinallee to Karl Marx Allee.

Murmansk Russia

Convoy PQ 16 left Reykjavik, Iceland on May 19, 1942, with thirty-five merchant vessels: twenty-five American, eight British, one Dutch and one of Panamanian registry. There were twenty-five military escort vessels of navies of Britain, Poland, Russia and the United States. Sailors were issued rubber suits with internal life vests. The convoy traveled at eight knots, the same speed a German U-boat could travel when submerged.

When Heinkel bombers dropped torpedoes on PQ 16, the convoy launched grenades to explode torpedoes before they could reach a vessel. Watching for a trail of a torpedo, and lobbing a grenade calculated to land ahead of the projectile course, was an art. Despite five days of sailing under fire, twenty-five merchant marine vessels delivered their cargo in Murmansk. Hitler was livid, when he learned of the Allied success. He vowed to annihilate the next convoy.

Convoy PQ 17 left Hvalfjord, Iceland in May 1942, in a fog. Of the thirty-five merchant vessels only eleven arrived safely in Murmansk. In the fog, convoy vessels were struck by mines in waters for which the convoy had no new maps of mine fields. The escort military vessels were ordered to scatter, based on intelligence of incoming enemy ships and planes. The pride of the German navy and air force was thrown at the defenseless convoy, in an effort to allow Hitler to pronounce a victory in the North Sea. The German battle ship *Von Tirpitz*, a Bismarck class battleship, the cruisers *Admiral Scheer* and *Admiral Hipper*, and seven destroyers were joined by U-boats, Heinkels and Stukas in pursuit of the convoy.

War Memorial

Convoy PQ 17, sans escort vessels, was located by German planes in the Barents Sea. One by one vessels were targeted and sunk. Survivors on rafts were sunk. The ships surviving through the barrage sailed to Novaya Zemlya Islands, where Barents himself sought shelter. There resourceful sailors lived by eating local birds. They opened shipping crates of tanks and placed the tanks, armed to shoot, on the decks. The odd convoy, with thirteen hundred surviving sailors, entered Archangel. Many survivors had only what they were wearing when rescued. The military commander found himself trying to clothe, feed and house an immediate infusion of sailors.

Of the 157,000 tons of cargo held by PQ17, only 57,000 tons arrived in Russia. Convoy sailors returning to New York were deposited on Staten Island. Those with no visible injuries were left to wander. There was no assistance for psychiatric distress in 1942. The Murmansk route closed.

In September 1942, Churchill renewed his press on Roosevelt to support Stalin, to avoid the Russians entering into a separate peace with Germany and thus allowing Germany to concentrate on control of France. The war effort once again focused on the Murmansk Convey. PQ 18 left New York harbor with forty merchant vessels, accompanied by fifty-one warships and two submarines.

PQ 18 met enemy fire northeast of Bear Island in Barents Sea. The following days into weeks, the convoy went further east into the Arctic, evading German aircraft and ships. The convoy risked becoming trapped in Arctic ice, as they sailed close to land, with the protective cover of inland fog. German planes and ships made a tight grid of the Arctic Ocean searching for ships. Meanwhile, Archangel was under constant German air attack. Eventually, twenty-seven of the forty cargo ships docked safely in port. Despite concentrated air attack, the convoy was a success.

Over the next two years, convoys faced fewer German aircraft. In 1944, a Murmansk bound convoy had forty-two merchant ships and a military escort of only nineteen warships. On November 12, 1944, the Royal Air Force located the *Von Tirpitz* at anchor in Tromsø, Norway. The scourge of PQ 17 was removed as a threat to Murmansk Convoys.

Russia gave military decorations to merchant seamen of the Murmansk Convoys. A total of sixteen million tons of cargo was delivered by their efforts. Ninety-eight ships and eight hundred and twenty-nine crew were lost in the effort. German troops never entered Murmansk, despite a ground offensive in 1941.

Seafarers' Monument

Modern Murmansk

Today there is little evidence in Murmansk of events in either world war. There are monuments to the efforts of civilian sailors and soldiers, who brought relief to Russia through the port. The prominent statue, Alyosha, overlooking Murmansk harbor today, is a compelling monument to Russian soldiers. A tribute to the Woman Who Waits, recalls effects on families looking for ships to safely return to port.

Russia harbors the Northern Fleet near, but separate from Murmansk harbor. At the Murmansk pier, nuclear-powered icebreakers of Atomflot can be spotted. The icebreaker Lenin is open as a museum to the era. In the plans for Murmansk, is regular service to Canada, leaving from the historic Customs House.

Monument to Murmansk Convoys in Archangel

Stalin Avenue, renamed Karl Marx Avenue, still runs to the statue of Lenin. New blocks of apartments fill landscape above the port. The Arctica Hotel is fully remodeled as the Azimut Hotel, the tallest building in the Arctic Circle. Still a bargain, the hotel has few frills. The best way to visit Murmansk is on a cruise ship. Temperatures in the Arctic Circle are unchanged. They are above zero only in June through September.

Murmansk is enjoying a twenty-first century purpose without a relationship to war. The city of three hundred thousand is a center for education in the Murmansk peninsula. It is touting itself as a bargain destination from which to view the Northern Lights. Murmansk is also a research base for study of the Arctic and a growing commercial port. After accomplishing so much in one century, Murmansk looks forward to the next 100 years.

Woman Who Waits

Entertainment Hall

Welcome to Archangel

Archangel's Marvelous Merchant Adventurers

English Merchant Warehouses Archangel

England was late to the scene in the Age of Discovery in which Portugal and Spain expanded their wealth by expanding their domain. The Dutch were quick to capitalize on new information and the English less so. English merchants brought wealth and exotic goods home through trade with secondary sources in Europe, the Mediterranean and North Africa.

In the beginning of the sixteenth century, English merchants awakened to their Viking heritage to dream about direct trade with the Far East by sailing north and east. A mélange of myth and mystery filled maps accumulated by anxious merchants in London. The Mystery Company and Fellowship of Merchant Adventurers for the Discovery of Unknown Lands was formed to act on their dream. The mission of discovery was a thinly veiled mission for commercial opportunities.

In May 1553, three vessels sailed out of the Thames for China, by the Northeast Passage, buoyed by optimism. Two ships entered lore of the Northeast Passage ending in tragedy. The third ship, captained by experienced navigator Richard Chancellor, spent the winter in the White Sea, and by fate, developed a relationship with Russian Tsar Ivan IV, before the tsar became Terrible.

English exploration of the Arctic did not end in the White Sea. The challenge to chart and sail a Northeast Passage from London to China, over the top of the world, was a dream realized after more than three hundred years of effort. Success was attained by a Swede at the end of the nineteenth century. That story of daring and discovery in the Arctic sails on past Archangel.

Archangel sits on both sides of the Dvina River as it spills into the White Sea. Location put Archangel at the confluence of history, in which England began a three hundred-year trade relationship with Russia from 1553 to 1853. In that period, there were two politically caused hiatus on trade, quickly remedied by success forged by the Merchant Adventurers, a company that evolved into the Muscovy Company. The Muscovy Company created the English model for international trade.

This is the story of Archangel, as discovered by the English, and developed by the Russians. Russia was opened to the west, despite its landlocked capital in Moscow, by the direct line to Archangel. Before St. Petersburg was the dream of Peter the Great, Archangel flourished as the trade capital of the Arctic. Overshadowed by technological advancement in transport in the twentieth century, and taking on a sinister patina in the Stalin era, Archangel is reemerging as a port from which to launch study of the Arctic. Its importance as a port has never diminished.

Travel now with the marvelous Merchant Adventurers in their pursuit of opportunities in the Arctic. This story diverges from the goal of a Northeast Passage to China, by stepping off in the port of Archangel and leaving the Northeast Passage to another story. Archangel also played a role in the post-World War I invasion of Russia, by British, French and American forces. The 1918 invasion has its own story. This story is the tale of the Muscovy Company in Archangel.

English Discovery of the White Sea

Merchant Ship Memorial

The English discovered the White Sea in 1553. It was not uncharted territory. Danish sailors were in the area in 1496. Russian fishermen and fur trappers frequented the Arctic. Since at least 1489, German merchants traded with Russians for fur. Vikings raided villages along Murmansk Nos, the North Cape, in the early eleventh century. For several groups of indigenous people, the length of Siberia was home. For the English captain who entered the White Sea in 1553, discovery was not the goal. The area provided a port in a storm, on the intended journey to warmth in the Far East.

Merchants in London were inspired to support discovery of a direct link to lucrative trade goods of silks and spices, that cut out middlemen Spanish and Portuguese traders. They needed a reliable route not blocked by Ottoman conquest of the Near East into Constantinople, and a route that avoided competition from the Hansa League of merchants based in Germany. Hansa controlled Baltic trade since the thirteenth century. Ottomans controlled Mediterranean traffic, otherwise known as an Ottoman Lake. The specter of increased profit made the Englishmen bold.

In 1551, a group met to form the Mystery Company and Fellowship of Merchant Adventurers for the Discovery of Unknown Lands. They brought in as a charter member the well-respected, eighty-two-year old Venetian sailor, with the anglicized name, Sebastian Cabot. Cabot had a resume of long service to the Spanish king, and served English king Henry VIII since 1548.

In 1553, three ships, holding a total of one hundred and three sailors, plus accompanying gentlemen, left from the Thames with the goal of reaching the Pacific and establishing a Northeast Passage. Leader of the expedition was the respected nobleman-knight, Sir Hugh Willoughby. Complimenting Sir Hugh, with a knowledge of sailing, was Richard Chancellor. On the ship with Chancellor, was Stephen Burrough, a talented navigator, who made his own mark in the Arctic.

Willoughby became disoriented, after a storm caused his two ships to lose contact with Chancellor, as they passed the North Cape. Lacking the skills of Chancellor and Burrough, Willoughby missed the entrance to the White Sea and spent a winter making a brave attempt to stay alive, until spring thaw allowed him to continue east. Willoughby did not survive the winter. His fate joined lore of the Northeast Passage.

Meanwhile, Chancellor looked for Willoughby at the rendezvous place, then sailed east as far as Novaya Zembla, the islands north of the Russian mainland. Deterred by ice, from a further search, Chancellor sailed into the White Sea. On the banks of the Dvina, not far from where Archangel is today, he and his mates spent the winter entertained by Russians. Chancellor made history, despite his other plans.

Russian fishermen and fur trappers encountered by Chancellor were generous in sharing food, fire and information concerning navigation of the area. They would not engage in trade without permission of their king. Somehow, Chancellor conveyed the desire to be taken to their leader. The result was a six-hundred-mile transit to Moscow and the court of Tsar Ivan IV.

Chancellor's timing was perfect. He landed at the White Sea monastery of Nikolo-Korelsky, not long after Ivan brought Siberia into his Russian domain. Ivan was a young man, born in 1530, and not yet Terrible, as he would become in later life, the result of mercury in his medications.[139] In 1553, Ivan was smarting from battles with Hansa merchants, whose navy laid siege around his trading city of Novgorod, on the Baltic. Ivan wanted new trade opportunities, with non-Germans.

Chancellor spent three months in Moscow, learning how to conduct trade with Russia. He thought Moscow primitive, although the court of Ivan was impressive. He was feted on gold plates. Ivan wore impressive jewels. The Tsar sent Chancellor home with an agreement to allow the English trading rights throughout Russia, without import tax, or export duty on furs, oil and items prized in England. Russian fur became high fashion in England. Merchant Adventurers, saddened by lack of news from Willoughby, were merry over news from Chancellor.

When the Merchant Adventurers learned of the fate of Willoughby, they quickly sent Chancellor back to the White Sea, to retrieve his remains and their two stranded ships. They also sent an official message from Queen Mary to Ivan, beginning diplomatic relations. Chancellor never returned to London. The two ships in tow were lost off the coast of Norway. In sight of Scotland, Chancellor's ship was caught in a storm and was dashed upon rocks. A hero to the end, Chancellor was able to save the life of the Russian ambassador, losing his life in the process.

---

[139] Medical examination of Ivan's bones in 2006 revealed bone disease treated with mercury, a common additive to medications. High mercury levels in the body renders the living to become irritable and eventually insane.

Archangel in the time of Ivan IV

Last of early English Company enthusiasm for a Northeast Passage was directed toward Stephen Burrough. As the Merchant Adventurers evolved into the Muscovy Company in London, Burrough sailed the *Searchthrift* to Murmansk Nos, where he befriended local fishermen. They directed him east to the Pechora River and left him with rough maps of Novaya Zemlya. In 1556, Burrough sailed the passage to the Kara Sea between Novaya Zemlya and Vaigach Island, before ice coming through the strait and a close encounter with a whale sent him back to the White Sea. As Burrough retraced his route, he saw Dutch and Norwegian ships capitalizing on English gains. Burrough had gone further east in the Arctic than any European explorer. It was his last effort.[140]

---

[140] Rayner Unwin, A Winter Away from Home, Seafarer Books, Sheridan, New York, 1995.

By 1555, the Dutch took advantage of trade with Russia established by Chancellor, once they saw 200% profits realized by the English doing business with Moscow. In that year, Raphael Barberini, an Italian sea captain, established an Antwerp to Russia route into the White Sea.[141] If the English did not wish to lose all benefit of pioneering success into Russia, they needed to reform their company with a priority to Moscow and divert effort from the Northeast Passage.

Muscovy Company 1555 – 1917

English House Archangel

In 1555, shareholders of the Merchant Adventurers formed the Muscovy Company, focused upon trade with Russia. It was the first joint holding company, preceding those of England, France, or Holland in the East

---

[141] Joseph Hamel, England and Russia: Voyages to the White Sea, Elibron Classics 2005 reprint of Richard Bently Publisher, 1854, at 124.

India Companies and West India Companies. The Muscovy Company not only established England's first foreign trade station, it became a model investment company.

In a joint holding company, the members pay a fee for a share in the profits of the whole. The company owns or leases ships to carry company trade goods, not those of individual members. Individual dealing dilutes company profit. Years later, competition weakened Muscovy Company. It became simply a regulated company carrying goods for individual merchant members.

The confluence of need and opportunity gave quick rise to the Muscovy Company. King Henry VIII commandeered the wealth of the Catholic Church, when he made himself head of the Church of England. He spent all he gained and more on war. He bequeathed a bankrupt country to his daughters. At a time when Vasco de Gama enabled 1000% return on investment to his Spanish royal backers on goods imported from the Far East, the English government was unable to back such exploits. The Muscovy Company marshaled private funds to accomplish that which its sovereign could not. Individual nobles could invest without directly becoming merchants.[142]

In the mid-sixteenth century, the English economy was in a trough. Cloth was not selling and those in the industry could not pay their rent. Merchants of London were desperate for new markets, not already controlled by the Hanseatic League based in Lübeck, Germany. Chancellor did not provide a route to the Far East, yet he did obtain a new and willing trade partner in Ivan.

From 1555 to 1561, the Muscovy Company went from having two warehouse-trading stations in Russia at Vologda and Colmogro, between the port and Moscow, to adding a third station in Moscow. Over the next five years, the Company added eight more company operations along the Volga River, such as Jaroslav.[143] They established a trading station at Novgorod, undercutting Hansa's former stronghold in Russia. Hansa over-stepped when it tried to

---

[142] Point made by Kit Mayers, Northeast Passage to Muscovy, Sutton Publishing Ltd., Phoenix Mill, 2005, pp. 3-20. Nobles could receive rents and profits from their land, but it was not legal for nobles to work, or be merchants.

[143] Muscovy trade stations were also located at Kazan, Nijni, Astrakhan, Pskov, Dorpat and Narva.

strong-arm Ivan by placing a siege on Novgorod. When Ivan had English partners, he no longer needed Hansa. The Hansa League began to decline as a regional power.

Treasure Box with intricate locking mechanism

Ivan developed a long-distance affinity for Elizabeth I of England. Their personal correspondence indicates the wily Ivan intending to gain English support in his desire to obtain weapons from England, for his use in attacking English allies. Swedes watched English ships closely to detect gun-running. Elizabeth denied all allegations. Her letters are discrete and evasive.

In 1570, an Englishman, jailed in England for fraudulent dealings and later doing business in Russia, convinced Ivan that Elizabeth would be an ideal choice for his seventh wife. Ivan's first wife died in 1547, and the five who came after her had short tenure. Wives either died under questionable circumstances, or were sent to a convent. Ivan sent a marriage proposal to Elizabeth. Elizabeth was clever in dodging the offer. She extended English hospitality should Ivan ever need a safe haven. He was not amused.

In 1570, Ivan suspended trading rights of the Muscovy Company. He soon had other more pressing problems. In 1571, the Tatar people, whose lands were previously conquered, rose to burn Moscow. Trade with England helped Russia to recover and rebuild. The English House in Moscow, which functioned as trading base of operations and ambassador residence, was rebuilt.

Fortunes of the Muscovy Company diminished when the exclusivity agreement was terminated in 1649. Tsar Alexi used the action to express his anger with England, when King Charles I was executed. The Company was already feeling the effects of competition from Dutch and other traders, as well as self-dealing by company directors. In 1571, the Battle of Lepanto, in Greek waters, began the decline of Ottoman control in the Mediterranean. Overland trade opened opportunities for the Levant Company of London, in which several Muscovy directors were also shareholders.

England and Russia maintained good trade relations until 1853 brought the Crimean War. Russia had long desired a warm water port on the Black Sea, since the days of Peter I, at the beginning of the eighteenth century. Catherine II (the Great) accomplished the feat when a Turkish fortress was captured. Turkey was an ally of England. Prime Minister William Pitt wanted to engage in war with Russia, an occurrence that was thwarted by deft action by Catherine's foreign minister Semyon Vorontsov.[144] Loss of support for Pitt in Parliament, began the decline of his career.[145]

In 1853, three hundred years of a trade relationship between England and Russia was severed when English troops arrived in the Crimea. Aggression between Russia and Turkey, on land surrounding the Black Sea, had abated

---

[144] The Vorontsov family appears in Cruise through History©, Itinerary XI – Ports of the Baltic Sea, St. Petersburg and Itinerary IV Ports of the Black Sea, Odessa.

[145] Catherine II's son and successor Paul was Grand Master of the Knights of St. John in Malta, when Britain occupied Malta. Instigated by France, Paul planned to invade India, another of England's allies. The invasion never occurred.

by the time of the arrival of England's troops. The harsh winter that followed, and the folly of battle, was memorialized in the poem, *Charge of the Light Brigade*.[146] The marriage of Queen Victoria's second son to the only daughter of Russian Emperor Alexis II only accomplished a little good will.

The Muscovy Company continued to function in a limited form until 1917. In later years, it served as a benevolent society. The Company retains importance today for historic value and as testament to the value of trade relationships across the globe.

Archangel's Opening to the West

Archangel was founded by Ivan IV, just prior to his death in 1584. He gave the city the name of its protector, the Archangel Michael, in deference to the monastery long established on the Dvina. The city now straddles the Dvina River. In its earliest days, the city developed across the river from where Chancellor moored his ship, on his first arrival in the White Sea.

Ivan IV is most remembered for that part of his life, when he became an insane despot, responsible for the death of thousands of people, mostly in Novgorod. In calmer times, he built the walls of the Kremlin and, as a tribute to the defeat of Tatars and expanding his domain, built St. Basil's Cathedral, the icon of Moscow. Ivan did not have time to build edifices in Archangel. He died while playing chess in 1584. Chess was popular in Russia, possibly associated with the end of Ivan.

Functioning as the entrance port to trading in Moscow, Archangel flourished in the sixteenth century. Despite Ivan's distain for German merchants, German and Dutch traders established outposts in the city. In 1668, they built a Merchant Yard, which can be visited as a museum today. Sited on the White Sea, below the Arctic Circle, Archangel provided a safe harbor and long season, made all the more accessible with advances in ship-building technology and ice-breakers.

---

[146] The poem is by Alfred Lloyd Tennyson. See the Bickering Brothers of the Light Brigade, in Cruise through History©, Itinerary IV Ports of the Black Sea.

Peter I looking over the Dvina

The seventeenth century was a tempestuous time for Archangel. Russia was often at war with its neighbors, making Archangel a strategic target. It was the site of battles in 1613 and 1619. In 1637, the Polish-Lithuanian army launched a campaign into Russia and burned the city. The port was rebuilt and made larger in 1693, as a staging point for Russian battles with Sweden.

Emperor Peter I (the Great) founded his great city on the Neva, St. Petersburg, in 1703, eclipsing the value of Archangel.[147] To promote his new European style city, Peter forbade any cargo traffic into Archangel except that necessary to local needs. The prohibition lasted to 1762. Despite the actions of Peter, Archangel looks kindly toward Russia's first modern monarch. His statue sits high above the sea wall today, at the beginning of a seaside promenade.

In the 1890s, the railroad connecting Archangel to Moscow insured its commercial life as a port for the export of timber, a function that continues today. At the close of World War I, when the revolution in Russia caused the royal family to be deposed, England, France and the United States invaded Russia. The point of entry was Archangel. That sad tale has its own story.

Stalin Era in Siberia

When Stephen Burrough realized that he could not pass into the Kara Sea in 1555, he returned to moor in the Dvina delta. During World War II, Burroughs's choice of landing was used as a Soviet nuclear submarine base. The location was not shown on maps until 1991, and the opening of Russia after dissolution of the Soviet Union. During the Soviet era, the train line from Moscow to Archangel became a passage to prison in Siberia, for those who fell on the wrong side of Stalin.[148]

The Soviet Era Gulag system of Stalin has been repurposed at Yertsevo, to a maximum-security prison. In the 1940s, Yertsevo was a hard-labor camp from

---

[147] Peter I is properly referred to as Emperor. He dropped the moniker Tsar as old-fashioned and not European.
[148] This is not to be confused with the 2005 film version Archangel.

which people were not expected to survive.¹⁴⁹ Despite its historic significance, do not expect the prison to be included in a shore excursion.

Domes of Solovetsky Island Monastery

The fascinating shore excursion from Archangel, into the era of Stalin, entails a side trip to Solovetsky Island, and a walk from the little pier to the Gulag Museum. Museum exhibits are candid and chilling. Russians ask why Stalin committed genocide of his own people.

Prior to the Gulag, political prisoners were housed in Solovetsky Island Monastery, a great walled complex, with its own fascinating history. There are three Orthodox Churches within the walls, two built into the wall, with beautiful frescoes, well preserved. This is residence to an active, although small, community of monks. Russian tsars supported the monastery and sent political prisoners in the seventeenth century to its thick-walled, cavernous

---

¹⁴⁹ See, Gustaw Herling-Grudzinki, A World Apart, Arbor House, London, 1951, 1980. (In Polish, 1953).

chambers. In the nineteenth century, British gun-boats lobbed cannonballs into the monastery, where they bounced off solid walls of residence buildings. Today, a small hotel on the island pier anticipates tourism.

Solovetsky Island Gulag Museum

Walled monastery from island interior

Painted dots represent English cannon fire of Crimean War and no damage

Gatehouse chapel of monastery

Today in Archangel

*Archangel Art & Architecture Promenade
with Radio Tower Building in background*

Today Archangel is evolving from a dark Soviet demeanor to a lighter and truly international appeal. The iconic, tall, rectangle building with the radio spire on top, formerly the tallest building in the city, is now a backdrop to a pedestrian mall. The landscaped mall is lined with reconstructed historic homes of the eighteenth and nineteenth century, punctuated with bronze sculptures of poets and storytellers. A bronze, life size woman is caught in the moment of spinning yarn, while a child plays at her feet.

At the end of the landscaped promenade, the street becomes an insight to pre-restoration Archangel. It is a private opportunity waiting to happen, to add shops and cafes, which will draw local people into the historic district and give impetus to preservation of wooden buildings of architecture uniquely Arctic Russia. Archangel is a work in progress.

Historic Archangel Tribute to Family

Fantasy Archangel

Storyteller of Archangel

The story of Archangel at the arrival of the Merchant Adventurers, soon joined by German and Dutch traders, is recalled in the Merchant Yard Museum on the Dvina River. This is part of Stone Town, the oldest section of Archangel. At the Port Authority offices nearby, Peter the Great, not Lenin, dominates the podium. Along the Dvina River, a river walk draws locals on nice days.

War memorials, are present in memorial square, in scale to the city. Memorable is the tribute to the Murmansk Convoys, dramatically displayed against the retaining wall of the Dvina. A tribute to seals rests along the river wall. People survived on seal meat during the wars. Along the river, a wide and inviting walkway is enjoyed by visitors as much as locals, with babies in push prams.

Tribute to Murmansk Convoys of WWII on Dvina River

The old city docks, within easy proximity to downtown, are accessible to small ships. Larger ships dock at the commercial harbor, on an island thirty minutes from the city. The ride into town allows views of the Russian frontier in centuries old, two-story apartment buildings of wood, begging for rehabilitation and restoration.

If Archangel can capture enough of its history, restore and promote its assets, curious visitors to this part of the Arctic will increase, weather permitting. Archangel was a safe harbor for Chancellor in the sixteenth century and is an intriguing harbor today.

Archangel Part II: 1918

Changes to Royal Medalion Archangel

In the winter of 1918, British, French and United States troops invaded Russia in an undeclared war. The action lasted eleven months. It ended with defeat and hasty departure of allied invaders. Often dubbed the Polar Bear

Expedition, military objectives of the North Russia Expeditionary Forces evolved from protecting Russia from Germany, up until the Armistice ending World War I, to active involvement in the Russian civil war between White Russian royalists and Red Russian communists. The Allied mission was to support a democratic Russia, free of Bolshevik control.

Archangel Lenin Square

When Armistice was signed on November 11, 1918, ending World War I, Allied forces in Archangel did not go home. The public reason for overstaying express military objectives was given as the inability to depart through winter ice in the Arctic Ocean. There was more underlying the decision to stay in Archangel. When troops in Archangel were joined by troops from Murmansk, it was obvious that battles arising during World War I, those in the far north Russian theater, were not over. This part of the story of military action in Archangel is 1918: Part II.

The story of 1918: Part I takes place in Murmansk, the staging area of the North Russia Allied military operations up to the Armistice. Allied forces were Britain, France and the United States, with substantial involvement of the Czech military and Japan, which offered its support. At the beginning of World War I, Imperial Russia was part of the Allied forces. By the end of the war Imperial Russia no longer existed. The question of what entity governed Russia was an open question. United States did not recognize the Soviet Union until 1933.

Wars are waged by governments at the expense of humans. When the human element is considered, there are more facets to the story than the number of flags on the field. In this story, outsized personalities of Winston Churchill, then Britain's Foreign Minister, Lloyd George, Britain's Prime Minister, United States President Woodrow Wilson and the rising Red stars of Vladimir Lenin and Leon Trotsky, figure prominently.

Battles on the field are won and lost by military leaders of varying skill. In this story, most distinguished were the leadership of thirty-eight-year-old British Colonel Edmund Ironside, who assumed command in 1918, for our story Part II, from U.S. Commander Frank Poole in Murmansk, who led the action in 1918: Part I. In the story of 1918: Part II, critical decisions of when to advance into Russia and when to extract forces, were made by distant civilians. Decisions were political more than strategic. Stunning was the civilians' lack of knowledge of Russian terrain and politics.

Often in war, an opponent is dubbed with a marginalizing moniker. Bolsheviks were viewed by the Allies as undisciplined wildmen and given the name *Bolos*. It is one matter to enthuse troops by marginalizing the enemy and quite another to base military decisions on such characteristics. Underestimating Bolshevik forces, their commander and their ability to perform in frozen terrain proved fatal.

Seldom does Cruise through History delve into war stories. In a visit to Archangel, it would be an oversight to talk of history without the chapter of events from November 1918, to September 1919. This seldom told, and little-known, story was never popular material for Hollywood movies. The soldiers who fought in this mission asked: *Why are we still here?* Historians ponder the same question. This is their story.

End of 1918: Part I

Archangel 1918

A little review of Russia's history going into World War I, sets the stage for circumstances in the fall of 1918, that Wilson referred to as the *cruel dilemma*. Changing alliances complicate the picture. When revolutionary Bolshevik gangs became the organized communist party of Russia in 1918, the question of what entity governed Russia was confusing, even for Russians.

Tensions rose when in 1908 the Austrian-Hungarian empire annexed Bosnia-Herzegovina. Independent Slavic Balkan nations, including Czechoslovakia, feared for their security and the fate of ethnic Slavs in Russia. Slavic nations annexed part of Russia. Adding to the mix was German aggression into France. Germany allied with Austria, and France allied with Russia, joined by Britain, in what became the Great War. Russia made a separate pact with Germany, then realized that to keep Germany from breaking the agreement and continuing into Russia, Russia needed assistance of the Allies of Britain, France, Czech forces and the United States.

The flash point, marking the beginning of World War I, was June 1914, when a Serbian assassinated Archduke Ferdinand, heir to the throne of Austria-Hungary. One month later, Austria declared war on Serbia. Germany aligned with Austria, and Russia entered adverse to Germany, even though reigning monarchs Nicholas II of Russia and Franz Joseph of Austria were grandchildren of Queen Victoria of England. Turf battles overcame family alliances.

Anti-German fervor was so strong, that St. Petersburg was renamed Petrograd, to give the city a more Russian moniker. Bolsheviks roused peoples' fear of Germans, while at the same time spreading anti-royal sentiment. In Russia, people who fought wars were tired of dying for the causes of an unpopular monarchy, despite distain for German aggression. In response to destabilizing Bolshevik actions, in 1915, five Bolshevik leaders were sent to prison in Siberia.

During this time, the Imperial family was under the spell of Rasputin, a curious mystic, who became the target of assignation by Russian leaders fearful of his hold over Nicholas II and his family. The Russian military decided they could no longer support the Tsar in the event of a revolution. Revolution came in February 1917. By the end of the month, the Tsar abdicated and the Imperial Family retreated to Tsarskoe Selo, palace of tsars, where they waited fate to turn.

A hastily formed provisional government of the Russian Socialist Soviet Republic included, but was not controlled by, Bolsheviks. This changed in October 1917, known as Red October.[150] Vladimir Lenin emerged as leader of the Bolsheviks, which evolved to the communist party. Lenin led the transition from unfocused anarchy to Marxism. Hundreds of thousands of starving people demonstrated in the streets. Communists deposed the provisional government, which it blamed for the financially bereft status of the country.

The country divided into civil war of Red Guards under Lenin and White Russians, who hoped to restore the monarchy, or establish a representative form of government.[151] Red Guards controlled Moscow. White Russian

---

[150] Under the Russian new calendar, the taking of power on October 25, became November 7. Russians remember Red October as Four Days in November, memorialized in Russian film.

[151] In 1881, Tsar Alexander II proposed a constitutional monarchy in the model of Britain. He was assassinated by anarchists.

forces amassed in the south and east of Russia. In Archangel, a White Russian stronghold, dreamy royalists and White Russian leaders-in-waiting gladly accepted sustaining support from the Allies.

Royal Customs House Archangel

Armistice ended fighting in World War I. It did not end civil war. On July 17, 1918, the Imperial family of Russia was executed in a secret location. On July 18, British Colonel Ironside arrived in Archangel to lead Allied action in northern Russia, with the mission of destroying the Bolshevik army. The *cruel dilemma* feared by President Wilson, too few troops for too large a mission, was about to take hundreds of lives among the Allies and thousands of lives in Russia, before it ended.

Why Are We Still Here?

To Allied soldiers remaining in fortified blockhouses and villages of northern Russia, shooting at Bolsheviks, not Germans, prior to and after the Armistice, it may seem arbitrary to draw a line in the story at the Armistice on November

11, 1918. To Bolshevik leaders, who tolerated with caution armed Czech soldiers and Allies up until the Armistice, offensive military actions of the Allied army after the Armistice was an invasion force in an undeclared war. President Wilson understood the delineation. Prior to the Armistice, he clearly committed US forces to aid Czechs in protection of Russia from Germany and Austria and to support a developing democratic Russian government. After Armistice, Wilson's public statements are duplicitous.

Historic Archangel

Late 19th century Archangel

20th century Archangel

Early 20th century Archangel

During Paris Peace talks ending the Great War, Wilson noted that for the United States to send an army against Bolsheviks would aid their cause by a display of imperialism. At that time, the majority of the forces in Archangel were Americans. Prime Minister George was more practical. It was his opinion that Bolsheviks could not be crushed without a major military offensive, something his country did not have the enthusiasm to support. Even as he spoke, the North Russia Expeditionary Force was under British command, with no orders to retreat. French President Clemenceau was honest in his declared support for anti-Bolshevik military forces. In the Allied first offensive post-Armistice, Bolsheviks decimated the French field force.

Winston Churchill was consistent in his views before and after the Armistice. For him, there could be no peace in Europe, while Bolsheviks controlled Russia. He advocated a strong effort to wage war until democracy-loving Russians took hold of their country. Unfortunately, Allied forces never ignited a ground swell of farmers to the cause. Democracy-loving Russians were few, if any. Caught between forces of battle, locals whose villages and crops were burned by successive armies simply wanted peace. Their biggest enemy was starvation. Those not fond of Romanov royals were equally displeased by the prospect of British royalists ruling Russia. Peasants had not yet met the depravations of communism. Churchill's elegant words were lost on people with basic needs.

In London, Paris and New York, the end of the war was celebrated. Troops began to arrive home by the end of 1918. Soldiers left in Archangel wondered why they had no orders to withdraw. Colonel George Stewart, commanding the 339th Company, wrote his superiors to advise that as of November 14, 1918, the original objective was met and that in order to leave the area prior to a freeze, immediate action was necessary. The troops saw the arrival of Commander Ironside in a haze of disbelief. He planned fresh offensive action for the winter of 1918 to 1919.

To answer troop questions, an official statement issued by military leaders was: to guard military supplies of use to the White Russian army; guard against an uprising by German and Austrian prisoners and sympathizers; and to support the White Army in removing threats to Russia from Bolsheviks. There were two White armies in the field at the time. One was in the south and the other in the east. The only soldiers encountered by Allied troops were Red Soviets, not Germans. The supply depot of the White Army was already empty. There was nothing and no one to guard.

An anonymous treatise, credited to an American officer upon returning from action at the front in Archangel, offers succinct reasons for overstaying a welcome in another country.[152] He noted that the British were royalists, hoping to restore the monarchy, with whom England established trade relations in 1553. The French motive is assigned to the fact that France held substantial sovereign debt of Romanov Russia, in default upon demise of the royals. Of the American incentive, the officer considered Wilson's statements dismissive of military ability of Jewish boys Nicolai Zederblum and Leon Bronstein, known after November 1918, to the world, as Lenin and Trotsky.

Battles of 1918 Part II: November 1918 to September 1919

Monument to Seals that Fed People During the Great War

---

[152] A Chronicler, Archangel: American War with Russia, A.C. McClurg & Co., Chicago, 1924. Credited to American officer John Cudahy by E. M. Halliday, The Ignorant Armies, Award Books, New York, 1964, 277-278, 293.

In the north Russia action, the Allies faced three enemies: Red Army, extreme cold and illness. Strength and resolve of the Red Army were continually underestimated. Winter temperatures reached minus 45°, presenting a challenge, even for winter-hardy soldiers from Michigan and Wisconsin. Commanders in Archangel found arriving troops suffering from flu contracted on the voyage. Another matter was ignorance of Siberia by the United States War Department. Relief intended for northwest Siberia in Murmansk, or Archangel, was sent to Vladivostok four thousand miles away. To the US War Department, Siberia was a single transversable place.[153]

Allies were emboldened by their initial engagement with Bolsheviks, the early Soviet Army, soon after the Armistice. Trotsky, Commander of the Sixth Red Army, withdrew his troops in the face of battle, the better to gauge enemy strength and intention. Allies pursued the Red Army into the swamps and forests of northwest Russia, as winter decreased ability of troops to survive in the open environment. The Red Army knew the landscape. They knew that if they were patient, the cold would fight the war for them.

Ironside inherited an army fighting on five fronts. He quickly condensed the forces to two fronts; one south of Archangel, on the Dvina River, and one progressing down to the railroad, with the intent of joining White Army forces, should they progress west through Red Army defenses. Then, Ironside focused upon capturing two towns, not for strategic advantage, but rather to obtain winter billeting for troops. Adjacent to the towns, Allied engineers supervised building blockhouses, which were ammunition storage for gun placements, designed to withstand shelling from the Red Army. Blockhouses provided additional shelter for Allied forces.

On January 19, a massive display of Red Army strength came at the Allies bunkered in the town of Nijni. Allies were blasted from their blockhouses and pursued through town streets. Troops moved randomly through snow north toward Archangel, for two days. To keep moving meant not only avoiding Red guns, it meant staving off frost. Frost claimed lives of troops with otherwise minor injuries.

---

[153] Troops sent to Vladivostok spent the war there, warm and well-supplied, without enemy engagement.

At the end of March, Trotsky led another major offensive, attempting to corral Allies into Archangel. Only discipline of Allied soldiers, cold and hungry, yet resolute in their training, kept the battle from becoming a rout. Trotsky pulled back short of a battle victory, out of concern that the White Army was approaching joinder with the Allies at the railway. Joinder never occurred.

As weather warmed, Ironside knew he must bring the troops into crowded Archangel. Absent icepack, Lake Onega was not passable. The Soviet Army had gun boats ready to deploy on the lake. On Dvina River, Allies were assisted by women from the Karelia Peninsula, displaced by war between Russia and Finland, in the strip of land north of St. Petersburg. They were expert boats-women, having braved all-weather to bring food to their men, who in peacetime had been farmers and fishermen. When faced with gunfire from Soviet boats on the river, the women rammed their boats into Soviet craft, upending the gunboats. Two women were given British medals of valor.

Meanwhile, in Britain, the Parliament that thought people would no longer tolerate military service, was surprised to have thousands of convalescing soldiers volunteer to rescue troops from Archangel. By the end of September 1919, Allies evacuated Archangel. By two weeks into October, evacuation of Murmansk was completed. By February 2, 1920, Soviets controlled Archangel. The White Army was no longer a fighting force. Months later, the civil war ended.

With evacuating Allies, came some White Army and royalist leaders, fearful of Soviet reprisal, a few Russian brides, and several Russian children. The children came at the behest of American infantrymen, who had spent much of the winter sharing rations with Russian families. Russian families in little villages of Siberia, who risked their safety to house troops in freezing weather, hopped the children would have a better life.

Aftermath of Battle

Returning veterans of 1918: Part II, the post-Armistice North Russia Expeditionary Offensive, did not receive the festive homecoming that met troops returning home the prior fall. They were the forgotten army of the unspoken war. Those who experienced front lines in snow, were irrevocably scarred. Post-traumatic stress was not recognized in the early twentieth century.

Memorial Square Archangel and Eternal Flame

In Michigan and Wisconsin, home to many of the United States troops of the 339th Company, the dead lying in Russia could not be forgotten. At their urging, Congress appropriated $200,000 in 1929, to send a delegation to Russia to retrieve remains. Despite the fact that the US did not then recognize legitimacy of the Soviet government, the Soviets cooperated in the retrieval. In 1934, another delegation brought home nineteen more coffins. Returning remains received the homecoming of heroes. In home states of the fallen, their service was acknowledged.

In speeches made in 1953, Winston Churchill was still advocating eradication of communists in Russia. By then, it was obvious that in addition to strategic, military and diplomatic errors of judgment in the North Russia Expedition, post Armistice, there were several missed opportunities to effectuate the goal of decimating Bolsheviks through non-military means.

General Ironside's evaluation of the action included the need to recruit and train White Army troops from among local Russians. This was never fully attempted. There had been no serious efforts to build a provisional Russian government, other than those of Lenin, in creating the Soviet ruling infrastructure. Even as the British were debating what currency to use in Russia, British pounds or Imperial rubles, the Soviets were printing their new currency. A new government does not emerge from supply depots. Lenin would never negotiate with White army leaders. He knew that their government did not exist outside of Allied supported Archangel.

In the future, Archangel played a role in battles of World War II, when Russia again joined the Germans, then the Allies, to Soviet advantage. Future efforts of democratic nations to deal with Soviet Russia were diplomatic, economic and through third nations. Never again did the Allies directly invade Soviet territory.

Promenade along Dvina River in Archangel

Today Archangel, not a major metropolis, has a memorial square, in a scale in relation to its size. The square is still impressive, with several monuments to service men and women. There is even a memorial to the seal, the source of food that kept residents alive during the worst of the war. To see memorials to the North Russia Expeditionary Force, a trip to Michigan is necessary.

ICELAND

IN REYKJAVIK CELEBRATE THE WORLD'S OLDEST DEMOCRACY

Iceland Vistas

Iceland is home to the oldest, arguably continual, democratic government in the world. Viking tradition of democracy inspired mass emigration from Norway to Iceland, in the ninth century, during the time of an overbearing king. Iceland became a major Viking domain, where raiding Vikings settled, becoming Norse farmers. Norse families adopted a democratic governing style.

In 927, a delegate was sent from Iceland back to home turf in Norway, to study law and return to educate fellow farmers. By 930, Viking democracy, evolved from practices in Norway, became fundamental to government in Iceland. In Iceland, with some hiatus, democracy as an institution was inseparable in culture, as a lifeway that has continually endured to the present day.

First to Settle Iceland Ingolfur Arnarson

Breadth and sophistication of Viking jurisprudence, in a representative democracy, throughout its social structure, gives a picture of Viking life, that is in stark contrast to visions of Vikings in raiding excursions. Raiding parties, or armed feuds, and representative government sessions were not mutually exclusive. Still, there were rules. Transgression of rules had consequences. In a world of verbal communication, everyone knew the rules.

A millennium prior to mass communication in telephones and television, Vikings developed a means for mass communication among the fjords. In a system to rival the Romans, a millennium prior, Vikings convened to learn the rules, settle disputes and become current on community affairs. So elegant was the system developed, that it continued into modern practice. Sessions are now held indoors, in rooms with electric lights and thermal heating. Form and content are little changed. Delegates to Iceland Parliament now arrive in cars, not by ship, or horse. The place of Iceland Parliament is on a grassy hill, home to Reykjavik city government and businesses.

Vikings had an appreciation for good real estate. Meeting places for legislative and judicial sessions were held on rising ground, giving pArcticipants constant view of their ships. Freedoms were important. Ships were a life-line. In Iceland, Thingvellir, a large National Park today, is the site of the original Icelandic Althing, the whole-island meeting, that began in 930.

Things, democratic meetings, were held in regions of Iceland, with the annual Althing event held in Thingvellir.[154] High point of this story is the vision of that critical place, where government and environment melded. Iceland has spectacular landscapes. Vikings made that landscape special.

Viking Democratic Tradition in Iceland

Vikings, the raiding parties of well-armed fighters in elegant ships, originated in fjords of western Norway, the Vesterland. Fiercely independent, as they were in desire for land, competition for land amid growing populations of farmers,

---

[154] Sometimes seen spelled as Ping, or with an Old Norse Character. The Iceland National Park is Thingvellir.

and a Norse king intent on unifying and subjugating the Norse of Vesterland, sent able sailors west in search of new turf. In the 870s, new domain was found in unoccupied Iceland. Norse of Vesterland were joined by Norse from Scotland, Orkneys, Isle of Man and Ireland. Celts of Ireland joined Norse neighbors in transition.

Ingólfr Arnarson led the first, organized, armada of about four hundred settlers from western Norway to Iceland. They landed near present-day Reykjavik and spread across the landscape, claiming land for farms. Much knowledge of their lives comes from *Icelandic Sagas*, including the *Book of Settlements*, which are individual stories of Norse families in the tenth and eleventh centuries.[155]

Landscape of Thingmen Farms

---

[155] Norse Sagas, including *Sagas of Icelanders and Modruvellir Saga*, a compellation of eleven stories of farm families, deserve their own story. Likely written by chiefs among fellow farmers, they tell of loves, lives, conflicts and peace agreements. Later *Sturlunga Saga*, of the twelfth and thirteenth centuries, tells tales of battles.

From the first landing party, Iceland society was unique in form from any other in Europe, including Scandinavia. Icelanders were universally farmers.[156] There were no royals. There was no demarcation by class, or hierarchy. Every farm family strove to stay alive on their land. Even the concept of slavery; captured enemies put to work in service to a family, ended quickly in Iceland. Slavery assumed an obligation of the family to house and feed slaves. There was no excess in production. Initiative and hard work kept people alive. Everyone worked on their farm.

Iceland did not develop urban centers until the nineteenth century. In prior centuries, until Danes controlled Iceland and exploited fishing for export, farmers fed their growing families. Still, as the population grew from immigration, competition for land, disputes between families over marriage and inheritance, as well as the occasional bloody encounter, required resolution to keep peace. In 927, farmers nominated a fellow farmer, Ulfljótr, to sail back to fjords of western Norway to become a man of learning in law.[157]

The system developed as a representative democracy in Iceland, surpassed its model in Norway. Norway became a form of constitutional monarchy, at times a vassal to other monarchs. Norse councils in Norway were local, or advisory to the monarch. In Iceland, in the absence of monarchs, or royals at any level, democratic council developed into a sophisticated social form of governance, without parallel in the ancient, or Medieval world.

Rather than ask all farmers to leave their farms, to meet several times each year, groups of farmers joined under a representative, who met in one of four regional meetings several times during the year. In one region, there was such dissention, that it split, rendering the number of regions five by the beginning of the eleventh century. A representative farmer was known as a godi and his group of farmers were the Thingmen of the godi. Godi were regarded as chiefs among fellow farmers, yet not a royal. To be a godi was an obligation of service, not a designation of royalty.

---

[156] See generally, Jess Byock, Viking Age of Iceland, Penguin, London, 2001.
[157] The likely destination for Ulfljótr was Gulathing, the meeting place on a western fjord of Norway.

Plural of godi is godar. Godar met in in a regional meeting known as a Thing. At certain times, the godar of all five regions convened in a single place. The all-Islandic meetings were known as Althings. The first Althing, and place of Althings for centuries, was at Thingvellir. Vellir is a plain. Thingvellir, now a national park, is a large open plain, coincidently at the edge of a great fissure in the earth, on the banks of the Axe River in central western Iceland. The site is imposing as a natural feature of the earth. Althings, regularly occurring on this bit of landscape, became profound in the formation of the later nation of Iceland and monumental as a model society.

Law Rock at Fissure & Site of Althing at Thingvellir

Governance in Iceland quickly developed into a three-level decision-making form, the sort of structure touted in twenty-first century graduate schools of business and government around the world. Decision-making gurus of today have Vikings to thank, for working out an effective system. The outer ring of farmers, Thingmen, met with their godi, one of thirty-six to forty-eight godar, to learn the law and suggest or agitate for new laws. Godar met in Things in five regions.

Regional Things convened quarterly, known as fjordungathing. A few Thingmen might attend with their godi. If a godi tried to exert undue advantage over their Thingmen, unhappy Thingmen could depart and seek representation under a different godi. Although godi are referred to by historians as chiefs, all Thingmen were farmers and a godi was an equal among Thingmen.

From among all godar, three were chosen for three-year terms to officiate at the Althing. One of the three was typically a descendant of Ingólfr Arnarson. One of the three was a supreme chief, who officiated the logistics of the Althing. With so many people attending at Thingvellir, some allocation of space for meetings, tents or turf lodges for the two-week event, and places for peddlers, brewers and ale sellers, was necessary. One of the three was the Law-Speaker.

At the Althing, high on Law Rock at Thingvellir, the Law-Speaker stood to recite one-third of the laws, each of the three years of his term. If his memory failed, there were helpful godar to assist, no doubt fueled with ale. Votes were taken on amendments to laws, new laws, and major decisions, such as treaties.

Althing occurred in June, when the weather was best for travel. A preparatory Varthing occurred in May. At the Varthing, the value of an ounce in trade goods was set, known as the *thinglaseyrir*. In a session known as the *skapthing*, dates for Althing and procedures were established. By June, the massive Althing was set for trade deals, introduction of young people to marriage prospects and all manner of decisions made in a peaceful, orderly environment.

Icelanders had a fully functioning judicial system, in tandem with the legislative process. Godi were the first line in dispute resolution for their Thingmen. Matters that remained contentious went to one of four regional courts. In 1005, the Althing created the supreme Fifth Court, convened during Varthing.

Cases put before the Fifth Court were heard by twelve farmers appointed by godar. This may be the first instance of a twelve-person jury. Although women did not function as godar, they could be appointed to decide court cases. The Fifth Court held two sessions: *sóknarthing* was for prosecution of criminal cases; and *skuldathing* was for civil actions for injury or debt. Penalty for causing harm could include payment in horses, or in the case of murder, exile. Determination of obligation for debt would include failed promises of marriage and rights to marital property, or rights to property in inheritance.

From the top of Law Rock to the River of boats

In Iceland, men and women were free to intermingle. Legitimacy of children was not an issue until priests arrived. Still, complex issues of family made for complex inheritance cases.[158]

In the twelfth century, a scribe wrote laws into a book created from pages of calfskin velum. Known as *Grágás*, which in Old Norse is Grey Goose, the book is more saga than text of law from Althings. *Grágás* does not distinguish law, as voted into effect at an Althing, which is legislative law, from understood social practice, which is common law.[159]

---

[158] Halldór Kiljan Laxness was awarded a Nobel Prize in Literature in 1955 for his novel, Atómstödtin (Atom Station), published in 1948, of social tension in Icelandic society. His character said she was taught to believe nothing in the newspapers, and everything in the Sagas.

[159] The book was found in the sixteenth century on a farm in western Iceland. It was kept in Denmark in the Old Royal Library in Copenhagen. At the time of the find, Denmark controlled Iceland.

There is a section in *Grágás* on choice of bishop and the relationship of the church in an otherwise secular society, where godar are also priests. By 1118, a church building appeared on the landscape at Thingvellir. Missionary priests from Norway brought a new dimension to Iceland.

Separation of Church and State

Viking Landing

In Europe, as it was in Norway, priests, pArcticularly bishops or archbishops, held power to rival a king. In Iceland, Christianity arrived with the first settlers from Norway, although some settlers were pagan. Christian Icelanders looked to their god in heaven, while retaining Norse gods of the sea and crops. The concept of religious and secular deity came naturally to Icelanders, while the idea of a priest, or bishop, as a noble fell outside their rubric of organized society. The Vatican and the Archbishop of Trondheim, supreme cleric of Norway, Iceland and eventually Greenland, had to accept a unique form of Christian practice in Iceland, if they wished to convert Icelanders.

Arrival of the church brought a need for taxes, or tithe. Godar extracted a small Thing tax from Thingmen to compensate for loss of time on the farm while attending Things. Churches held land, in competition with farmers, and required a tithe to support the bishop, the local priest, the church building, and for distribution to the poor. Tithe was not distributed in equal amounts.

Norse farmers accepted Christ readily, although they balked at loss of land and payment of tithe. Church administration was not democratic. In the institution of the church versus Icelandic democracy, democracy prevailed.

In 1173, Archbishop Eystein, sitting in his palace at Nidaros in Trondheim, refused to accept as priests any godar of Iceland, who had ever killed a man in battle. In one edict, Eystein defrocked most godar of their dual role as Thing delegate and priest. In addition, Eystein declared that a priest could not also advocate in a court or legislative process. Godar appointed judges, however, their role was administrative, not an elevation to royalty. The ability to defend their property in court, or advocate for Thingmen, was inherent in the role of godar. In 1190, Archbishop Eirik Ivarsson flatly refused to ordain any Iceland godar as priests. The line was drawn.

At the next Althing, delegates began to unwind church ownership of property in Iceland. In 1195, Pall Jonsson, a priest, was elected Bishop of Iceland, at an Althing, not by a convention of priests.[160] Pall was a choice reflective of the times. He was an illegitimate child, which in Iceland carried no stigma. Pall was also married and the father of several children. When he traveled to Norway, Bishop Pall was given a warm welcome by Norwegian King Sverre. Sverre has his own story of elevation to king of Norway by force of will, rather than by family inheritance, as was custom.

---

[160] For more on Bishop Pall, see the story of Vikings Playing Chess in this itinerary.

By the thirteenth century, King Haakon unified Norway and sought extension of his domain, placing Iceland in the path of conquest. Norway successfully made vassals of Orkney, Faroes, Shetlands and Greenland, while Iceland held itself independent. Haakon sent Snorri Sturluson, as his agent, to prompt Iceland to the Norwegian fold. Snorri was part diplomat, part rabble rouser. He is also known as an author of Norse Sagas, including *Sturlunga Sagas* of the battles of Norway and Iceland. Snorri was not a neutral observer. He was of the Sturlung Clan, that by its notoriety in saga gave the name Sturlunga Age to the time of war and loss of democracy in Iceland.[161]

At the Battle of Orlygsstadir, in 1238, in northern Iceland, Sturlung clansmen led one thousand warriors against seventeen hundred independent Icelanders. Icelanders held back invasion of their land by the king of Norway. King Haakon of Norway tried another tactic.

At the time of the battle, the godar system was breaking down. A few men of a single family held several godar positions. They manipulated Thingmen to their advantage, as the few families dominated control of land. By dominating many Thingmen, fighting forces were formed, which were previously impossible in subsistence farming. While Snorri wrote Norse Sagas, complimentary of King Haakon, the king pursued the winning Icelandic warrior, Gizur Thorvaldsson. With the king as a patron, Gizur organized Iceland, used his family crest as the island seal, and became the first jarl, that is earl, of Iceland.

King Haakon died in battles in an attempt to attain the Hebrides and Isle of Mann. Snorri died in one of those battles in 1241. Snorri's nephew continued to write sagas. Haakon's son became King Magnus, giver of a new Law Code in 1271. Iceland remained under control of Norway, when Norway became dominated by Denmark. In 1814, when Norway went from Denmark to Sweden, Iceland remained territory of Denmark. Danish control of Iceland ended in 1944.

---

[161] See, Gunnar Karlsson, A Brief History of Iceland, Mal og menning, Reykjavik, 2016, pp. 16-17.

Institution of Democracy as Integral Icelandic Tradition

Skuli Magnusson Government House (prison 1813)

It would be a mistake to assume that Things ended upon Gizur becoming an earl. Placement of a royal representative was important to the king of Norway. The position meant little or nothing to Icelanders. Things and Althings were ingrained in Icelandic social systems of peace keeping, justice and regulation of property. Things were also conduits for community information, trade fairs and places of social interaction. If Things were of no political importance to kings of Norway, they held meaning for Icelanders.

There are no sagas written that record a list of Law-Speakers after 1271, when King Magnus of Norway gave a constitution of sorts to Iceland. Of record is the 1845 decree of King Christian VIII of Denmark, which allowed Things to be advisory to the resident Danish governor of Iceland. In 1873, an Althing resolved to ask the Danish king for a new constitution. A statue in front of the historic government house in Reykjavik, also residence of Danish royal representatives, shows King Christian giving Iceland a constitution, which allowed the Thing as advisory to the Danish Minister for Iceland. Icelanders did not need political decrees of foreign nations, to know their identity. Personal freedom and local decision-making emanated from established practice.

Norway became part of the Kalmar Union, a triumvirate of Norway, Sweden and Denmark, in which Denmark took control. From the 1480s to 1944, Iceland was part of Denmark. Denmark ruled Iceland as a source of fish, crops and wool to exploit for benefit of Denmark. From 1602 to 1874, Iceland was divided into trade districts, in which only Danes could pArcticipate in trade.

Foreign ships brought disease to Iceland. In 1707, there was a small-pox epidemic and in other years there was plague. In 1751 to 1758, there were crop failures and famine, during which exports to Denmark of fish and grain continued. In 1783, there was a massive volcanic eruption, followed the next year by extensive earthquakes and a haze over the sky, which brought more famine.

Iceland Parliament

By the beginning of the nineteenth century, there were forty-thousand Icelanders in the population. Hundreds of farms perished in volcanic activity and earthquakes. Through political overlords, environmental disaster and introduction of disease, Icelanders persevered. They maintained farms, Norse language, and their heritage of independent democratic society.

In 1918, Denmark agreed to home rule for Iceland. By 1920, a national court system was in force. Althings moved indoors to the Parliament Building in Reykjavik. The Parliament Building has an Art Deco style typical of the time in Europe. Women heads of households were voting members of Things since 1882. By 1911, women had equal rights to education. In a 1920 census, the urban population exceeded rural population. Reykjavik had a population of twenty thousand.

June 17, 1944 is National Day in Iceland. On that day, Denmark gave Iceland complete independence. A celebration of independence was held at Thingvellir, now a National Park.

Thingvellir National Park

Visiting Reykjavik Today

Skolavoustigur Street

Iceland needed no political capital of the realm when all legislative and judicial business was transacted in Things and at Althing in Thingvellir. In a land of farmers, there were no urban centers. Urban centers developed in Iceland, at the direction of Danish kings for use as ports.

As proof of the ongoing existence of Things, and their continual importance to Icelanders, in 1751, Skuli Magnusson and a dozen like-minded farmers requested approval at a Thing for the establishment of a commercial enterprise. *Innrettinger*, the New Enterprises, proposed to establish a factory near the fishing harbor in Reykjavik, where wool would be woven for export.

The first commercial homestead in Iceland, near the place where the first settlers landed eight hundred years earlier, became the beginning of Reykjavik as an economic capital of Iceland. At its height, the factory employed sixty to one hundred people.

In 1786, Denmark opened a window of opportunity to Icelanders. Monopoly of trade was eliminated. The wool export business of Icelanders flourished. Skuli Magnusson is regarded as the father of Reykjavik. Icelanders consider 1786 as the date the city was founded. By 1800, there were five shops in Reykjavik. The population grew to more than three hundred residents.

Harpa at the Harbor in Reykjavik

Blue Lagoon

Today, the inner harbor of Reykjavik is serene, the small fort is overshadowed by the Harp, a stunning concert hall. A monument at the seawall is dedicated to Looking Out to Sea, a tribute to lives, spent in the rough and beautiful, unspoiled Icelandic landscape. Above the harbor, a forest of cranes mark sites of a boom in hotel construction. Mainstreet is still a row, or two, of low profile, wood buildings from the harbor to the lake. Around the lake are lovely estate homes.

Parliament sits at the top of a grassy hill, where the Old Government House is at the bottom. Buildings are heated by thermal steam, a natural feature. To see the steam at the source, travel to Thingvellir National Park, where the landscape looks today as though an Althing could arrive at any time. Nearby are astounding waterfalls, geysers and the popular Blue Lagoon, the thermal swimming spot, with a poolside bar and restaurant. A lucky few will view Northern Lights.

Reykjavik Cathedral

Eric and Leif

US Monument to Leif Erikson in Reykjavik

Thus far, the story of Iceland has not included exploits of Eric the Red and his son Leif Erikson. Names so familiar to those in the United States, as to be considered synonymous with history of Iceland, are out of touch with Icelanders, who consider the men a rogue sidelight in their history. Eric the Red was born near Stavanger, Norway in 950. When he was ten, Eric's father, Thorvald Asvaldsson, committed a murder for which he was exiled to Iceland. The thought of Iceland, as a repository for criminals from Norway, has never found much appreciation in Iceland.

By the time Eric's family came to Iceland, all the good farmland was occupied by families arriving decades earlier of their free will. Eric managed to marry into a respectable family and inherit good farm land. Eric also inherited his father's temper. After causing the death of two men, Eric was sentenced by a court at a Thing to three years exile in Greenland, from 982.

Contrary to renditions of typical American history accounts of Eric, he did not discover Greenland. The Icelandic Sagas give credit to Gunnbjörn Ulfson for discovery of Greenland. Greenland's own story follows.

Eric returned to Iceland from exile, extolling the virtues of land available in Greenland, a name he gave to the island to make it sound appealing. As head of a large, now respectable family, Eric led a convoy to settle Greenland. One of the family group emigrating with Eric, was his twelve-year-old son Leif. As an adult, Leif made two haphazard sailings from Norway to Greenland, bypassing Iceland. He also sailed with able Viking mariners to forage for timber in North America, which is part of the final story of this volume.

Looking Out to Sea

In 1930, the United States commissioned a statue of Leif Erikson, by sculptor Alexander Stirling Calder, to commemorate a millennium of democratic government in Iceland, from 930. Choice of subject has always been a curious decision for Icelanders. They accepted placement of the large statue at the entrance to the US military compound. When the land reverted to Reykjavik, the city moved the statue to a traffic circle and used the former military area for a beautiful cathedral.

Travel is an experience that opens the mind and the senses. For those traveling to Iceland, lasting impressions will include experiences in amazing landscapes, of thermal pools, dramatic waterfalls and broad vistas. Hiking through Thingvellir National Park is an experience at the cusp of a fissure in the earth, that has been home to enduring democratic government since 930. Eric who? Leif who? It really does not matter. Photos taken with Ingólfr Arnarson in front of the Icelandic Parliament will be memorable.

Gullfossi near Thingvellir

GREENLAND
Mapping Greenland in the Fram

In the late nineteenth century, news of exploration of Greenland was as exciting as anticipating moon exploration almost a century later. Greenland, like north and south polar regions, was the last unexplored wilderness on the planet. Norway, like Canada, was a newly independent nation at the beginning of the twentieth century. As the two nations looked to sovereignty and expansion, between them lie Greenland, a vast opportunity, with territory still unmapped, with unknown potential.

Completing the map of Greenland in the nineteenth century required explorers of skill and experience in polar regions. Today questions of landscape are resolved by imagery conveyed from satellites. In the 1880s, knowledge of Greenland entailed skiing thousands of miles over unchartered territory and sailing through ice. Few explorers had the ability, or desire, to do so.

Otto Sverdrup skied Greenland from east to west coast with Fridtjof Nansen, with whom he later sailed Arctic seas on the *Fram*. Enduring months of depredation, in a frozen solid, totally white landscape was not new to him, when he captained the *Fram* for the third great expedition of the legendary ship to the unchartered west coast of Greenland. For his achievement, Sverdrup was received as a hero in Norway.

Norway had little time to trumpet Sverdrup's accomplishment. Canada quickly claimed as its territory all known and unknown land from the east coast of Greenland, north into the Arctic. Norway demurred to Canada. Consequently, Sverdrup's name and story are little known beyond his home country. Honor for a lifetime of accomplishment was bestowed in 1930, the year he died.

Greenland remains a little-known, massive, space on maps, of priority to many travelers only when filling in last gaps of their traversed world. Vikings are given credit for discovery of Greenland, as if surviving on the coast was conquest of the whole island. Denmark claimed Greenland, as part of booty with Iceland, when Denmark took control of Norway in the thirteenth century. For centuries, monarchs holding Greenland as territory seldom sent ships to its shores.

To know Greenland, and appreciate the skill of Inuit, who mastered life on Greenland, is to know the story of Otto Sverdrup. His story is of a time, not so long in the past, when explorers triumphed over nature, without the aid of technology. This story is a tribute to Sverdrup and his dedication to completing a map of the world. Always a modest man, he would give credit to Inuit.

Drawn to Unknown Greenland

Deck of the Fram

Eighty percent of the surface of Greenland is covered year around in ice. Inuit lived on the ice, in small family units, surviving on fishing. They did not venture south to ice-free terrain. They were not farmers. In spite of massive ice coverage, exposed land of Greenland, from the tip of Cape Farewell, up the west coast to where Nuuk, the capital, lies today, is about the size of Sweden.

Though it is known today that Greenland has rich iron deposits, iron was not evident on the surface to Norse settlers arriving in 985 with Eric the Red. Settlers noticed the absence of trees. From the first arrival of European settlers, it was obvious that life on Greenland could not be self-sufficient. Imports of wood, metal and grains were necessary to survive.

Early Norse settlers established two areas of settlement. Among habitable fjords of the southwest tip of Greenland, isolated farms comprised the Eastern Settlement, or Eystribyggo. Four hundred miles north, up the west coast, site of Nuuk today, was the Western Settlement, or Vestribyggo. A third area of settlement was begun between the two, but was soon abandoned. All settlement was below the Arctic Circle, in the southern quarter of Greenland.

Leif Erikson is credited with bringing a priest from Norway to Greenland in 1001. Leif, a dedicated pagan, performed the service as a deathbed request of King Olav.[162] Greenlanders paid church tithe in walrus ivory and animal skins. Pope Martin IV demanded gold, not animal hides, which was all people had. Testament to Christianity of Greenlanders are seventeen churches built in the Eastern Settlement and two in the Western Settlement, outsized to the small population.[163]

In the late thirteenth century, a Little Ice Age descended on the world. Life was pArcticularly harsh for Norse settlers. The Western Settlement was abandoned by 1342, while the Eastern Settlement was diminished. From across Canada, Thule people, Inuit ancestors of modern Inuit, came to Greenland. Hunting seal and walrus brought Inuit south to the area of the Eastern settlement.

---

[162] King Olav Tryggvason, was prior to Olav II, Saint Olav.
[163] Hvalsey Church, near present-day Qaqortoq had a glass window from Europe, rare in Greenland of the time.

Conflict for food was not an issue between Norse of Greenland and Inuit. Their tastes in meat differed.[164] Norse looked to ships from Iceland, or Norway, and later Denmark, to supplement their diet. In an effort to stay in touch with Europe, graves of Norse of Greenland, excavated in the early twentieth century, by Danish archaeologists, reveal people dressed in rough cloth, made into styles of fifteenth century Europeans.[165] People of the Eastern Settlement died young, growing into stunted and malnourished adults, before burial in graves marked with rune stones. In this unforgiving environment, their thoughts were of home in Iceland, or Norway, generations past.

Diminishing circumstances of the people beg the question of why they did not migrate west. The west was unknown territory. Their heritage was as farmers. Although there were no royals in Greenland, where the democratic system of Thing assembly continued in the style of Iceland, farm land was a measure of status in the community. To adopt a nomadic hunter-gather life, which served the Inuit, was a foreign and unacceptable concept to Norse farmers.

From 1000 to the 1350s, Greenlanders made regular sailings to Markland, their word for woodland, known today as Baffin Island and Labrador. By the 1350s, too few people, of too little strength, were able to sail for wood. Without wood and metal for nails and anchors, shipbuilding ceased.

Absent regular contact from Iceland, or Norway, Greenlanders were marooned. Three events resulted in total demise of Norse settlement of Greenland. The factors were: economics, disease and politics.

In 1294, King Eric VI of Denmark, sovereign ruler of Denmark, Norway, Iceland and Greenland, gave Norway a monopoly on trade with Greenland. Walrus ivory from Greenland was in demand in Europe, once walrus herds of Iceland were depleted. When Norwegian sailors located walrus on Arctic islands, closer to home, sailing to Greenland was unnecessary. By 1300, Hanseatic League sailors found sources of walrus ivory, supplanting Greenland sources and Norwegian traders. Then in 1349, the Black Death struck Norway,

---

[164] Inuit ate seal and walrus. Norse ate very little fish, despite abundance.
[165] Excavated grave goods and human remains from Greenland, were deposited in the Danish National Museum Copenhagen.

depleting its population over a two-year cycle of disease. Few Norwegian merchants sent ships far out to sea. Greenland's five thousand residents were left stranded.[166]

Finally, when later monarchs of Denmark became consumed with war and matters closer to home, the little income received from Greenland gave it a low priority. Denmark royals took Greenland off the schedule for sailing ships. Only random whalers, in violation of Danish law, made the occasional landing in fjords of the Eastern Settlement, until there were none.

In 1492, when Pope Alexander VI divided the known and unknown world between Spain and Portugal, prompted by the return of Columbus from the New World, he expressed concern that the Vatican lost touch with the bishop of Greenland. Bishops of Greenland, first appointed in 1124, were absent from Vatican contact by the early fifteenth century. The last record of a ship landing in Greenland is found in Icelandic Sagas of an event in 1406, when a ship headed to Iceland from Norway was blown off course. The last recorded marriage in Hvalsey Church, in the Eastern Settlement was in 1408. A Hanseatic merchant vessel, sailing from Hamburg to Greenland in 1541, returned to report there was no sign of life on the island.

In 1728, Hans Egede sailed to Greenland. Experienced as a Lutheran missionary, who came from Denmark to foster religion in Icelanders, he envisioned a quest to locate marooned European Greenlanders and renew their faith. As he sailed among the islands and fjords of southwest Greenland, he did not see evidence of Norse habitation. Homes, barns and all indicia of life to the early fifteenth century was eroded into mud, or collected by scavenging Inuit.[167] Not until twentieth century archaeologists made extensive investigation of the area, was it confirmed that prior Norse life on Greenland expired in the first decades of the fifteenth century.[168]

---

[166] Size of the population is a matter of debate among archaeologists, as is the number of first ships and settlers arriving with Eric the Red. It is uncontested that by the thirteenth century, when Greenland requested a bishop, the only bread known to people was communion wafers. See Sean McLachland, The Vikings in Greenland, Charles River Editors, Columbia, SC, 2020, no page number supplied.

[167] There is no evidence that Inuit attacked Norse settlers, or prompted their demise.

[168] Blue-eyed, fair haired Inuit are descendant from interaction of Inuit and eighteenth century settlers.

Egede met only Inuit in his travels in Greenland, so he amended his mission to converting Inuit to Christianity. By 1733, a missionary house was built, which became the anchor of a second wave of European settlement of Greenland. The second era of migration consisted of a broader sampling of Europeans. Danish government, culture and architectural design dominated the land.

Qaqortoq, Greenland was founded in 1775, as a destination for Danish settlers. Buildings of Danish design were brought by ship as prefabricated sections. They joined log and tar buildings, which sprang up around the harbor. In this iteration of settlement of Greenland, fishing, not farming, was the economic mainstay of residents.

Denmark looked upon Greenland as a colony for the benefit of Denmark. Royals financing establishment of settlements, expected return on investment. By 1850, Greenland was a two-tier social environment. A century of settlement created a local population, mixed to some extent with Inuit, in a blend of Danish-Scandinavian-Inuit people. Danes, of recent arrival, controlled government and commerce. Danes became wealthy on Greenland resources of fish and seals, while locals lived impoverished.

Toward the end of the nineteenth century, little more was known of the great mass of Greenland, than was known to Vikings almost a millennium earlier. In the 1870s and 1880s, scientific expeditions consisting of ski treks across the width of Greenland, disclosed breadth of the land, and the absence of any hidden pockets of habitable land. An 1870 ski expedition ended at Disko Bay, on the west of Greenland, which was found to have iron deposits.[169]

Disko Bay is a place of floating icebergs from nearby Baffin Islands glaciers. A place of hunting expeditions of Inuit and Norse, in the early Western Settlement, it is as barren today as it was in the nineteenth century. Part of Disko Bay is now preserved as home of Ilulissat Icefjord, a World Heritage Site.

---

[169] Disko is sometimes recorded as Disco.

Sverdrup and Fram Expedition to Greenland 1898-1902

Sverdrup's Fram in Fram Museum Oslo

Otto Neumann Knoph Sverdrup was born in northern Norway, in Bindal, just south of the Arctic Circle, in 1854. His family tree, for several generations before him, and in his time, was studded with politicians, inventors, theologians, scientists and academic scholars, representing a broad academy of Norwegian intelligencia. He married a cousin, and their son became an artist.

Otto Sverdrup, and his accomplishments, should not be confused with scientific contributions to oceanography of Harald Sverdrup, a third cousin.[170] At the height of Otto's efforts to map Greenland, he was confronted by fellow Norwegian Roald Amundson, who was embarking on a quest to be the first to reach the North Pole, before Robert Peary, and wanted no competition from Otto. In Amundson's group, at the time of the meeting, was Harald, who was recording Arctic data. Amidst a family of accomplishment, Otto was pleased to devote himself to study of the Arctic, a place with which he was familiar from birth. His accomplishments, though great, have often been lost in the shadow of family fame and fame of his friend, Fridjof Nansen.

Otto was introduced to Fridjof Nansen by Nansen's brother, a friend of Otto. Sverdrup and Nansen, seven years his junior, became a team, in which exploration of the Arctic became the passion of their lives.[171] Of interest to the two Arctic explorers was the unknown mass of Greenland.

A map of Greenland, dated to 1818, in aid of Danish resettlement of the island, names places on the east coast, also noted as unreachable, due to ice flow. Places from Cape Farewell at the southern tip of Greenland, indicated as an island on the map, and progressing up the west coast to Disko Bay are noted. The map shows a strait, the Olhunlongri Strait, from Disko Bay on the west coast to the east coast, as if an open waterway existed. Actually, the area is the deepest point of the ancient ice field that covers Greenland.[172]

Swedish Arctic explorer, Adolf Erik Nordenskjöld, made his attempt to cross the ice of Greenland, from Disko Bay eastward in 1870. An able skier, Nordenskjöld turned back after trudging a quarter of the distance across Greenland. In 1878, he turned his attention to crossing the Northeast Passage in his ship, the *Vega*. He has his own story of accomplishment in this itinerary.

---

[170] Harald Sverdrup, born in Norway in 1888, and died in Oslo in 1957, was director of Scripps Institution of Oceanography in San Diego, California from 1936 to 1948, and the Norwegian Polar Institute as of 1948.

[171] Fridjof Nansen was born in 1861 and died the same year as Sverdrup, 1930. He was awarded a Nobel Peace Prize in 1922, for work after World War I, to exchange and bring to their homes, 400,000 prisoners of war between Russia, Germany and Austria; and later to bring starving Russians, out of Russia, during a famine. Nansen was High Commissioner of Refugees for the League of Nations in 1922.

[172] John Gertner, The Ice at the End of the World, Random House, New York, 2019.

In 1888, Nansen invited Otto to join him on a cross-island exploration of Greenland. Their mission was to determine if open land existed in the sheet of ice. They sailed from western Iceland down the east coast of Greenland and back north along the coast to Umivik, Nansen Harbor today. In August, they skied two hundred and sixty miles, over eleven weeks, viewing nothing but white ice in every direction. When the small party reached the west coast at Amerikalikfjord, they built a boat and rowed to the Danish settlement at Godthab.

While overwintering at Godthab, the pair stayed with Inuit families and learned to eat from the land in frozen territory and to handle dogs for sledding across the ice. Lessons learned that winter became life-saving skills in future expeditions. The two men, now eternally bonded as an exploration team, returned to Oslo in May 1889, as national heroes.

Life on Fram

Nansen as expedition leader and Sverdrup as captain of the *Fram*, sailed the purpose-built Arctic exploration ship from 1893 to 1896, in an effort to sail to the North Pole. Their experience is a separate story. During the expedition, Nansen left the *Fram* to ski to the Pole and return to the ship. Missing the *Fram* by hours, he and his companion skied to civilization. No doubt, the skills learned from Inuit in Greenland were useful for survival on the adventure story of his life. Nansen was once again received as a hero, had numerous places on the map named for him, and had a statue of him erected in Oslo. Sverdrup's contributions slid into the background.

In 1898, Sverdrup was given the *Fram*, as captain and leader of a mission of his design, to map the north of Greenland, where no ship had gone before him. Numerous explorers had sailed up the east and west coast of Greenland, none making a comprehensive map. The map of northeast Canada was filling in, with a large blank spot around Ellesmere Island and Greenland. For four arduous years, from 1898 to 1902, Sverdrup mapped the High Arctic, where other captains lacked his skill in the Arctic and his marvel of a ship, the *Fram*.[173]

With sixteen men and eighty dogs, Sverdrup used his Arctic skills, learned with Nansen in Godthab, to traverse the unknown and map Ellesmere Islands. During their expedition, the men ate musk ox and polar bear, living like Inuit to survive in extreme cold, which reached minus sixty Fahrenheit. As the planned three-year expedition approached a fourth year, the doctor for the trip committed suicide. Life in the Arctic tested explorers, some past the point of an ability to endure.

During almost four years mapping the last remaining unknown land of the earth, between the Arctic continents, Sverdrup collected scientific specimen, improved on maps of those before him and determined whether areas were islands or peninsulas. As he headed home, job done, ice blocked the exit, even for the *Fram*. One more winter was spent in Gasefjorden, near the site where one hundred and thirty men, on two ships, perished in 1845. Crew of the *Fram* left notes in rock piles along their route, should the worst occur and searchers have need to find them.

---

[173] Before departing to unchartered water, or land, Sverdrup met Robert Peary, on his way to the North Pole. Peary was in a competition with Amundson and wanted no further competition from Sverdrup.

On September 18, 1902, the *Fram* sailed in the harbor at Stavanger to a hero's reception. Officials boarded the *Fram* before it sailed into Oslo harbor, with an escort of hundreds of small craft and thousands of spectators on the shore. This time accolades for three hundred thousand kilometers, that is one hundred and eighty-six-thousand square miles of land mapped went to Sverdrup.

Sverdrup, and those who trekked the landscape with him, spent seven hundred and sixty-two nights in tents on ice. The *Fram* traveled eighteen thousand kilometers, that is eleven thousand two-hundred miles. The team collected fifty thousand plant and two thousand animal specimens. From soil samples collected, oil and gas exploration focused on new areas on the map. Thirty scientists spent the next twenty years analyzing material, resulting in five volumes of reports and dozens of scientific dissertations. A generation of Arctic scholarship was informed by efforts of Sverdrup and his crew.

Fram Museum Oslo

Sverdrup wished to claim the previously unchartered landscape in the name of his mother country, Norway. Norway was part of Sweden at the time. Norway was unable, and Sweden was unwilling, to make the land claim. In 1905, Norway was independent of Sweden. It still declined to claim land of the Arctic on the far side of Danish Greenland. Sverdrup moved to Cuba.

In Cuba, Sverdrup invested in banana, cocoa and coffee plantations, until dry weather caused his venture to end in financial failure. He moved to Alaska and bought into a forestry venture, until World War I interrupted business. In 1914, at the age of sixty, Sverdrup was back in the Arctic, leading a team of a hundred reindeer, pulling sledges, as he commandeered a heroic rescue of two Russian naval, polar explorer ships.

The final challenge met by Sverdrup came in Oslo, where he championed preservation of the *Fram* and the legacy of he and Nansen. Sverdrup and Nansen died in 1930, the year Canada claimed Ellesmere Islands, without opposition from Norway. In 1936, the *Fram* Museum opened in the Oslo harbor, where the original ship is housed in a purpose-built museum building. Maps today show Sverdrup Island off the northern tip of Greenland.

Greenland Today

Greenland remained a Danish colony until 1953. It had a closed economy, dependent upon Denmark until World War II. Home rule was established in 1979, and the Greenland parliament became fully self-governing in 2009. Today, Greenland is a constitutional monarchy, in which the Danish monarch presides. The capital of Nuuk, near the Viking Western Settlement, is a city of seventeen thousand among a national population of fifty-six thousand.

Today Qaqortoq is a city of three thousand residents, the largest in southern Greenland. Although Inuit/Danish in historic culture, a second era of Norwegian influence is seen in colorful small buildings on the landscape. Dots of color stand out from white rocks and red algae in the summer landscape, from which Inuit derived the city name, which means white rocks.

Qaqortoq has an early nineteenth century historic cluster, which includes the 1804 blacksmith shop. Rock carvings seen around the city and surrounding hills, are the work of contemporary artisans, channeling ancient designs. Greenland is quaint, a bastion of environmental preservation, and a place of evolving cultural expression.

Greenland economy today is largely based on fishing, oil and tourism. Three-quarters of oil extracted is sent to Denmark. Greenland remains a bit of Denmark in the north Atlantic.

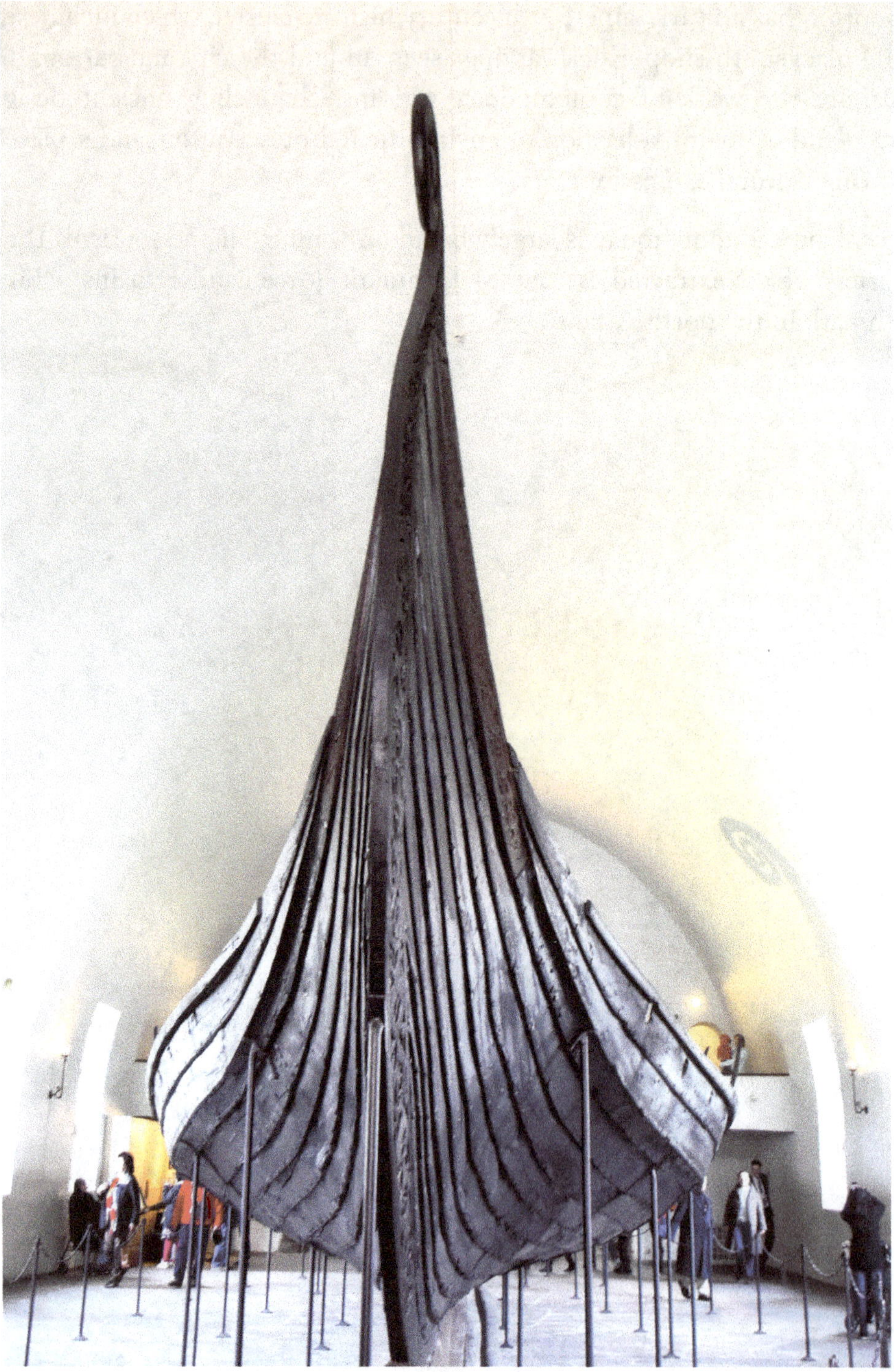

Viking Engineering

Discovery of the End of the Old World and Beginning of the New World

From the ninth to eleventh centuries, Vikings were the dominant sailors of the north Atlantic. No more violent, or mercenary, than soldiers of European lords, Viking superior technology in ship-building and choice of fine weapons, together with a healthy population of extra sons of land-based farmers and lords of western Norway, gave the Viking Age notoriety for ships and a reputation for raids, the scourge of coastal Europe, England and Baltic domains. In actual fact, Vikings added to exploration of the north Atlantic, to an extent not replicated for five hundred years.

Vikings emanated from a society of farmers, who were also great sailors. Living in the fjords of western Norway, the so-called Vesterland, meant small farms of coastal settlements, that hardly qualified as villages. Lives, trade and communication with other settlements, were conducted by conduit on the water. Viewed today, Viking ships, preserved in tombs, or risen from sunken ships at sea, are a marvel of engineering. To create such finely crafted ships, with only crude tools, amidst a small population, where specialized skills were rare, is a marvel of the Medieval world.

Some Vikings farmers were pressed to sea by scarcity of land in the growing population of Norway. They were also imbued with Viking democratic principles, which drove them from impending subjugation under Norwegian kings. Curious and risk-taking, confident in abilities to traverse great bodies of water, Viking sailors were never reluctant to seek the next island in search of land, or, as opportunities presented, the next easy target in a monastery full of silver and English coin.[174]

---

[174] Sean McLachlan writes in, The Vikings in Greenland, Charles River Editors, Columbia, SC, 2020, that more English silver coin of the age has been recovered in Scandinavia than in the British Isles.

A cruise itinerary across the sub-Arctic, north Atlantic, begs the popular question of who discovered North America. Does credit go to Leif Erikson, or Christopher Columbus? The two sailors are separated by five hundred years and thousands of miles of sea between routes. Vikings interested in locating trees to build ships, or on raiding excursions, did not keep detailed records, although they kept logs for which they receive little credit. Columbus engaged in years of study, to determine the extent of knowledge of the world, before he set sail. His maps are of record.

This little story sails from Greenland to the extent of the known Old World, to forays into the New World. During the Viking Age, Norse sailors headed west in search of new land. This itinerary of stories ends at the farthest extent of the Norse world from the North Sea to the west.

Sailing West in the Tenth Century

Coastal Settlement

In June 793, after crops were planted, a rowdy bunch of exuberant young men sailed off from western Norway, looking for excitement. The coast of England was an easy few days sailing. In summer weather, with long days and clear skies, navigating west presented little challenge.

Summer winds and ocean currents took the flotilla of ships from the southern fjords of Norway to beaches of the east coast of Britain. Before the mainland lie islands, known as Holy Islands for the monastery founded by monks from Iona. This was Lindisfarne. In the Lindisfarne Priory monks copied manuscripts and attended to religious duties.[175]

Lindisfarne Priory

Ships on the beach were of no concern to the monks. Pilgrims came to Holy Island, although June was not a month of a pArcticular celebration. Surviving monks later recorded streaming hordes of pagans rampaging through the priory. Shocked and defenseless, the number of Vikings landing on Lindisfarne that day seemed a great number. The actual number is unknown.

---

[175] Lindisfarne Priory today is a ruin of its early Middle Ages. The castle on the hill was built in the sixteenth century.

The attack on Lindisfarne is regarded as the beginning of the Viking Age. Not all Norse were Vikings. Those Norse that went *a-viking*, that is out for adventure and pillaging, found the monks easy prey, yielding a great deal of unprotected treasure. Results of the random adventure were too attractive not to repeat. The Viking Age continued for about two centuries, until Viking leaders found homes in new lands more attractive than summers at sea. Some Vikings became Christian.

Over the ninth century, Vikings landed further north on coasts of the British Isles. Coastal settlements were raided around Scotland, the Orkneys, Faroes, and Shetland Islands. In a few places, Vikings maintained camps, from which to stage raids further inland. Vikings were sailors, not an army. Inland raids were not deep incursions. As their infamy spread, and settlements became guarded, or occupants fled with valuables, once ships with rows of colorful shields appeared, Vikings continued ever westward. They landed in the Hebrides, stopped at Iona, and continued to Isle of Man. In 841, Vikings arrived in Dublin. They liked it there and some stayed.

Other westward Vikings went from the Faroe Islands to Iceland. Norse settlers were established in Iceland by 870. In the tenth century, travel to Iceland became routine. Entire communities in the fjords of western Norway were depopulated, when communities left for Iceland. Some people left fjords of Norway for fjords of Iceland, to find farmland for growing numbers of families. Others left Norway, either to avoid becoming vassals of the king, or having fought on the wrong side in battles of royal succession. So many villages of western Norway were depopulated during this time, that the king instituted an emigration tax.[176] To avoid the tax, people left in secret.

By 930, Iceland society was fully functioning as a social network, independent of Norway. Icelanders farmed and fished, rendering themselves self-sufficient in place. At the beginning of the eleventh century, when going a-viking lost most of its allure, Iceland was an island unified, not under a king, or by a religious leader, rather by a democratic alliance governed in Things.

---

[176] Assumptions that Iceland was populated by murders in exile is not supported by historical facts. Exile was a common method of punishment in extreme cases. Thousands of people, entire families, left Norway for Iceland in a few decades.

Seekers of new land continued to sail west. Around the west fjords of Iceland, ice floes came each spring. By summer ice was sufficiently dispersed to allow ships to sail to the east coast of new territory. Arctic current carried ships south, along the east coast to the tip of the land mass and around to warmer coves. The southern tip of Greenland, Cape Farewell, is the entrance to coves and inner fjords of islands, warmed by northern flowing Atlantic current. As yet unnamed, Greenland was known to Icelandic sailors, as a treeless, unoccupied, foreboding place.[177]

Norse sagas give credit to Gunnbjörn Ulfson for the discovery of land to the west of Iceland. This does not mean that he landed on the new territory, or explored its attributes. Assuming all land to be much like home, in the heavily wooded fjords of Norway, or Iceland, the new land was thought to be a future home for expansion. Until then, it was an opportune place to banish exiles.

Eric the Red

---

[177] Greenland is only above freezing temperatures in July.

Eric the Red was an Icelander, born in Norway, who came to Iceland as a youth, when his father was exiled for murder. Continuing family history, Eric, as hot-headed as his father, left two men dead. In a court hearing, during a Thing in 982, Eric was banished to the new land, for three years.

At the time the family was sent to Greenland, Eric's son Leif was of about the same age as Eric, when his family came to Iceland. Eric made history as the first European to land in Greenland. Eric was fortunate to sail from western Iceland and become caught in the same southern currents, which carried Ulfson around Cape Farewell, to warm turf in southwestern coves of Greenland.

Though Eric found no timber and no metal, the two critical components of Norse sailing ships, he found ample grass for his herd of cattle.[178] Eric did not remain long enough to notice that the grasses became depleted year to year. He returned to Iceland, triumphant with news of a place he called Greenland. He envisioned himself, the son of an exile, an exile himself, as leader of a colony in a new land.

Eric returned to Greenland in 985 with twenty-five ships, transporting a total settler group of about seven hundred people.[179] Inuit people appeared, dispelling any idea that the place was uninhabited. Inuit were peaceful people, who lived near the sea and survived from fishing. The new arrivals from Iceland brought cattle and survived on meat and dairy.

Settlers quickly realized that growing season was short. They supplemented their diet from grains brought from Iceland. They also realized that they needed to find sources of wood, for building homes and ships, as well as for fuel. If they were to survive, someone must continue to sail west to find sources of what they lacked in their new home. Eric quickly lost esteem among settlers.

---

[178] Iron deposits were found in 1870, in Disco Bay, by geologist Nils Otto Nordenskiöld, skiing across Greenland.

[179] Some Sagas give Eric credit for leading fourteen ships with about four hundred settlers. Eric is a controversial figure in the Norse world.

New Found Land – The Saga of Leif

Leif Erikson

Leif, son of Eric, does not have his own saga. His tale of travels comes down through time in the *Vinland Sagas*, a compellation of Norse Sagas, which includes the *Greenlander's Saga*, likely written at the end of the twelfth century and *Eric the Red's Saga*, written in the mid-thirteenth century. When recalling the story of Leif, the two sagas differ. Historians typically find the earlier saga a more credible account of discovery of new land by Leif. Later sagas become couched in terms giving the ancestors of a nominated bishop greater acclaim for discovery of new lands.

Contender for discovery of north American land is Bjarni Herjulfsson. In 985, Bjarni was sailing from Iceland to Greenland, when he overshot Greenland and next saw land of a hilly, wooded place. The best candidate for the sighting is Labrador. Bjarni did not land. He sailed north to glaciers, known today as Baffin Island, before heading east to Greenland.

An eleventh century collector of information of world travelers, Adam of Bremen, wrote all he knew of Norse travelers in 1075.[180] That treatise was relied upon by Ari Thurgilsson, also known as Ari the Learned. Ari wrote *Islendingabók*, Book of the Icelanders, in 1120. Ari's text informed Greenlander's Saga, further preserved in the 1367 text *Flateyjarbók*. Perhaps the writers knew how controversial were the travels of Leif during his lifetime. They assumed, correctly, that controversy would persist through the ages.

Leif was known in his time as a traveler. He was not known as a great navigator. He was in Norway, in service to the king of Norway until death of the king brought him home in 1001. Leif made two sailings from Norway to Greenland, bypassing Iceland. The sagas give him no credit for sailing skills, or ability as a navigator. He survived both sailings by luck.

The Greenlander Sagas, giving credit to Leif for leading the first European landing in north America, are careful to distinguish Bjarni for a sighting, not a landfall. Bjarni is credited as an experienced sailor and talented navigator. Leif followed the route of Bjarni, in reverse. He left west Greenland and easily reached glacial Baffin Islands, which Leif named Helluland, Land of the Flat Rocks. Leif made a point of landing on a few rocks before he sailed further.

---

[180] Adam of Bremen was German, as was a sailor with Leif, who found the vines of Vinland.

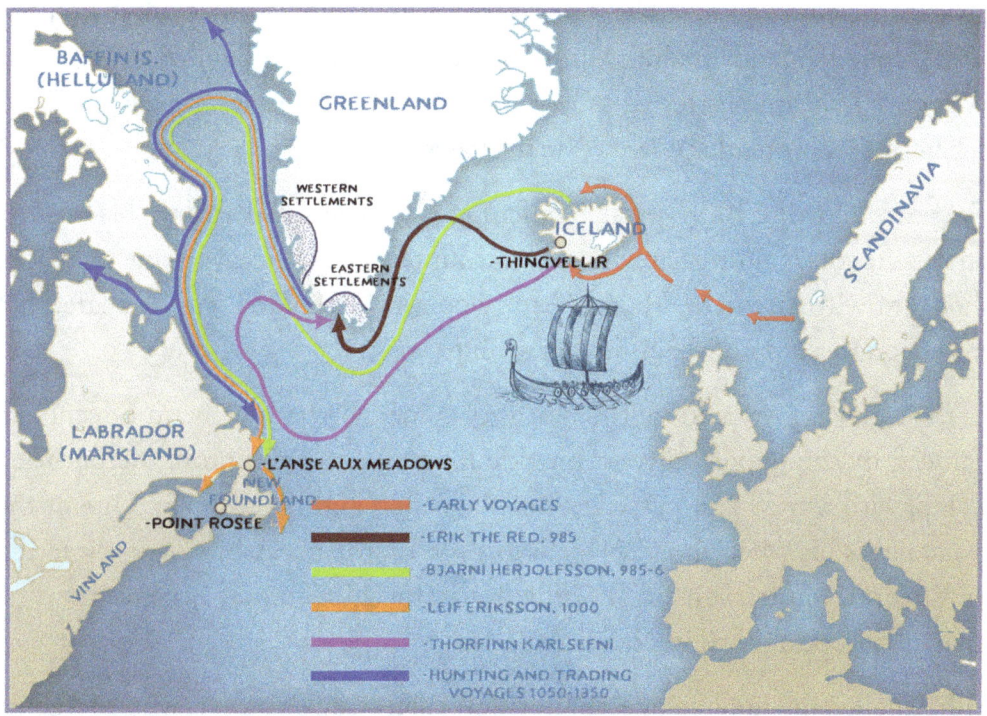

As Leif sailed southward he came to a land, where plentiful trees were visible from the sea. He named the land Markland, old Norse for Forest Land. From descriptions and maps created over the centuries thereafter, Markland is the area now known as Labrador. Greenlanders in need of wood, made repeated trips to Markland.

From Markland, the sagas tell us that Leif sailed northeast then south for two days before he landed in Vinland. In this place Leif built a large house, which in the next years he rented to other Greenlanders, including his brother and sister. Leif described his choice of landing as a place between an island and a large promontory. From descriptions of salmon and sailing positions, in addition to later maps, the landing is attributed to Labrador and L'Anse aux Meadows in Newfoundland.

A German sailor in Leif's crew trekked a distance, while the remaining crew built the longhouse and fished for salmon. The man returned with berries, which the group understood to be from vines. There were no Norse-German interpretors in the group. Leif called the land Vinland.

Sixteenth century map-makers put Vinland in Labrador. Twentieth century writers put Vinland further south, where grapes are known to grow today. Whether Leif ate berries or grapes, the mystique of Leif's travels spawned debates of who first discovered North America.

The year following Leif's establishment of a campsite at Vinland, his brother Thorval made a return trip. Thorval encountered local natives, one of whom shot him with an arrow. The need for wood in Greenland was so acute, that the encounter did not deter further sailings west.

In the following year, a wealthy Norwegian ice merchant came to Greenland. Enticed by the opportunity to provide lumber at a great profit, he outfitted a ship, with a crew and passengers of sixty men and five women. One of the women was his wife, who gave birth to a son on the trip, while over-wintering in Vinland. Snorri, son of Thorfinn Karlsefni and Gundi, became the first known European born in North America.

While collecting lumber, one of Thorfinn's men struck a native, who had come to trade furs. Thorfinn reinforced his homestead with a defensive wall. A large group of natives returned, possibly for trade. Thorfinn's men expected a battle and killed numerous natives.[181] If Greenlanders had hopes for expeditions further south or inland, their encounter with natives compromised plans.[182]

---

[181] Natives encountered by Thorfinn were likely Algonquin.
[182] Eric the Red's Saga includes exploits of his daughter Freydis. The next summer after Thorfinn's encounter with natives, he remained in Greenland, while Freydis joined ships with two brothers, Helgi and Finnbogi. Once in Vinland she refused to share the lodge she rented from her brother Leif. Left in the cold, the two men collected lumber. One morning Freydis visited Helgi and offered to buy his ship. She returned home and told her husband the two men attacked her. To avenge Freydis, Helgi and Finnbogi were killed. Their ships were loaded and Freydis claimed the cargo, she then sold to Thorfinn. Thorfinn wasted no time leaving Greenland for Norway.

Detail Clinker Built, Nails & Oarlocks

Viking Legacy Today

Early Settlement

In 1960, archaeologists located the long house of Leif Erikson near L'Anse aux Meadows on Newfoundland, corroborating the *Greenlander's Saga*. The turf lodge had a capacity for seventy to ninety occupants. Efforts of some theorists to consider the site a settlement, supporting a population of up to five hundred residents, lack credibility, when the population of Greenland at the time of Leif's travels was about four hundred to five hundred people. For ninety adult males to sail from home for more than a season, possibly overwintering in the new land, put the entire base community at risk. Obtaining wood was worth some risk. The number of sailors was limited.

Using the description of Leif, and accounts of the sagas, to compare sites described to places south of Labrador is problematic. Creative speculation places travels of Leif anywhere from Cape Cod and New York, to Florida. Beyond Labrador is likely out of range of Leif's two-day sailing.

This story now returns to the original question of whom to credit with discovery of the New World. Informed by the travels of Leif, Greenlanders had mastery of sailing the Labrador Sea. Sagas and recent archaeology agree that Greenlanders came to Newfoundland for timber. They neither settled the area, nor went further south. After conflict with natives, Greenlanders went no further than Markland for lumber, until the early fifteenth century, when they ceased sailing.

Columbus had access to knowledge of the world known to Europeans of his day. He corresponded with those who could fill in blank spots on his map prior to sailing. Neither Columbus, nor the later sailing captains Champlain or Hudson, had maps of North America. Prior to Columbus, Europeans had no knowledge of the western hemisphere, other than the far north, or the breadth of the Atlantic.

Algonquin and Mi'kmaq natives encountered by Leif and his siblings do not join in this debate on discovery. They had no question of the existence of their domain. Violent encounters, ending in death of natives, begun by Thorfinn, were just the beginning of their troubled history with Europeans. That history, begun in this itinerary, continues in another itinerary, with more stories.

INDEX

A

Abel, Niels Henrik, 123
Age of Discovery, 257, 259, 303
Algonquin, 382
Althing, 339, 342-344, 346, 348, 351, 353
Amundsen, Roald, 115, 155
Archer, Colin, 112
Architectural style
    Amsterdam Renaissance, 12, 83, 90
    Art Deco, 350
    Art Nouveau, 177, 242
    Brick Gothic, 30
    Dutch Renaissance, 73, 77, 83
    English-Romanesque, 220
    Gothic, 22-23, 29-30, 159, 217-218, 220, 238
    Neo-classical, 73, 77
Arnarson, Ingólfr, 340, 343
Asbjørnsen, Peter Christian
    Soria Moria Castle, 178
Asleifarson, Svein, 278
Astrup, Nikolai, 166
Asvaldsson, Thorvald, 110
Attila the Hun, 194

B

Barents, Willem, 163
Battle of
    Bulge (Bastogne 1944-1945), 32, 40
    Drøbak Sound (1940), 154
    Golden Spurs (1302), 24-25
    Hastings (1066), 107, 198, 278
    Houplines (Christmas 1914), 39
    Lepanto (1571), 312
    Orlygsstadir (1238), 347
    Passchendaele (1917), 32, 39, 55
    Portland (1653), 81
    Somme (1916), 179
    Stamford Bridge (1066), 107, 183, 218
    Stiklestad (1030), 196, 218, 226, 231
    Tsushima Strait (1905), 269
    Waterloo (1815), 32, 38
    Ypres (Ipers) (1914-1917), 39, 49
Beguinage (Belgium), 23
Bering, Vitus, 264-265
Birchlegs, 12, 15, 181, 185-187, 191
Birchlegs America (Ski Race), 191
Bleuet de France, 54
Blücher, Gebhard von, 38
Bolshevik, 291, 324-330
Bragi the Old, 175
Breydel, Jan, 24
Brimeu, Marie (Princess Chimay), 88
Brun, Bishop Johan Nordahl, 153, 165
Brunel, Oliver, 263
Bull, Ole, 164, 167, 169-170
Burrough, Stephen, 261, 306, 308, 315

C

Cabot, Sebastian & John, 259
Castles and Palaces
    Akershus Fortress (Oslo), 109, 155
    Bergenhus Fortress (Bergen), 203, 205, 211
    Cranenburg House (Brugge), 25
    Fort Oscarsborg (Oslofjord), 153-154
    Fredriksten Fortress (Norway), 129, 148-149
    Ghent Castle, 35

Hotel Refsnes Gods (Oslofjord), 151
Rosenkrantz Tower (Bergen), 190, 210
Slottsfjellet Tower (Tønsberg), 149
Steinvikholm Castle (Trondheim), 224
Topaki Palace (Istanbul), 93
Town Hall (Brugge), 30
Chancellor, Richard, 261, 304, 306
Chelyuskin, Semion, 265

Churches
Abby of Saint Omer (Calais), 27
Basilica of the Holy Blood (Brugge), 21-22
Fredrikstad Cathedral (Oslofjord), 149
Hvalsey Church (Greenland), 363
Lindisfarne Priory (England), 375
Munkeliv Monastery/Abby (Bergen), 160
Nidaros Cathedral (Trondheim), 215, 217, 220, 222-227, 231-232, 281
Noorderkerk (Amsterdam), 87, 90
Nykirken (Bergen), 163
Our Lady (Brugge), 29
St. Clements's (Trondheim), 231
St. Donation Cathedral (Brugge), 21
St. Mary's (Bergen), 163, 201
St. Mary's (Trondheim), 219
St. Olav's (Trondheim), 219
Westerkerk (Amsterdam), 83-84, 90
Zuiderkerk (Amsterdam), 77, 83-84, 90

Churchill, Winston, 289, 293, 325, 330, 334
Cicignon, Major General Johan Caspar, 227
Clusius, Carolus (Charles de L'Escluse) *Historia*, 95
Columbus, Christopher, 13, 27, 94, 258, 274
Cominek, Pieter de, 24
Convention of Moss, 152

D

da Vinci Bridge, 154
Danish Theater (Bergen), 162
Dark Ages, 11, 17, 30, 181
Dolk (Lundgren), 168
Dutch East India Company, 57-58, 60-61, 77, 83, 92, 94, 96, 100
Dutch West India Company, 57-58, 66, 68, 100

E

Egede, Hans, 363
Eisenhower, President (General) Dwight David, 40
Engelbrektsson, Archbishop Olav, 226, 240
Eric the Red, 110, 278, 355, 361, 363, 377-378, 380, 382
Erikson, John, 136
Erikson, Leif, 13, 110, 355-356, 361, 374, 379, 384
European Union, 36
Eystein, Archbishop Trondheim, 217, 220-224, 226, 238, 240, 284-285, 346

F

Flemish Primitives, 26
Frederick III (Denmark), 148
Frobisher, Martin, 262
Frommer, Arthur, 37

G

Gad, Cille, 159, 161
George, Prime Minister Sir Lloyd, 329
Gomez, Estevan, 260
Grágás (Grey Goose), 344-345
Grieg, Edvard Hagerup, 165
Grieg, Johan Nordahl Brun
Freedom, 23-24, 58, 76, 166, 229, 349
The Ship Sails On, 165

Grimkell, Bishop of Nidaros, 219
Gruuthuse, Louis, 28
Guerin, Anna, 53
Gupta Empire, 274

H

Hansa Riot 1455, 159-160
Hanseatic League (Hansa), 36, 199, 310, 362
Helmer, Lieutenant Alexis, 49
Hepburn, James, 4th Earl of Bothwell, 239
Herjulfsson, Bjarni, 380
Heyerdahl, Hans
    Girl at the Window, 151
Heyerdahl, Thor
    Kon Tiki, 105, 116
Holberg, Ludvig
    Gynaicologia, or a Defense of the Female Sex, 162
Holy Blood, 21-22
Hudson, Henry, 67-68, 258-259, 262
Hugo, Victor, 139

I

Ibsen, Henrik
    Peer Gynt, 177
International Peace and Arbitration Association, 142
Inuit, 360-364, 367-368, 370, 378
Iron Age, 151
Ironside, Colonel (Field Marshall)

J

Jonsson, Bishop Pall, 284

K

Kalmar Union (Tre Croner), 203, 208, 222, 349

Keyser, Hendrick de, 73, 83, 90
Kings, Queens & other Royals
    Albert I (Belgium), 38
    Alexander II (Russia), 137, 327
    Baldwin Iron Arm (1st Count Flanders), 19
    Black Knight (England), 37
    Caesar, Julius (Roman), 19
    Canute (England, Denmark, Norway), 196, 198, 218, 221, 237, 277
    Catherine II, the Great (Russia), 162, 312
    Charlemagne (Franks), 32, 37
    Charles II (England), 68
    Charles the Bald (France), 19
    Christian I (Denmark), 205, 208
    Christian II (Denmark), 209-210
    Christian III (Denmark), 224, 239
    Christian V (Denmark), 227
    Clovis (Franks), 37
    Derek of Alsace, Count Flanders, 21
    Edward I (England), 189
    Edward III (England), 37-38
    Elizabeth I (England), 37, 311
    Eric I, Bloody Axe (Norway), 108, 149
    Eric III Norway), 205
    Eric of Pomerania (Poland), 204-205
    Eystein I (Norway), 184, 206
    Franz Joseph (Austria), 326
    Frederick II (Denmark), 148
    Frederick VI (Denmark), 110
    Haakon III (Norway), 187
    Haakon IV (Norway), 187-188, 191, 210
    Haakon the Good (Norway), 108
    Haakon V (Norway), 110, 189
    Haakon VII (Norway), 110
    Harald I (Fairhair, Norway), 149
    Harald II (Norway, England), 108
    Harald III (Norway), 107
    Harald V (Norway), 222
    Henry VIII (England), 310

Inge I (Norway), 185
Inge II (Norway), 188
Ivan IV, the Terrible (Russia), 13, 274
James II (England), 68
Karl XII (Sweden), 149
Louis XIV (France), 35
Magnus (Norway), 157, 159, 183, 185-186, 198
Magnus II (Norway), 181, 183-184
Magnus IV (Norway), 185-187
Magnus V (Norway), 188-189
Maria of Burgundy (Hapsburg), 25, 28-29
Mauritus (Prince of Netherlands), 57, 61
Maximilian (Hapsburg Austria), 25, 28
Maximilian II (Holy Roman Emperor), 88
Nicholas II (Russia), 269, 290, 327
Olaf II (Norway), 109
Olav III (Norway), 181, 183, 193, 198, 206, 213, 220, 225
Oscar II (Norway), 111
Pepin (Franks), 32
Peter I, the Great (Russia), 164, 312, 314-315
Philip II (Spain), 37, 58-59
Suleiman the Magnificent (Ottoman), 93
Sverre (Norway), 185-187, 198, 220, 238, 240, 246
Victoria (England), 313, 327
William (Duke of Orange, Dutch), 59
William I (the Conqueror, England), 198, 274
Kinsky, Bertha (Countess von Chinic, von Suttner)
  Lay Down Your Arms, 142
Kittelsen, Theodor Severin, 166, 177
Kjaer, Nils, 244
Klippfisk, 241
Knights of Saint John, 23, 27, 29

L

Laptev, Dmitri, 265
Law of Lübeck, 20, 24
Lenin, Vladimir (Nicolai Zederblum), 291, 325, 327
Lewis Chessmen, 272, 278-279, 281
Lindisfarne, 195, 237, 375-376
Linnaeus, Carl, 88
Little Ice Age, 194, 361

M

Margret the Adroit, 284
Matines of Bruges, 25
McCrae, Lieutenant Colonel John
  A Song of Comfort, 47
  Anxious Dead, 50
  In Flanders Fields, 11, 31-32, 35, 38-40, 43, 46-47, 49-51, 55
Memling, Hans
  Mystic Marriage of St. Catherine, 28
  Reliquary of Saint Ursula, 27
Memorials
  Alyosha (Murmansk), 288
  Essex Farm (Flanders), 39
  Menin Gate (Ypres), 40-43
  Murmansk Convoys (Archangel), 13
  Tyne Cot Cemetery (Passchendaele), 43
  Wimereux Cemetery (Boulogne-Sur-Mer), 50
  Woman Who Waits (Murmansk), 299, 301
Mi'kmaq, 385
Michael, Moina Belle
  The Miracle Flower, 52
Moe, Jørgen, 117
Munch, Edvard
  The Scream, 118, 151
Murmansk Convoys, 13, 289, 292-293, 298, 300, 321

Museum
　Anne Frank House (Amsterdam), 89-90
　Bergen, 12, 14-15, 109, 150, 157-171, 181-191, 193-196, 198-199, 201-206, 208-211, 213, 217, 220-221, 235-240, 242-243, 249-250, 253, 255, 279, 281
　British (London), 223, 272, 278, 281
　Cement (Oslofjord), 154
　Coster Diamonds (Amsterdam), 104
　Cultural History (Oslo), 110
　Emanuel Vigeland Studio (Oslo), 130
　Flanders Fields (Ypres), 38, 43
　Flåm Railway History, 253
　Fram (Oslo), 12, 105-106, 111, 114-116, 268, 365, 369-370
　Frogner Park (Oslo), 121-122, 126-127, 129-130
　Groeninge (Brugge), 28
　Gruuthuse (Brugge), 28-29
　Hansa (Bergen), 12, 190, 193, 198, 201-203, 206, 208-211, 238-239
　Henie-Onstad Cultural Center (Oslo), 118
　Iceland National (Reykjavik)., 339
　KODE (Bergen), 169-170
　Kon-Tiki (Oslo), 12, 106, 117, 155
　Kristiansten Fortress (Trondheim), 229
　KunstLab Children's (Bergen), 170
　McCrae House (Guelph, Ontario), 46-50, 52, 55
　Memling (Brugge), 26-28
　Merchant Yard (Archangel), 313, 321
　Munch (Oslo), 117, 151, 169
　National Gallery (Oslo), 151
　Natural History (Bergen), 169, 266
　Nobel Peace Center (Oslo), 119, 134, 141, 144
　Rembrandt House (Amsterdam), 78
　Rijksmuseum (Amsterdam), 90
　Ringve Manor Museum of Music (Trondheim), 229
　Royal Treasury (Copenhagen), 154, 224
　Scottish National Museum (Edinburgh), 272, 278, 281
　Swedish National Museum of Natural, 266
　The Hague (Netherlands), 98, 264
　Tower of London, 34, 54-55
　University of Bergen History, 169, 206
　Vigeland Sculpture Arrangement (Oslo), 127
　Vigeland Studio (Oslo), 126
　Viking Ship (Oslo), 12, 105, 110, 149-151, 155, 373
　Westerkerk Tower (Amsterdam), 90

N

Nansen, Fridtjof, 111, 349
Nidaros Cathedral Restoration Workshop, 231
Nilsson, Olav, 12, 190, 193, 211
Nordenskjöld, Adolf Erik, 265, 366
Norse Sagas
　Eric the Red's Saga, 380, 382
　Flateyjarbók, 380
　Greenlander's Saga, 380, 384
　Islendingabók, Book of the Icelanders, 380
　Modruvellir Saga, 340
　Orkney Saga, 278
　Sturlunga Saga, 340
　Vinland Sagas, 380

P

Patton, General George S., 40
Pershing, General John J., 39
Poole, Commander Frank, 325

Popes
    Alexander III, 109
    Innocent II, 186
    Innocent IV, 187
    Martin IV, 361

R

Reichborn, Johan Joachim, 162
Rembrandt Harmenszoon van Rijn
    Anatomy Lesson of Dr. Nicolaes Tulp, 77, 96
    Aristotle Contemplating the Bust of Homer, 81
    Blinding of Samson, 77
    Claudius Civilus, 82
    Frans Banning Cocq (Night Watch), 79
    Parade of the Civic Guard Led by Captain, 79
    Return of the Prodigal Son, 82
    Stoning of St. Stephen, 76
    Syndics of the Cloth Draper's Guild, 82
    The Conspiracy of the Batavians under, 82
    The Jewish Bride, 82
Remembrance Day, 55
Royal Geographical Society, 111
Rudbeck, Olaf, 134
Rundstedt, Field Marshal Gerd von, 40

S

Saints
    Catherine of Alexandria, 28
    Olaf (Olav), 109
    Ursula, 27-28
Sampaio, Lopo Vaz, 94
Scheel, Hans Jacob, 129, 149
Scott, Sir Walter, 281
Ships
    Admiral Hipper (German), 297
    Admiral Scheer (German), 297
    Blücher (Germany), 152, 154
    CSS Monitor, 136
    Fram (Norway), 106, 112-116, 168, 360, 365, 368-369
    Gokstad (Viking), 110, 149-150
    Half Moon (Dutch), 68
    Kon-Tiki (private), 12, 106, 116-117, 165
    Lenin (Russia), 290, 299
    Maud (Norway), 154-155
    Oseberg (Viking), 107, 110, 149
    Searchthrift (England), 308
    Sibirakov (Soviet), 269
    Tune (Viking), 108, 111
    USS Merrimac, 136
    USS Northwind, 269-270
    Vega (Sweden), 267-268
    von Tirpitz (German), 298
Sigusdatter, Sister Birgitta, 160
Silk Road, 13, 17, 34
Sivle, Per, 245
Skyss, 243
Sobrero, Ascanio, 137
Stewart, Colonel George, 330
Sturluson, Snore or Snorri, 218, 277, 347
Stuyvesant, Peter, 68
Suez Canal, 133, 137, 139, 270
Sverdrup, Otto, 112, 359-360, 366

T

Tall Ships Race, 149
Thing (Gulathing, Øyraping), 223
Thingvellir, 339, 342-343, 345, 350-351, 353, 357-358
Tolkien, John Ronald Ruel
    Lord of the Rings, 178
Trans-Siberian Railway, 269, 290
Treaty of
    Armistice WW I (1918), 54, 324, 328
    Brest-Litovsk (1918), 291
    Kiel (1814), 152

Paris (1855), 136
Utrecht (1579), 59-60
Utrecht (1713), 83
Trondson, Kristofer (Rustung), 239
Trotsky (Bronstein), Leon, 325
Tulipomania, 12, 92-93, 97

U

Ulfson, Gunnbjörn, 356, 377
University of Copenhagen, 161-162

V

Van Gogh, Vincent, 83
Van Houten, Coenraad Johannes, 100
Vauban, Marshall, 35
Verenigde Oostindische Compagnie (VOC), 57, 61
Veterans of Foreign Wars (VFW), 53
Vigeland, Emmanuel (Adolf Gustov Thorson), 122
    Tomba Emmanuelle, 130

W

War
    American Civil, 136
    Anglo-Dutch, 69
    Austrian Succession, 32
    Crimea, 136, 312
    Napoleonic, 23, 32, 70, 152
    Spanish Succession, 32, 38
    War of 1814, 152
    Winter War, 165
    World War I, 11, 13, 32, 35, 38, 40, 45-46, 48-49, 116, 153, 179, 244, 289-293, 315, 324-328, 366, 370

World War II, 11, 13, 18, 32, 45, 54, 90, 101, 126, 152, 178, 190, 199, 229, 235, 239, 252, 289-290, 292-293, 315, 335, 370
Way of St. Olav, 216, 221
Welhaven, Johan Sebastian, 165
Wellington, Duke of, 38
Willums, Sigbrit, 209
Wilson, US President Woodrow, 325
World Heritage Site
    Beguinage (Brugge, Belgium), 23
    Brugge (Belgium), 11-12, 17-21, 23-30, 33-35, 40, 47, 209
    Bryggen Hansa Docks (Bergen, Norway), 160
    Canals of Amsterdam, 73
    Cloth Hall (Ypres, Belgium), 33, 40
    Geirangerfjord (Norway), 242
    Ilulissat Icefjord (Disko Bay, Greenland), 364
    Solovetsky Monastery (Russia), 316
    Thingvellir National Park (Iceland), 350, 353, 357

Y

Young Men's Christian Association (YMCA), 52
Ypres Salient, 38-39

Z

Zeeuwse chocolate, 100

www.ingramcontent.com/pod-product-compliance
Lightning Source LLC
Chambersburg PA
CBHW081739100526
44592CB00015B/2232